"199+ Emergency Traps & Survival Hunting Tricks To Capture Any Game:"

"199+ Emergency Traps & Snares And Other Hunting Tricks To Capture Any Game!"

Published By Joseph A. Laydon Jr.

Website------------------------------**http://www.survivalexpertbooks.com**

E-Mail--------------------------------**wwwsurvivalexpert@yahoo.com**

MOST IMPORTANT NOTE: The *"199+ Emergency Traps & Snares And Other Hunting Tricks To Capture Any Game!"* is for INFORMATION USE ONLY!

Published By Joseph A. Laydon Jr.

Website------------------------------**http://www.survivalexpertbooks.com**

E-Mail--------------------------------**wwwsurvivalexpert@yahoo.com**

Copyright

Copyright © 2017 by Intensive Research Information Services And Products (IRISAP).

All rights reserved. No part of this book may be reproduced in any form or by any electronic or mechanical means including information storage and retrieval systems – except in the case of brief quotations in articles or reviews – without the permission in writing from its publisher, Joseph A. Laydon Jr. All brand names and product names used in this book are trademarks, registered trademarks, or trade names of their respective holders. We are not associated with any product or vendor in this book.

IRISAP DISCLAIMER STATEMENT

The author of *"199+ Emergency Traps & Snares And Other Hunting Tricks To Capture Any Game!"* and owner of Intensive Research Information Services And Product(s) (IRISAP) is exercising his right under the First Amendment to self-publish and co-author this informational product to better educate the public with respect to International Hunting applications. The author is publishing this information based upon his *"intensive research"* and his very own experiences with traps & snares and hunting experiences.

"199+ Emergency Traps & Snares And Other Hunting Tricks To Capture Any Game!" is designed to help the reader become more aware of the number of ways to hunt for all types of game from insects, small game, big game,…

The information within *"199+ Emergency Traps & Snares And Other Hunting Tricks To Capture Any Game!"* are for educational purposes only. Professional advice from *"qualified experts"* is ALWAYS and HIGHLY recommended. Advice is neither implied nor intended. IRISAP and authors\writers of resource materials are not responsible for the purchaser's and third party activities and is in no way responsible for sickness or death or successes.

THE PURCHASER OF THIS SPECIAL REPORT IS SOLELY RESPONSIBLE FOR THIRD PARTY DISCLOSURE AND RESPONSIBLE FOR THEIR ACTIONS AND ANY PRIVATE OR PROFESSIONAL ACTIONS TAKEN FROM THIS INFORMATIONAL PRODUCT.
This Special Report is Copyrighted and VIOLATORS WILL BE PROSECUTED!
If the consumer DISAGREES with ANY portion of this DISCLAIMER STATEMENT, the consumer MUST immediately (upon receipt) return this entire informational product for a full refund.

Table Of Contents

Contents

"199+ Emergency Traps & Snares And Other Hunting Tricks To Capture Any Game!" 1
"199+ Emergency Traps & Snares And Other Hunting Tricks To Capture Any Game!" 2
Copyright 3
Table Of Contents 4
Introduction! 12
"199+ Emergency Traps & Snares And Other Hunting Tricks To Capture Any Game!" 14
    Trap And Snare Consideration 14
    Trap And Snare Construction 17
    Triggers 17
    Traps & Snares And Hunting Tricks 18
    01-Mile Long Range Shooting 19
    1st Antelope Lure 21
    2nd Antelope Lure 21
    1st Cree Indian Geese Decoy 21
    2nd Cree Indian Geese Decoy 22
    1st Hypnotizing Chicken Trick 24
    2nd Hypnotizing Chicken Trick 26
    3rd Hypnotizing Chicken Trick 27
    4th Hypnotizing Chicken Trick 27
    5th Hypnotizing Chicken Trick 28
    6th Hypnotizing Chicken Trick 30
    1st Hypnotizing Frog Trick 31
    2nd Hypnotizing Frog Trick 31
    3rd Hypnotizing Frog Trick 32
    Hypnotizing Other Small & Big Game 32
    Hypnotizing – Stunning Humans 33
    Hypnotizing Lizards 33
    1st Lion Repeller 34
    2nd Lion Repeller 34
    3rd Lion Repeller 35
    4th Lion Repeller 35
    1st Super Bait 36
    2nd Super Bait 36
    3rd Super Bait 37
    4th Super Bait 37
    Acerrano Under Rock Vittles 38

Advancing Crouch	38
Alligator Defense	40
American Woodcock Worm Catcher	40
Animal Frying Pan	41
Antler Fight	42
Ants Follow The Light	43
Apache Blood Stew	43
Apache Foraging	43
Apache Food	44
Apache Sling	45
Aztec Deer Stalking	46
Aztec Duck Hunting	47
Aztec Duck Sticks	47
Aztec Fishing	48
Aztec Long-Range Weapons	48
Aztec Pitfall Trap	49
Aztec Short-Range Weapons	50
Bacon Fat (Grease) Shelf Life	50
Basket Fish Trap	54
Bear Hunting	55
Bear Parts	55
Beavers	58
Beaver Bank Trap	59
Beaver Blow Holes	60
Beaver Dam Traps	60
Beaver Deadfall	60
Beaver Drowning Trap	61
Beaver Ring Trap	61
Protective Beaver Fur	62
Old Bachelor Beavers	62
Bird Pit Trap	63
Black Bag Big Game Pitfall Trap	64
Black Bag Dip Net	67
Black Bag Fish Trap	68
Black Bag Shelter Trap	69
Blood Pudding	70
Bola	71
Bottle Trap	72
Branch Snare	73
Bread Of The Desert	75
Buck's Travel Corridor	76
Buffalo Waste Not Want Not	77
Caged Gill Net (Triple Catch)	79

5

Caribou Hunting	81
Catching Scorpions	81
Caw Caw Caw	83
Chipmunk Call	83
Cloth Sling	85
Civil War Rat Vittles	86
Coatimundi	87
Cold Water Diving Reflex	89
Hypothermia Water Survival Table!	90
Comanche Favorite Food	91
Critters Big And Small You Gotta Know About	92
Beavers	93
Grizzily Bear	95
Mountain Lion	96
Raccoon Hunting	98
White-Tailed Deer	100
See	102
White-Tailed Deer Track Size	103
White-Tailed Jackrabbit	103
Concussion Fishing	105
Congo Dual Fishing Lures	106
Congo Fish Baskets	106
Critters Survive Killer Desert Temperatures	107
Crow's Natural Enemy	108
David's Sling	109
Debilitating Rabbit Sticks	111
Deer Encirclement	112
Deer Hunting With A Costume	112
Deer Snare	113
Delicious Peanut Butter Deer Bait	116
Delicious Peanut Butter Emergency Food	118
Nutritious Survival Food Could Save Millions & You Too	118
11+ Peanut Butter Facts!	119
Delicious Peanut Butter Emergency Fire-Starting	123
Den Trap	124
Diaper Decoys	126
Dip Net Fishing	126
Djonga Crocodile Call	127
Djonga Crocodile Trap	127
Drunk Birds	128
Dry Land Fishing Pole	128
Duck Feeding Call - Splashing Boots	129
Duck Feeding Call - Splashing Fingers	129

Duck Feeding Underwater Trap	129
Eagle Vittles	130
Easy Antelope Vittles	130
Easy Buffalo Catch	131
Easy Seal Vittles	132
Eel Pot Trap	132
Elephant Hunting	133
Eskimo Bad To The Bone - Slow Killer	134
Eskimo Bird In The Hand Trap	135
Eskimo Bird Net	135
Eskimo Blind	136
Eskimo Caribou Supplies	136
Eskimo Caribou Weir	137
Eskimo Duck Bolas	138
Eskimo Feather Alert	138
Eskimo Flightless Geese Round	139
Eskimo Gull Fishing	139
Eskimo Hookless Lure	140
Eskimo Pitfall Trap	141
Eskimo Polar Bear Baits	141
Eskimo Polar Bear Teacher	141
Eskimo Seabird Sausage	142
Eskimo Seal Imitation	143
Eskimo Snow Pit Ambush	144
Eskimo Tracking	144
Eskimo Waterfowl Snares	145
Eskimo Wolf Lick Killer	146
Exploding Mice Concoction	147
Exploding Seagull Concoction	147
Explosive Flavor	148
Faceless Hunter	148
Fat-Laden Termite Trap	148
Figure Four Deadfall	149
Fishing Bonfire	151
Fishing Hook & Stunner	151
Fish Spear	151
Fish Stake-Out	153
Floating Platform	155
Floating Duck Snare	157
Flutter Kicks	159
Foot Load Index	160
Forked Walking Stick - Staff	161
Frostbite Remedy	163

Gambel's Quail	163
Georgia Wild Boar Stunner	163
Giant Water Weir	164
Gill Net	166
Goose Final Approach	169
Great Lakes Ice Fishing	169
Ground Squirrels	170
Grouse Are Dumb?	171
Guayaki Camoflage Paste	172
Guayaki Coati Hunting	172
Gulag Blood Food	173
Gurico Gum	174
Hadzabe Leopard Bait	174
Hadzabe Night Hunting	175
Hallet Crocodile Escape Technique	176
Here Kitty Kitty Kitty Kitty	177
Herter Mud Soup	178
Herter Pond Scum Soup	179
Hippopotamus Traps	179
Hogging	180
Hooking Eyes Trap & Snare	181
Hooking Traps & Snares	183
Hooking Waterfowl Snares	185
Hopi Snake Catching	187
Hot Gear	188
Hotter Gear	188
Human Traps	189
Hunting The King Of The Jungle	189
Hunters Harvest	190
Hypnotize Venomous Snakes To Avoid Their Deadly Bite	191
Hypnotizing Alligators	192
Walking Staff Defense	194
Headlocking An Alligator!	194
Hypnotizing Alligators!	195
900+ Japanese Soldiers Mass Slaughtered And They Never Saw Em' Comin'!	196
Hypnotizing Castoreum	197
Hypnotizing Lobsters	199
Imitating Duck Call	200
Ice Support Measurements!	201
Indian Appetite Suppressant	202
Indian Bad To The Bone - Slow Killer	202
Joachim's Traps & Snares	203

Jacking	204
Jigging Pole	205
Juicy Cooking	207
Kalahari Antelope Snare	207
Kalahari Bird Snare	208
Kalahari Glue Snares	210
Kalahari Smoke-Out	211
Kalahari Tsama Trap And Snare	211
Kalahari Underground Fishing	212
Kephart – 'The Dean Of Camping'	213
Kephart's Baited Snare	213
Kephart's Branch Snare	215
Kephart's Deer Drag	217
Kephart's Deer Dressing	217
Kephart's Mosquito Trap And Drowner	221
Kephart's Runway Snare	222
Kissing For Blue Quail	224
Lakota Rattlesnake Hunt	225
Laydon Static Bola Snare	225
Lichen Emergency Food	230
Lift Pole Snare	232
Lions Hunt For You	234
Lobster Trap & Snare	234
Lobster Trap Stats!	234
Log Drop Trap	237
Long-Range Boomerang	239
Man Against Anaconda	240
Man Against Python	241
Man Trap	243
Marten Vittles	244
Massai Blood Food	245
Massai Lion Hunting	245
Metal Gill Net	246
Minnow Trap	246
Montagnais Moose Vittles	249
Moose Tracking	249
Musk Oxen	250
Naskapi Indian Blood Pudding	252
Noodling	252
No Weapon Duck Hunting	252
Nowlin's Fish Stunner	253
Nowlin's Pike Net Fishing	255
Nowlin's Fish Stunner	256

Ojibwa Bird Pole	257
Ojibwa Deer Hunting	259
Onoda Jungle Fowl Trap	259
Onoda Rat Trap	260
Onoda Sock Rat Trap	261
Onoda Wild Cat Trap	262
Ostrich Imitation	263
More Ostrich Imitation	264
Pacific Coral Fish Trap	265
Pacific Moa Snare	265
Pacific Mutton Bird Trap & Snare	266
Pacific Rat Traps	266
Pacific Seal Hunting	267
Pelican Fish Stunner	267
Penguin Vittles	268
Penobscot Brown Bear Killing Trick	268
Pioneer "Bark The Squirrel" Hunting	269
Pioneer Beaver Trap	269
Pioneer Deer Hunting	270
Pioneer Wolf Trap	271
Pounding Stick	272
POW Fly Trap	272
Pronghorn Coyote Trap	273
Pronghorn Snow Trap	273
PRSC	274
Pueblo Indian Dead Falls	276
Pueblo Coyote Dead Falls	276
Pueblo Prairie Dog Dead Fall	277
Pueblo Rabbit Dead Fall	278
Punji Traps	278
Pygmy Fat-Laden Termite Trap	280
Pygmy Human Meat	281
Quail	282
Rabbit Dead Fall	282
Rabbit Round-Up	283
Rabbit Squealing Bloody Murder	284
Rabbit Sticks	284
Rabbit Stopper	286
Rat Dinner	286
Rat Vittles	286
Salmon Harpoon	287
Salt Lick Ambush	288
Sauna In A Can	289

    Secret Mountain Man Caches 297
    Seminole Hypnotizing Alligator Trick 299
    Shadow Decoys 300
    Shallow Water Blackout 300
    Shining 302
    Simple Snare 302
    Small Game & Fish Paralyzing Stunner 303
    Snake Alert 304
    Snake Fence 305
    Snake Trap 305
    Snow Drift Traps 305
    Squirrel Pole 306
    Super Duck Decoys 307
    Swimming Cramp Remedy Point 308
    Tangling Bird Catcher 309
    Tapping 309
    The Deer Is Over Here 309
    The Wrath Of Mother Nature - Blizzards 310
    Trash Basket Decoys 313
    Treadle Spring Snare 313
    Twitch-Up Snare 316
    Waiting Snake Trap & Snare 317
    Wampanoag Deer Snare 318
    White Pelican Corral Fishing 319
    Woodrat Food Cache 320
    Worming 321
    Worm Stick 322
    Zuni Crow Snare 323
    Zuni Hunters 324
    Crows Can't Count 324

"Laydon's Emergency Survival Employment Instructions!" 326

"300,000 Plants On Earth – Edibility Test!" 327

Survival Acronyms! 328

Points Of Contact! 348

More Kindle E-Books And Paperback Books For YOU! 360

About The Author 366

Take Notes 369

Introduction!

Welcome to *"199+ Emergency Traps & Snares And Other Hunting Tricks To Capture Any Game!"*

I used the word *'Emergency'* to protect myself against any lawsuits. Many of these survival applications, techniques and tricks may be illegal. However, in a survival situation where your life is on the line, in my humble opinion, 'you could throw all them laws out the window.' However, *"199+ Emergency Traps & Snares And Other Hunting Tricks To Capture Any Game!" is FOR INFORMATION USE ONLY. See DISCLAIMER.*

"199+ Emergency Traps & Snares And Other Hunting Tricks To Capture Any Game!" is designed to teach the novice to the professional hunters – emergency hunting tricks that are guaranteed to put vittles on the dinner table.

"199+ Emergency Traps & Snares And Other Hunting Tricks To Capture Any Game!" includes proven international hunting applications, techniques and tricks used by the REAL SURVIVORS throughout history and throughout the world.

"199+ Emergency Traps & Snares And Other Hunting Tricks To Capture Any Game!" also includes several hand-picked & proven emergency survival tricks that can save your life if you get into trouble with Mother Nature and all She possesses.

"199+ Emergency Traps & Snares And Other Hunting Tricks To Capture Any Game!" should be read multiple times so you can find your favorite hunting tricks.

Fishing is part of hunting too. I could have added a couple hundred *'international fishing trucks'* but only included several in this book. I highly recommend that you take a look at **"269+ International Fishing Tricks And More!"** at **www.survivalexpertbooks.com**

MOST IMPORTANT NOTE: Before you start reading this book, please read **PRSC** (see Table Of Contents) right now. Nobody uses *PRSC* except military combat patrols. *PRSC* (civilianized version) could save your life!

"199+ Emergency Traps & Snares And Other Hunting Tricks To Capture Any Game!"

Are you still hungry? Not satisfied with eating the plant life, all those insects, or tasty water treats? You're a meat and potatoes type of survivalist? I don't know about the potatoes, but I can tell you about getting some wildlife meat! Throughout this book, we'll talk about traps & snares and how to employ them to get that small game and even the big game! Traps & snares require a bit of unique knowledge before understanding them and employing them. Let's start with *Trap And Snare Consideration*.

MOST IMPORTANT NOTE: I started this book with *Trap And Snare Considerations* because there are Traps And Snares throughout this book. So when you read about any Trap And Snare, consider coming back to this segment for a re-read. OK, let's get started.

Trap And Snare Consideration: For an unarmed survivor, constructing traps and snares may be your only alternative for food procurement.

a) Several well placed traps and snares have the potential to catch enough game to sustain your health till your rescue. To be effective with any type of trap or snare you must be familiar with:

b) Species of animal you intend to catch.

c) Proper construction of a particular trap. The trap and snare should be constructed so that it will be triggered by the wildlife it is intended to catch and not triggered by a gust of wind, or other wildlife.

d) Signs that may alarm the animal of your presence. You must remove or mask the human scent on and around the trap and snare that you set. Nearly all animals depend on their sense of smell than they do their sight. Removing the human scent is probably more difficult to remove than masking it.

In order to mask your scent, you can use the urine bladder from previous kills; mud, especially from rotting vegetation; smoking the parts of trap and snare; rub charcoal (from your fire) on all the parts of the trap and snare; and you may also rub your hands in mud or rub them with charcoal prior to touching any parts of the trap and snare or anything at the trap and snare site.

DO NOT use freshly cut vegetation for construction of your traps and snares. Freshly cut vegetation will bleed *"sap"* and alert the prey. Attempt to camouflage the site prior to leaving the area.

e) There are no catch-all traps you can set for all wild game. You must determine what species are in a given area and set your traps specifically with those critters in mind. Look for the following:

f) Runs and trails. A run is small and not as distinguishable as a trail. A trail will show signs of use by several species.

g) Tracks. If you can identify tracks from the wide variety of animals, then you can better pick your trap and snare for that particular animal along with the bait if it's readily available.

h) Droppings. Droppings (scat) are another clue to time the animal was in the area and the type of animal.

i) Chewed or rubbed vegetation. These are signs of a feeding area. They may also indicate the time the animal was last at the feeding site and the size and type of animal.

j) Nesting or roosting sites (size of site).

k) Feeding and watering areas.

l) Channelization. Traps and snares should be placed on a game run or trail and channelized. Build a barrier so that the prey is steered toward the trap and snare. Channelization should be inconspicuous so that the prey isn't alerted. Camouflage the channelization as to blend in with its surrounding area.

m) Bait. To increase your chance of catching small or large game, bait must be used. Give your prey a reason to wander into your trap and snare.

Even though the bait should be something the animal knows, it may not be readily available. Intestines from previous kills, peanut butter, scraps of food, and even shiny objects, empty small packages or packets (some animals are curious).

Trap And Snare Construction: Traps and snares crush, choke, hang, entangle, trap, and snare all types of prey. A single trap or snare may incorporate two or more of these principles.

The **tension** to provide the power to trap or snare the intended prey may come from the struggling prey, gravity, the tension of a weight, the tension of an overhead branch or sapling, or a combination of these.

Triggers: The most important part of any trap and snare is the **triggering device**. The triggering device can be a number of things to include a y-shaped piece of branch, a straight piece of stick... triggers can be carved and slightly burnt so that it is **so sensitive** that in most cases simply dropping a ball point pen can set off the trigger (standards for Army SERE students).

Triggers

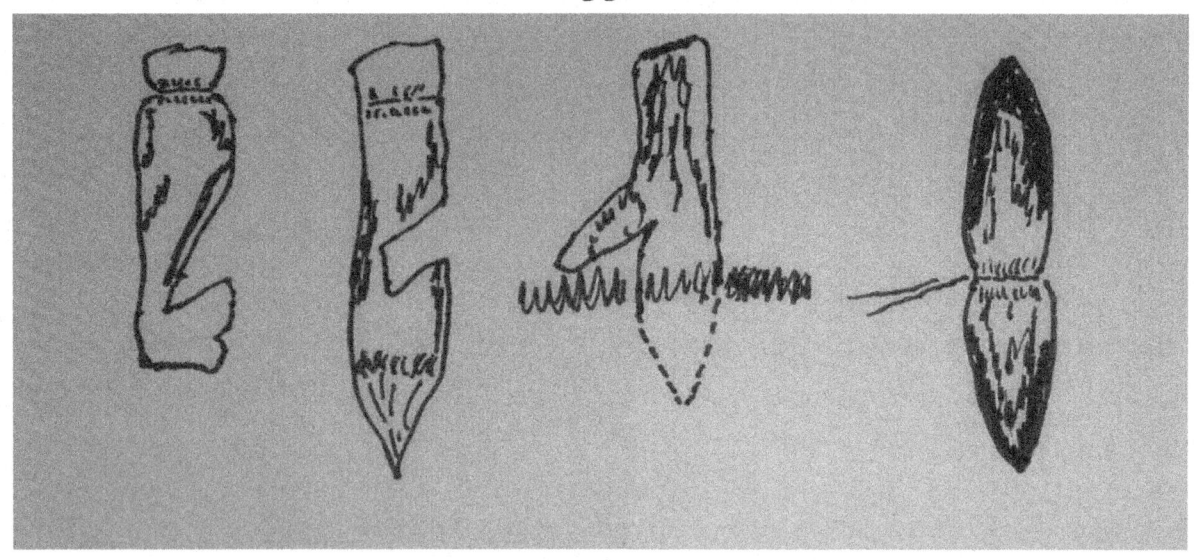

Prior to constructing any trap and snare, consider how you want it to affect the intended prey, the source of tension to trap and snare the intended prey and type of trigger to effectively set off the trap and snare (if a triggering device is needed).

Traps & Snares And Hunting Tricks: The following are traps & snares and hunting tricks you may consider to use if you feel your life is threatened due to starvation or threatened by wildlife. These traps & snares and hunting tricks **should NOT be used to capture wild game for fun**. Most or all may be illegal to use in non-survival situations.

Besides international traps & snares, this book includes international hunting tricks used throughout history to the present day. Let's start with *01-Mile Long Range Shooting*.

01-Mile Long Range Shooting: Buffalo hunters of the 1800s engaged buffalo at ranges no 10 arrow combined could reach. To engage the buffalo after buffalo without the heard stampeding off, the buffalo hunters shot upwind into each buffalo. Shooting upwind, the buffalo couldn't smell the human scent or gunpowder with their super sensitive nose that warned them of danger. To steady their rifles, they secured their rifles on forked sticks that were securely held in the ground. The barrel lay on the joint of the forked stick complimenting the hunters other marksmanship fundamentals that were a necessity to engage buffalo at long ranges.

To reach their target at long ranges, many buffalo hunters initially used a 07-pound* Sharps weapon they called the *Big Fifty* or *Old Poison Slinger*. It fired a 50. caliber (1/2-inch wide) bullet that had a maximum range of 05-miles with a maximum effective range of approximately 01-mile. The bullets used were factory loaded but buffalo hunters that re-loaded their own bullets turned out to be better marksmen. The $80 to $100 rifle was top of the line and their marksmanship was second to none. Hey, with kazillions of buffalo to shoot at they had plenty of practice.

*The Sharps heavy caliber rifle was continuously improved and final models in that era weighed up to 16-pounds.

1st Note: Some US Army Special Forces snipers use a set of 03-sticks secured together at one end where they are folded out to form a stand. The 03-legs are secured in the ground and the barrel rests on top of the 03-sticks where they're joined.

2nd Note: The 2nd sniper school I (author) attended, we were taught to reload our own ammunition that was TAILORED specifically to our own sniper system. Turns out the tailored ammunition shot better than issued National Match ammo.

3rd Note: And while I'm at it, here's how we used rice to improve marksmanship. We took about 02 to 03 cups of rice and secured it in a loose plastic bag (waterproofing). Then we put that bag of rice in an OD green sock and tied a knot on the sock that formed a ball. When taking up the prone firing position, the bag of rice is placed under the stock. Minute changes of elevation (increase or decrease) are done by barely squeezing the bag or manipulating it. Rice is used because it molds and holds to changes during the engagement process. Plus it can be used as an emergency food source!

4th Note: OK, one more trick to help out your engagement process. Eye Relief. Eye Relief is the distance between your rear sight and your eye. To keep the same exact Eye Relief for all shots, we were taught to mold and secure Eye Relief Patch (cloth and OD Green 100mph tape) to the stocks of our weapon. Once it was secure we'd press our face against it and mold the impression of our face while we're looking through our telescopic site or rear iron sight. That Eye Relief Patch insured our Eye Relief was exactly the same distance each shot for years! Every little bit counts when it comes to pinpoint marksmanship. I can go on with more marksmanship tips but that's for some other time. Let's start this book with *1st Antelope Lure*.

1st Antelope Lure: Indians lured antelope into point blank range by taking advantage of their curiosity. Staying out of sight, they got within sight of the antelope. They carefully tied a batch of feathers to the top of a bush. The winds moved the feathers back & forth which caught the very acute vision (big eyes) of the antelope even at great distances. The curious antelope advance on the fluttering feathers till they get within an acceptable engagement range of the hunter.

2nd Antelope Lure: Like the antelope lure above, the Indians had their tricks to lure in those tasty curious antelope and the white man had their own tricks and here's one of them. Instead of using a set of feathers, they used a white cloth (handkerchief) that stood out against the landscape. The curious antelope would try to figure out what the heck it is and advance on the white fluttering object. It advanced till it was within an engagement range for the hunter.

1st Cree Indian Geese Decoy: Cree Indian hunters (what is now Canada / US – Great Lakes area & northward) used an ingenious trick to compel Canada geese to land within point blank range of their hiding spots (blinds). Cree used other geese – but dead geese. The freshly dead geese were spread out in an open field (facing upwind for landing and takeoff - remember, more times than not, all birds, like planes, land into the wind for a controlled landing and take-off into the wind for lift and controlled flight). The dead geese were placed on the ground in a sitting position facing into the wind.

Their heads were propped up in an erect fashion using a stick. When flocks of geese flew overhead, their super keen eyesight saw their brothers and sisters on the ground below socializing, eating, resting,... and saw no signs of predators (man or beast). So the flock swooped down turning and turning, heading into the wind for a controlled landing. Well within range there they were met by Cree hunters in their blinds who used shotguns to shoot the unsuspecting geese. See *Goose Final Approach*.

Note: Geese, ducks,... tend to migrate at the west side of streams, lakes ponds,... when breeding.

2nd Cree Indian Geese Decoy: I know what you're asking: *"What if I don't have and fresh dead geese for decoys in the 1st place? What am I going to use as decoys? C'mon I'm starving here!"* OK, OK - Cree hunters also used another decoy to compel them Canada geese critters to land within point blank range of their blinds. It's time consuming but it worked. All they did was take a pile of long brown twigs and patiently built a geese look-a-like decoy. That's it. I'm sure they had more than a few twig decoys, but that's all they did - weave fake geese using a bunch of twigs! And insure the decoys are facing into the wind. See *Goose Final Approach*.

1st Note: Famous bad ass mountain man Jedediah S. Smith and fellow mountain men came across a tribe of non-aggressive Indians he called Sacramento Indians. He noted that they made duck decoys that were so realistic, they even fooled the experienced eyes of himself and fellow mountain men. When initially sighting the decoys, these savvy mountain men were fooled by the decoys and took shots at them.

2nd Note: Anthropologist have uncovered evidence that prehistoric man fabricated feathered decoys to lure in and capture fowl game.

3rd Note: Keep in mind that a flock of ducks, geese,... may overfly your decoys for a quick look and come back around turning into the wind before landing near your decoys. So if they see anything out of place, they'll leave the area real quick. Insure you take a re-look at the POCs I just mentioned.

4th Note: Geese, ducks,... tend to migrate at the <u>west side</u> of streams, lakes ponds,... when breeding.

1st Hypnotizing Chicken Trick: Now let me tell you how to hypnotize a chicken for a silent and humane kill!

a) First of all you'll need a green stick about 02 1/2 feet long and 3/4 of an inch wide that won't break very easily.

b) Clear-out a small area of all debris and vegetation. You'll need this to draw a clear line in the dirt with your stick.

c) Secure your chicken - gently hold it to the ground and point its head to the area of the area you cleared of debris and vegetation.

d) Take your stick and draw a straight line directly from the chickens head (its head should be fairly close to the ground) and away from it about 02 1/2 feet out. Do this several times till you can see that the chicken is frozen by the line drawn in the ground.

e) Once the chicken is hypnotized and is FROZEN in place, GENTLY let it go and take your drawing stick and GENTLY place it over the chicken's neck. As you are facing the same direction as the chicken, place your left-foot on the left-side of the stick and your right-foot on the right-side of the stick.

f) Your full weight is now on the stick and has the chicken pinned to the ground. Bend down and grasp the body of the chicken and **forcefully pull-up** while still maintaining all your weight on the stick that is on the chickens neck.

g) The chickens body should easily separate from the chickens head. Immediately release the chicken and let it flop around. The chicken has all sorts of fleas, parasites, bugs... on it, and since the chicken's body temperature is dropping, all those fleas, parasites, bugs... are looking for a new host - YOU!

h) So let it flop around and lay there about 20-minutes before you dress it.

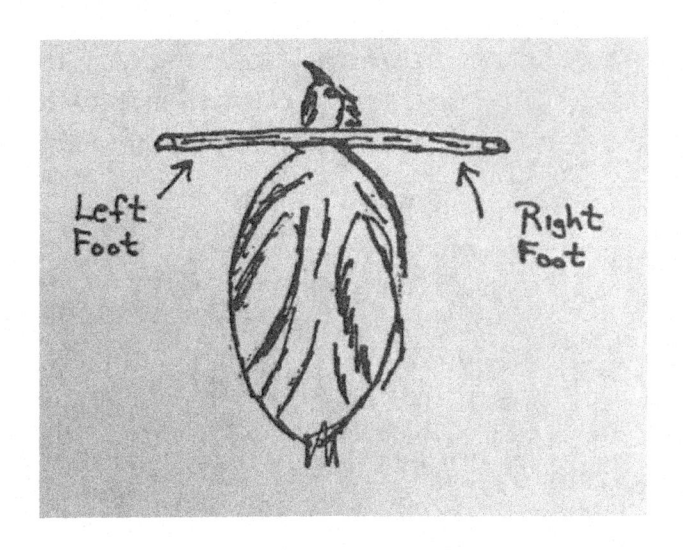

2nd Hypnotizing Chicken Trick: Place the chicken on its back. Secure one of the wings and give the chicken a good spin. The spinning will dizzy the chicken very quickly but it will not last forever so take action to sever the chickens head as quickly as possible.

3rd Hypnotizing Chicken Trick: Secure the chicken and place it on its side in some soft dusty dirt. Wave your hand in front of the chicken's face so to get its attention. Then draw a 01 to 02 foot arc with your finger or a stick in the dirt next to the chicken face. This will stun the chicken for several seconds to a few minutes depending if there are any distractions nearby that would snap the chicken out of this hypnotized state. Take immediate action to sever the chicken's head as quickly as possible.

4th Hypnotizing Chicken Trick: This next technique is called The Oscillating Finger Method. Place the chicken on its side with its wing underneath its body. Gently hold the bird down with one hand. With the free hand, take the index finger and move it back and forth from in front of the chicken's beak to about 04-inches away and back again over and over. Insure the tip of the finger stays on the same level as the chicken's beak.

Keep oscillating the finger back and forth till the chicken is hypnotized. This will stun the chicken for several seconds to a few minutes depending if there are any distractions nearby that would snap the chicken out of this hypnotized state. Take immediate action to sever the chicken's head as quickly as possible.

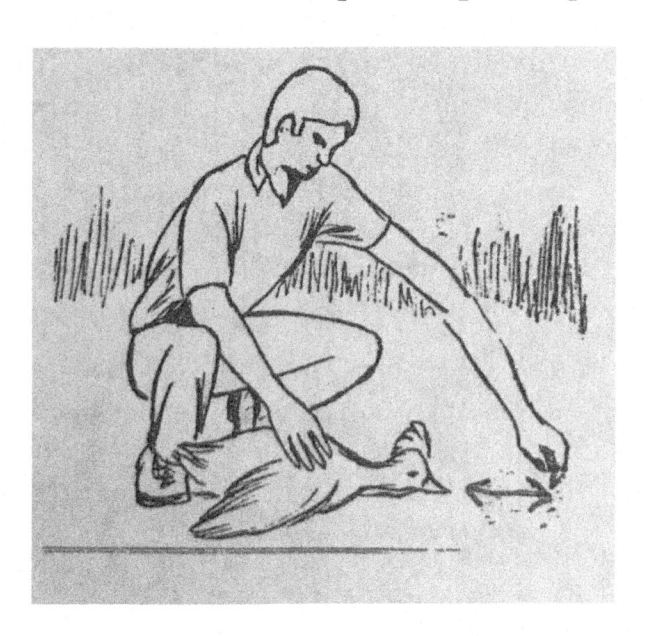

5th Hypnotizing Chicken Trick: The last technique is called the Sternum Stroke Method. Secure the chicken on its back and gently hold it in place. Gently and lightly massage the birds sternum area (chest) using the index finger and thumb slightly separated. This will stun the chicken for several seconds to a few minutes depending if there are any distractions nearby that would snap the chicken out of this hypnotized state. Take immediate action to sever the chicken's head as quickly as possible.

Now you know a total of 05 ways to hypnotize a chicken for a quick, SILENT and humane kill. Plus with that meat not tensed-up, it's relaxed, it should taste better.

1st Note: The chicken has all sorts of fleas, parasites, bugs... on it, and since the chicken's body temperature is dropping, all those fleas, parasites, bugs... are looking for a new host - YOU! So let it flop around and lay there about 20-minutes before you dress it.

2nd Note: Many times when I or my students hypnotized and dressed-out the chicken for cooking; we found eggs in them. Now these eggs are the freshest eggs possible. But when you go to the store to buy your eggs, how do you know if they're really fresh? When cracking open the raw egg in the frying pan, a fresh egg will not spread out all over the frying pan and will keep its mass in one tight circular form. On the other hand, an older egg will tend to spread out more-so in the frying pan. Why?

Cause as the egg ages, it loses its protein which helps bind all the egg matter together. Now that you know how to tell the difference between a fresh egg and older egg, let's carry-on with more hypnotic theory that gets you more than eggs.

6th Hypnotizing Chicken Trick: You already know 05 ways to hypnotize a chicken and here's a 6th - only from IRISAP. I was talking to a soldier who served over in Kosivo on a peace-keeping mission back 1999. This hypnotizing trick is used in a slaughter house in Kosivo. Chickens are placed on a wooden chopping block to get their heads cut-off. But this is a special block of wood for it has a long groove cut-out in the block of wood. This groove hypnotizes - stuns the chicken. It's head is placed on the block of wood and directly in front of the chicken's eyes is a 07-inch long groove about 1/2-inch wide and 1/4-inch deep. And in a short second or two the tasty chicken is zapped - paralyzed for a silent kill!

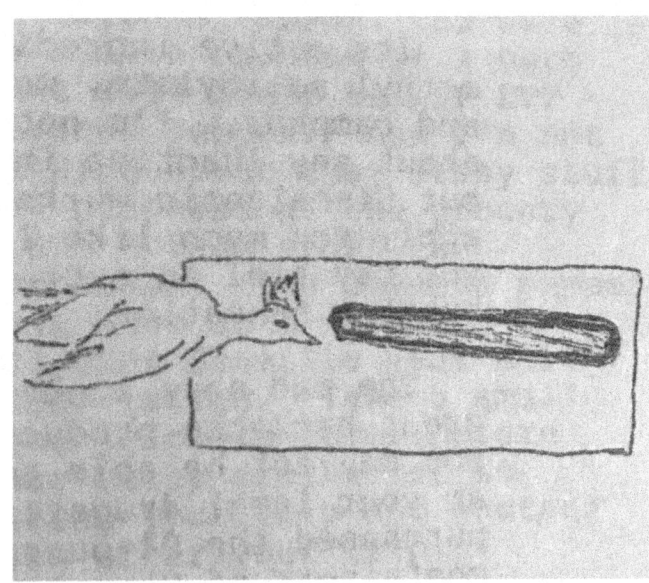

Now you know 06 ways to hypnotize chickens. And don't forget, other animals can be hypnotized - stunned too.

1st Hypnotizing Frog Trick: Lots of folks hop around after eating frog legs because they're lip-smacking delicious. But how do you catch frogs. One technique that compels frogs to get *"hooked"* is the color scarlet. Scarlet is a bright reddish orange color. Take a small piece of scarlet-colored cloth and place it on a hook and cast your line in the water where there's evidence of frogs (sounds, sightings,...). For some reason, frogs are compelled to scarlet like fish are compelled to the color red & white. Once you capture a few of them hopping critters, their legs are what you're after. So dress em' up and fry em' up for dinner vittles!

2nd Hypnotizing Frog Trick: Also called Frogging, this technique is done at night. Once you spot a frog, shine your bright light from your flashlight directly in its eyes. The frog will be absolutely stunned and confused and will not move like shining does to deer at night. Maintaining the light on its eyes so it's still stunned, quietly walk over and pick it up and secure it in a bag and carry-on with the next frog. The bright light in its eyes just screws em' all up so they're paralyzed. Dress em' and fry em' as needed.

1st Note: A 1,000,000 candle power flood light ought to do it. They're very affordable and rechargeable. INSURE you have a back-up flashlight

2nd Note: Since frogs don't have diaphragms, another technique to put a frog in a sleep-like state, see *Hypnotizing Lizards*.

3rd Hypnotizing Frog Trick: I'm going out on a limb here, but here's a technique to stun frogs during daylight hours. You already know light stuns frogs at night. Why not use light to stun them during daylight hours. How? By using a mirror to reflect direct sunlight into their eyes. Facing into the sun, use your mirror to aim & reflect the super bright rays of the sun directly into the eyes of the frog. Like snakes, this should temporarily stun them so you can close on em', dress em', and fry em' up! For proof, see *Hypnotize Venomous Snakes To Avoid Their Sickly & Deadly Bite*.

Hypnotizing Other Small & Big Game: As I stated before, I sincerely believe other small game fowl like grouse, prairie chickens, prairie hens, sage hens, turkeys, guinea fowl (cousin to domestic chicken),... and probably other non-fowl small & big game can be temporarily HYPNOTIZED by using color, spinning, light, held upside down, smell, sound,...) so to temporarily control them for a quick, SILENT, and humane kill instead of beating the poor critter to death. And now there's initial proof as **I suspected long ago** that animals other than chickens can be hypnotized.

Dr. Doris White, a professor at William Paterson College, NJ, states *"Pheasants go out faster than any other wild bird. Wild pheasants are very nervous and high-strung, and usually very easy to hypnotize."* Dr. White has successfully hypnotized several species of fowl and tabulated data on all her test subjects.

Hypnotizing - Stunning Humans: Can humans be stunned or hypnotized so they have absolutely NO CONTROL over their actions or lack of actions? I would certainly say so. Us humans have 05 senses (hearing, sight, smell, touch, and taste). Plus our body is an electrical grid. Plus our brain is still a mystery to us even today. Our brain, 05 senses, and our *"electrical"* body can be manipulated so it's stunned or controlled. How? You got me, all I know is that it can be controlled. I'm sure there are a few scientists somewhere in the world trying to figure out how to absolutely control or temporarily shut off the human body via sound, light, frequencies,... without permanent damage. And here's another hypnotizing trick you have to know so you're ready Anytime Anywhere.

Hypnotizing Lizards: Once you grab a lizard, it can be rendered docile so to control for an easy kill. By just placing the lizard on its back, a lizard can be rendered harmless, putting it in a sleep-like state. You see, lizards (all reptiles?) have no diaphragms like us humans.

Without our diaphragms, us humans would suffocate real quick. As for lizards, they use the muscles in their body to help them breathe. When they're placed on their back, breathing is difficult. So their body's self-preservation mechanism kicks-in real quick and the lizard goes into a sleep-like state.

1ˢᵗ Lion Repeller: Bushmen camping at night or in their small villages repelled lions and other predators by insuring fires burned throughout the night. Most animals want nothing to do with any fire. Plus it helped as a navigational beacon (for late or lost bushmen), mosquito repellent, kept them warm,... See *3ʳᵈ & 4ᵗʰ Lion Repeller*. See note below.

2ⁿᵈ Lion Repeller: To protect themselves and their cattle, African villagers may build a fence of brush that is dense with super sharp thorns. The fence encircles the village. The fence may be several feet high. See *3ʳᵈ & 4ᵗʰ Lion Repeller*.

1st Note: During the dry season, roaring lions can be heard up to 02-miles away. The roaring may indicate that they're sounding-off protecting their territory. However, while stalking prey, they're not likely to give away their current position. During the wet season, sounds may be muffled. Also as I stated before sound travels much farther in colder temperatures than warmer temperatures.

2nd Note: Lions in contact with their human prey may stalk their human prey like they do other prey but probably with far more patience. Lions may smartly decide to stalk their human prey at night rather during daylight hours to take advantage of limited visibility to humans but not to their keen night sight. Lions may stalk their human prey by circling them several times attempting to pick-up as much data, weaknesses, and defensive strong points as possible. And other predators may stalk their human prey in a similar manner. NEVER underestimate your opponent (humans, insects, small & big game, terrain, vegetation, weather,...). See *The Ghost And The Darkness* in the POC Section.

3rd Lion Repeller: If you can repel lions with this concoction, it's gotta work on other angry attacking critters! I got this concoction from an experienced world traveler who spent a lot of time in the heart of Africa. He stated that he carried formaldehyde on him. He said one time one of those *"kings of the jungle"* critter was right behind him and he used the formaldehyde from a spray bottle. It stopped the lion in his tracks, it rubbed its face and went the other direction. Hey, if formaldehyde will work on the *"king of the jungle"* it's gotta work on other attacking angry critters.

Note: You can acquire these chemicals - ingredients at hardware stores, drugstores, grocery stores, agriculture outlets, department stores,...

4th Lion Repeller: This next concoction came from the same subscriber who gave me *3rd Lion Repeller*. He stated an old African native told him if he ever woke-up to find a lion in his tent, he is to calmly **"spit in the lion's face."** I asked him *"Why?"* He didn't know and I got to thinking about it all that night and it came to me. I called him up and told him by spitting in the lion's face you're simulating the *"attack of a spitting cobra!"* Makes sense uh! In different parts of the world there are spitting cobras and injecting cobras. Those lions know about spitting cobras and know better than to mess with them. So by spitting in the lions face, the lions thinks you're a spitting cobra and he's outta there!

1st Super Bait: Chinese fishermen and hunters have used this proven bait for centuries. It's called Rhodium Oil. Rhodium Oil is extracted from the true lignam rhodium. 80-pounds of wood will yield 09 drachms (ancient Grecian unit of weight) and a resinous old woods will yield 02-ounces of rhodium. Rhodium oil is a light yellowish color but may be the color of red when stored. Another source of rhodium oil is from the root of the rose-wort, rhodiola rosea and the oil is also yellowish in color. 01-pound will yield 01 drachm.

Rhodium oil is a super-compelling bait for fish (freshwater & saltwater), rats, and all sorts of small game like beaver, muskrat, raccoon,... - it compels the small game to come to the baited trap. To use Rhodium Oil, place a couple drops of Rhodium Oil on your fish bait and they'll be compelled to get hooked. You can also use Rhodium Oil on traps and snares for other small and medium game.

But you don't have to get Rhodium Oil the hard way, you can get it from a Murray's Lure's and it's real cheap - only $3.50 for 01-ounce. Remember, just a couple drops or so will do to compel that critter to come to you Anytime Anywhere! See *Murray's Lure's* in the POC Section.

2nd Super Bait: Take a fish and cut it up in small pieces and put everything in a closed jar. Place the jar in the hot sun for days. The contents of the jar will rot and an oily residue will form. Use this super-scented oil for a great scent to smear on your bait whatever it is. Fish will be attracted and compelled to take the bait.

3rd Super Bait: Take the organs (heart, liver, lungs, kidneys,...) of just about any critter and chop them up. Better yet puree the organs to a liquidy paste and place them in a closed bottle to age. After several days to weeks, you'll have a scent a bear with a sinus infection could smell. This scent can be used to scent traps, bait,...

Note: If you don't want to make your own scented bait as prescribed above, go to your local WalMart stores. In the Sporting Goods area, you'll find ready-to-go scents for your next hunting trip.

4th Super Bait: One of the most dangerous animals to hunt are bear. And one of the best baits bears just love are fresh fish covered with honey.

1st Note: And don't forget about another great Super Bait - see *Hypnotizing Castoreum*.

1st Warning: Bears are still legally hunted in parts of North America and are protected in most of the US and Canada. However, bears are still a serious threat to all outdoor lovers. Insure you check with the local Forest Ranger for <u>all</u> potential threats and like I've said before - ALWAYS carry a weapon with you at all times, even if it's only a Forked Walking Stick.

2nd Warning: No matter what bait you're using, it may invite dangerous predators like other bears, bobcats, coyotes, mountain lions, wolves,... to your exact location so keep an extra good lookout cause them ornery critters are experts of experts at sneaking up on their prey (YOU).

2nd Note: On 08 October 2003 (Wednesday), Fox News reported that a man writing a book on bears was killed by a bear at his isolated campsite located in Alaska. I guess he failed to carry a self-defense weapon that I've told you about multiple times in previous AASNs. See *Counter Assault* and *Universal Defense Alternative Products* in the POC Section. Plus I'd carry a high-powered rifle. But <u>MOST IMPORTANT</u>, leave them ornery critters alone! You're on their turf, you're now in the food-chain, especially at an isolated campsite located in Alaska where help is miles & miles away, no roads, no trails, no 911 - it's just you, thousands of square miles of wilderness, and them ornery critters (my kinda place)!!!

Acerrano Under Rock Vittles: Aquatic insects can be found under rocks in shallow fresh water streams and just off shallow fresh water shores. To get the insects, place your fine net on downstream side of the rock. Uplift the rock, this should release the insects into your net. These insects can be eaten after they're thoroughly cooked. And these same insects are great fish bait. See "*300,000 Plants On Earth - Edibility Test!*" at the end of this book.

Advancing Crouch: When a kid, remember playing cowboys & Indians, playing Army, or sneaking up on the neighborhood cat or dog? Remember you crouched while advancing? Why not walk upright? Kalahari bushmen crouched while advancing on the downwind side of their favorite big game - the Eland antelope.

The giant Eland was a favorite for the bushmen because it had a lot of meat and a lot of fat especially surrounding the heart. Bushman crouched while advancing upwind on their favorite prey. And when available they used vegetation to hide their movement. The closer they got to their prey, <u>the lower they crouched</u>. Why crouch while advancing or in a static position? Crouching hides the human stature. It disguises you from being human from both animal and other humans which delays warning to your prey. The 02-horned Eland is the largest antelope species in the world. It clocks-in at 06-feet tall and weighs up to 1,800-pounds.

The *Taurotragus oryx* or and *Taurotragus derbianus* - Eland antelope has a light-brown or grayish coat with 02 spirally twisted horns. It once populated Central and South America, but today its numbers are substantially reduced. Its status as a far as an endangered species is unknown. Eland wouldn't be as vulnerable if their human predators walked upright and that goes for all game and even humans. But remember a few important facts *"Movement attracts the eyes"* and *"Camouflage camouflage camouflage"* and *"Be aware of your scent scent scent."*

Note: I'm telling you crouching really works for stalking and advancing on both humans and animals. I've had plenty of folks trying to sneak up on me. They never snuck up on me at point blank range but they got in a lot closer while crouching versus walking upright. Walking upright immediately BROADCASTS HUMAN HUMAN HUMAN to both animal and man. See *Faceless Hunter*.

Alligator Defense: Yeah I know what you're saying *"There ain't no alligators in Canada or Alaska!"* Yes, not in these modern times. But to the south, their southern Indian cousins used this technique to defend and capture alligators for tasty meals and other uses using most parts of the alligator. To control the alligator, a few brave Indians would secure a long durable pole and shove it in the alligator mouth and down its body. The pole in the alligators mouth not only controlled the alligator but made it impossible to bite anyone. And the pole was used to turn the alligator over on its most vulnerable belly where it was speared to death. The alligator was either cooked whole over a fire or dressed-out. From the very beginning, I've always told you to have a walking stick to aid you in walking and as a weapon to enhance your security. Do you think you can use this same *"alligator technique"* to protect yourself against other attacking critters?

Here's a neat trick to call those all-teeth critters. It was told to me by an international traveler, a WWII Silver Star recipient. He stated the sound of a French horn had them all-teeth critters coming to the noise. He told me a man playing the French horn was tree'd by some alligators responding to that sound. Why they responded to the French horn sound is unknown. Don't try this unless you're prepared for the consequences!

American Woodcock Worm Catcher: I just told you about the healing wonders of HSOs and I joked - *"never seen a sickly earth worm."* Remember I told you about using *Worm Sticks*. Well the American Woodcock has a unique trick to get them worms to climb towards the surface so it can be plucked out of the dirt.

The American Woodcock is also known as the bogsucker, timberdoodle, hookumpake and night peck. It's 10 1/2 to 11 1/2-inches long, complimented with a long bill, rounded wings and has a dead leaf pattern on its upperparts, rusty color on its underparts, and its crown has black bars. And in-flight, its wings whistle. The American Woodcock is found in the eastern half of the United States and habitates in moist thickets and brushy fields. It eats all sorts of insects to include earth worms. To get the earth worms to climb to the surface, it vigorously thumps its feet on moist ground. Then it plunges its beak into the moist ground retrieving the earth worms. See *Worm Sticks*.

1st Note: YES, there's another species of bird that has a similar technique. Dang if I can't remember the name of this bird, but it beats it's beak on the ground to simulate rain drops hitting the ground. The worms don't want to drown so they maneuver towards the surface. The worms come to the surface where they're retrieved.

2nd Note: Can YOU stomp your feet for a batch of earth worms? Hey, it's worth a try.

Animal Frying Pan: Here's a cooking technique you can use when you have no frying pan or simply rather not clean-up after yourself. Once your big game is dead, go to the hind quarters or other section where it's meaty and cut out a section of meat in a circular pattern at least as large as a dinner plate. Insure you cut into the hide to capture as much meat as possible. Cut out the entire section of hide & meat in a circular section.

Next place the meat in the fire with the hide down against the fire and make sure the center section of the meat is lowest so it when it cooks, all the cooking juices and fat are contained within the section of cooking meat. The meat will cook in its own fat juices which can't spill over and it no doubt adds great taste to the meat along with additional nutrients and the fat grams you need in a survival situation. Cook till you have it rare, medium, or well done like you want it - Mmmmmmmm! But my recommendation is to cook it well done!

Antler Fight: One neat trick to lure them big bucks (male deer) is to take a set of antlers and rub them, strike them back and forth against each other for about 20-minutes as if two bucks were fighting over turf and a harem of does (female deer) - make some noise. It's best used by two hunters facing each other and imitating the sounds of 02 bucks fighting with their antlers in their original position as if they were still attached to a deer's head. To help this technique succeed, look for deer signs that will indicate they are in the area like their droppings (scat), antler scratches on trees (polishing antlers, practice fighting,...), food source. Also consider the most likely time of year when bucks fight which is during rut (does and bucks mate) season.

Ants Follow The Light: Pygmies had a technique to get ants, moths and other insects for food. At night they go static on a slope with a torches. Waiting there with lit torches; ants, moths, and other insects congregated to the lights where they were gathered for food.

Pygmies are noted to eat all types of insects like large white worms found in palm trees, caterpillars, grasshoppers, snails, termites, tree slugs, water insects, wood beetles,... and other small wildlife like crayfish, frogs, mice, mollusks, snakes,... See *"300,000 Plants On Earth - Edibility Test!"* at the end of this book.

Apache Blood Stew: Their stews of meat, water, vegetables were thickened by adding blood from the animals they killed - especially the few buffalo. And as I've stated before, blood is a liquid food loaded with water and much needed nutrients in a survival situation.

Apache Foraging: Apache women were experts at foraging. They were plant experts. More than 1/3rd of their diet consisted of gathered acorns, mesquite beans, nuts, onions, potatoes, roots, sunflower* seeds, vegetables, wild grapes, wild mulberries, wild strawberries,... Some Apache tribes grew crops. They also accumulated food, other supplies and even slaves through raids on pioneers and other Indian tribes.

Apache Food: As far as meat (small & big game), Apaches hunted and ate coyotes, deer, dogs, grouse, horses, jackrabbits, mules, prairie chickens, wolves, jackrabbits, wild fowl, wild turkeys, wood rats, buffalo,... And almost nothing of these animals was wasted especially the buffalo. All parts of the buffalo had ingenious uses to help them survive in their unforgiving wilderness environment. The meat was maxed-out with fat and protein and eaten raw or cooked in a variety of ways or dried, smoked for a future food source. It was also made into pemmican (see Eskimo & Other Northern Tribe Survival Tricks in this Book.

The brains, eyes, hearts, internal organs, tongues, were eaten. The blood of the buffalo was used in puddings, soups, stews, and other dishes. Fetal calves were a delicacy. Buffalo bones were roasted and broken to retrieve the tasty & nutritious bone marrow. Bones were also used to make sewing needles, scrapers, digging tools, eating utensils, spearheads, arrowheads, knives,... The hooves were used to make glue and tools. Lungs were boiled with vegetables. Udders were grilled over a fire and eaten. The hide was use as a robe, for bedding, shields, moccasins, teepees,... Buffalo hair was woven into bags, belts, blankets, cords, halters, lariats, medicine pouches, ropes, scarves, wallets,... Other items made from the buffalo were bags, bone ladles, boxes, dog saddles, horns, ornaments, parfleches, rattles (scrotum), straps, thread (sinew), trunks,...

Again, you won't run into any buffalo, but there are many other critters that are not only a food source but their parts have many many other uses to help you satisfy the *8 Elements of Survival* (Fire, Water, Shelter, First-Aid, Signal, Food, Weapons, and Navigation) to survive Anytime Anywhere.

Apache Sling: When you hear the word Apache, the famous Indian Chief Geronimo comes to mind. The Apache lived and roamed the areas of Arizona, southeastern Colorado, southern Kansas, northern Mexico, western Oklahoma, New Mexico, and western Texas. They were feared by neighboring Indian tribes as well as white pioneers, US Cavalry,... And speaking of the US Cavalry, man for man, they were no match against Apache Indians. Apaches were well seasoned in the *"art of suffering"* and knew how to eat, drink, and sustain themselves in the killer unforgiving wilderness environment of the dry desert southwest.

The Apache's weapons for fighting and hunting were both from nature and man-made. One weapon was the *Apache Sling*. The *David's Sling* and the *Apache Sling* are very similar and employed the same way. The difference is the *Apache Sling* has 13 small opaque-shaped apertures cut into the pouch. These apertures may be placed there to rid the pouch of dirt, water drainage, reduce drag while being rotated through the air.

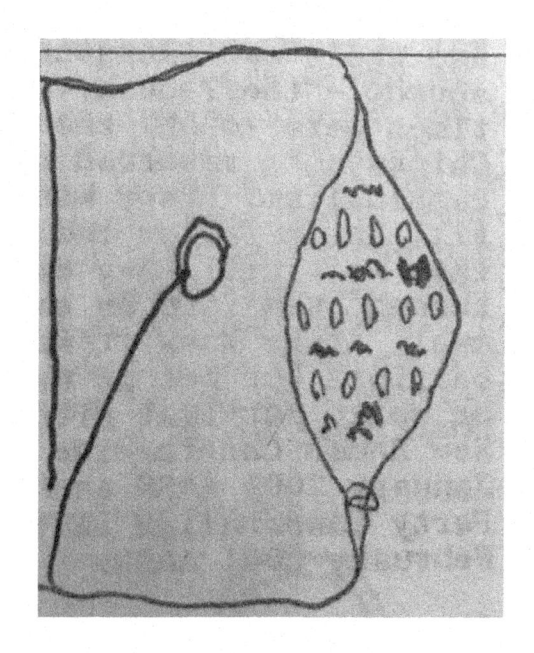

Aztec Deer Stalking: Aztec killed peccary (60-pound pig-like animal) and white-tailed deer at point blank range. How did they do it? They covered themselves in deer skins. Once the deer were spotted they moved towards the deer while they were hunkered under their deer skin. No doubt the deer saw them and weren't alerted. The Aztecs stalked right up to the deer launching their arrows or spears into the unsuspecting deer.

Note: Deer don't habitually look up in trees searching for predators and neither do other North American non-predator big game animals like horses, donkeys, antelope,... Take this into consideration on your next hunt. But keep in mind, the hunter's movement and scent must be absent so not to alert the big game.

Aztec Duck Hunting: Aztecs had a neat trick to hunt plenty of ducks. From the months of October thru March, huge flocks of migratory ducks, geese,,... landed to winter in the warmer climate. The savvy Aztec hunters let them eat, rest, and socialize all they wanted during the day. But at dusk, the Aztec hunters were hunkered down nearby hiding.

On cue, they'd rush the huge swarms of ducks and geese making a lot of noise. The swarms of ducks and geese would naturally and immediately take-off upward to the safety of the skies. But the savvy Aztecs already had a suspended horizontal net made from plant cordage set-up above a small section of the unsuspecting ducks, geese,...

Upon take-off, plenty of ducks and geese flew right into the net where they were tangled, or damaged their wings and fell back into the water. Each day at dusk, the savvy Aztec hunters used this same hunting trick to catch plenty of dinner vittles.

Note: Ducks, geese,... tend to migrate at the <u>west side</u> of streams, lakes ponds,... when breeding. See *Tangling Bird Catcher*.

Aztec Duck Sticks: You've heard of rabbit sticks to capture rabbits and other small game. Well why not use the same stick for ducks and call it a duck stick? And that's exactly what Aztec hunters did. They hunted ducks, geese, and other fowl by throwing a *"curved sticks"* at them. They were made this way for not only for flight but to cause injury on impact to at least incapacitate the prey. You can bet the leading edge of the duck stick was sharp instead of blunt for penetration - punch. See *Rabbit Sticks* and *Debilitating Rabbit Sticks* (Choinumne Indians).

Note: Ducks, geese,... tend to migrate at the <u>west side</u> of streams, lakes ponds,... when breeding.

Aztec Fishing: Aztecs made nets from the maguey plant. And with the net, one of the tasks used by their nets was fishing. They made a unique fishing net with pole that looks like our modern day butterfly nets. All they did was simply dip the net in the water where fish were seen or suspected and retrieved the fresh water fish ranging in size from 08 to 12-inches. The fish were cooked whole over hot coals or sauteed over a sauce (ingredients unknown - but try plain ol' butter). For more proof of this fishing technique, see *Dip Net Fishing*.

Aztec Long-Range Weapons: Aztec long-range weapons were the javelin, bow & arrows, and the sling.

a) Javelin: The javelin was light-weight spear propelled by an atlatl. The spear's point was fire-hardened or had an obsidian (volcanic glass) arrowhead. Some javelins had more than one point and had a cord attached to it for retrieval.

b) Bow & Arrows: Bows were no more than 05-feet long. The arrow tips were fire-hardened or they had bone or obsidian arrowheads.

c) Slings: Slings were made from weaved cotton and the ammunition were egg-sized stones. When the sling wasn't being used, it was tied around their head.

d) Atlatl: An atlatl is a device that uses leverage to propel a javelin, spear,... much farther than the thrower could ever throw it himself. The Aztec's atlatl was a 01-foot to 02-foot flat piece of wood. Down the long center was a long grove to accommodate and secure the javelin. At the rear end of the atlatl was a peg that butted up against the rear end of the javelin. At the other forward end of the atlatl were two loops to accommodate the throwers 02 fingers (index and middle fingers). With the thrower securing the atlatl and the javelin in a horizontal position, he propels the atlatl forward and rotating forward. The javelin is forced forward but its velocity dramatically increases as the atlatl is rotated forward.

Aztec Pitfall Trap: Aztecs used pitfall traps for big game. Pitfall traps were dug according to:
- Recent animal activity
- Game trails
- Size of animal (dug for width, length and depth to accommodate animal)

The pitfall trap was camouflaged with a matt of grass and twigs. The depth of the pitfall trap is important so the prey doesn't escape.

Several sharp pointed stakes may be secured within the floor and walls of the pitfall trap so to finish off the animal as it falls into the pitfall trap.

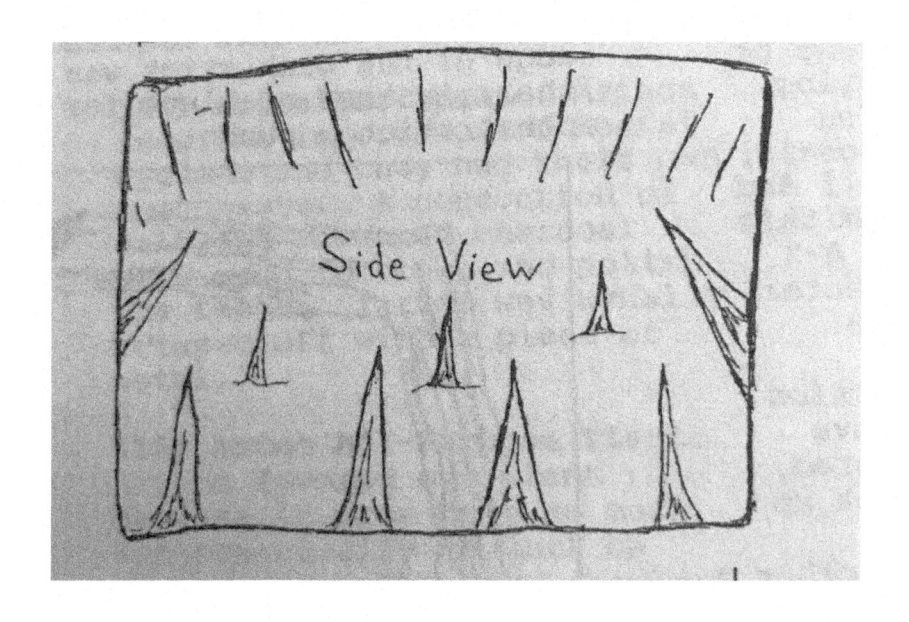

Side View

Aztec Short-Range Weapons: Aztecs had a vicious short-range weapon. It's a 36-in long sword carved from wood. In the knife blade edges were embedded many pieces of sharp obsidian (volcanic glass). The obsidian sword was so vicious, it could cut down a horse. When a piece of obsidian lost its sharpness, it was replaced by another. Aztecs had other short-range weapons like lances, thrusting spears (06 to 10-feet long), knob-headed wooden club, and hatchet.

Bacon Fat (Grease) Shelf Life: The following data comes from one my books: *"Basic, Advanced & Ultra-Advanced Emergency Fire-Starting TOTAL Package!"* I'm sure it will complement the hunting tricks in this book.

Last April 2014 I tried to find out the shelf life for bacon fat (grease). I couldn't find any 1st hand testimonials. So on 15 May 2014, I started my own R & D. I cooked-up some bacon and did my R & D for the shelf life of room temperature bacon fat and the shelf life of refrigerated bacon fat. See the video for my findings.

001) Bacon Fat R & D Notes:

Bacon R & D - Room Temperature

On 151516C May 2014, I took a 16-ounce pack of Hormel Black Label Bacon (12 slices) - Thick Cut and cut it in-half making 24 slices due to the size of the skillet. I cooked all 24 slices of bacon collecting 6.9 ounces of bacon fat. This bacon fat was placed in a 14-ounce can, covered with its own top and placed in a spare room at room temperature. The bacon fat is inspected every week to check if it's gone rancid (smell).

Bacon R & D - Fridge

On 151736C May 2014, I took a 16-ounce pack of Hormel Black Label Bacon (12 slices) - Thick Cut and cut it in-half making 24 slices due to the size of the skillet. I cooked all 24 slices of bacon collecting 5.9 ounces of bacon fat. This bacon fat was placed in a 14-ounce can, covered with a section of Glad Press n Seal and placed in the fridge. The bacon fat is inspected every week to check if it's gone rancid (smell).

Room Temperature Bacon Fat R & D

On 151314C November 2014, I re-checked the bacon fat for any ill smells - nothing. It's been 06-months into the R & D so I decided to give the "Room Temperature" bacon fat the ultimate test. I put a tablespoon of this bacon fat in a frying pan and made scrambled eggs (03 eggs). It was tasty. I had NO ILL effects from eating this 06-month old *Room Temperature"* bacon fat.

Room Temperature Bacon Fat R & D

On 161300C February 2015, I re-checked the bacon fat for any ill smells - nothing. It's been 09-months and 01-day into the R & D so I decided to give the "Room Temperature" bacon fat the ultimate test. I put a tablespoon of this bacon fat in a frying pan and made scrambled eggs (04 eggs). It was tasty. I had NO ILL effects from eating this 09-month old *"Room Temperature"* bacon fat.

Room Temperature Bacon Fat R & D

On 171000C February 2015, I re-checked the bacon fat for any ill smells - nothing. It's been 09-months and 02-days into the R & D so I decided to give the "Room Temperature" bacon fat the ultimate test. I put a tablespoon of this bacon fat in a frying pan and made scrambled eggs (04 eggs). It was tasty. I had NO ILL effects from eating this 09-month old *"Room Temperature"* bacon fat.

Room Temperature Bacon Fat R & D

On 151408C March 2015, I re-checked the bacon fat for any ill smells – nothing. It's been 10-months into the R & D so I decided to give the "Room Temperature" bacon fat the ultimate test. I put a tablespoon of this bacon fat in a frying pan and made scrambled eggs (04 eggs) with diced-up red potatoes, and bits of sliced ham. It was tasty. I had NO ILL effects from eating this 10-month old *Room Temperature* bacon fat.

Room Temperature Bacon Fat R & D

On 041200C June 2015, I re-checked the bacon fat for any ill smells – nothing. **It's been 01-year and 20 days into the R & D**. Cooked 06 eggs with a tablespoon of the bacon fat. Ate 03 eggs with sprinkle salt & pepper. A couple hours later, no ill effects.   END OF R & D.

Bacon R & D - Fridge

On 041230C June 2015, I re-checked the bacon fat for any ill smells – nothing. It's been 01-year and 20 days into the R & D. This bacon fat will probably be good for another year in the fridge.

SEE *'Updated Refrigerated Bacon Fat.'* for the final R & D.

Basket Fish Trap: A The basket fish trap consist of a twenty foot anchor line; several sticks, vines, wire, or chicken wire; that are woven into an oblong cone shaped basket that is approximately two feet long and approximately ten inches wide at its widest point in the center.

The basket fish trap has just one entrance; which has several pointed sticks facing toward the interior of the fish basket. This is so that once the fish enters the basket, it can't leave because it will continuously run into the pointed sticks or wire. Insure to mask the scent of all working pieces of the basket fish trap, including your hands. Bait and channelize as necessary. Secure the anchor line to the basket fish trap and to the shore.

Basket Fish Trap

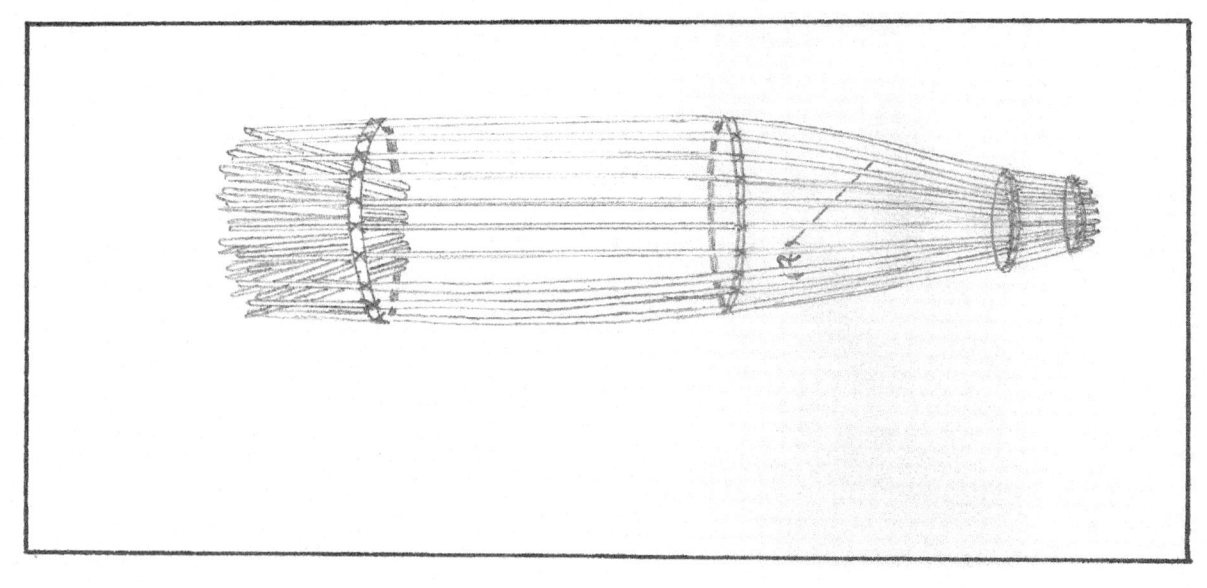

Bear Hunting: In this book, you'll learn how Indians, pioneers, mountainmen,... hunted various species of bears and other animals. This technique differs from all the others. First, in the fall months, the Indians tracked the bear to its hibernation den where it would stay for the winter. Remembering this exact location, the Indians would return months later during the winter months. One technique to wake the sleeping bear and coax it out of its den was to imitate predator birds (eagles, hawks, vultures,...) at the entrance to the den. The squawking of predator birds usually meant a fresh kill which the bear would confiscate. It's not unusual for a bear to temporarily come out of winter hibernation for a snack. The bear would wake-up and sleepily head for the entrance to the den. Arriving at the entrance, it was ambushed by several Indians who clubbed it in the head till it was dead.

Bear Parts: The Naskapi Indians (Labrador Peninsula which is east of the Hudson Bay in Canada) used almost all the parts of the bear. Some parts were forbidden only to be used for sacred worship. However, the following is a list of bear parts and their life-saving uses or concoctions made up of bear parts.

a) Blood Pudding: Blood pudding was made from the bear but specific instructions were not given. However see *"Buffalo Waste Not Want Not"*.

b) Fat Pudding: About 03 - 04 feet of the large intestine were cut-out with the fat adhering to it. A thin stick was placed down the intestine sack where it was tied to the stick.

The thin stick is then pulled through which inverts the large intestine sack inside-out with the adhering fat now inside the large intestine sack. If available, berries are stuffed into the intestine sack. Both ends are tied and the whole intestine sack with contents are boiled in water for an hour. After boiling it is cooled and is eaten cooled as a desert.

When In Rome Do As The Romans Do!

Pioneer folks during the gold rush days of the 1800s, were supplied with the same food they ate from their homeland but they still deteriorated and died. Why? In their cold weather environments their body lacked the nutrients it needed like fat. Fat is actually needed to transport nutrients throughout the body, it's also a good fuel source for your body to help keep you warm. And fat is a very IMPORTANT part of the Naskapi diet as well as all the other northern tribes throughout the world. If those gold seekers had the necessary amount of fat in their diet, they would have survived.

c) Bear Soup: To make bear soup all they did was heat some bear grease. Some say bear grease has a sweet taste to it and of course is full of fat and other nutrients.

d) Bear Head & Neck: The bear's head and neck were placed on a spit and roasted. Surprisingly it provided a lot of meat. However, the women and children were forbidden to eat these parts of the bear.

e) Leg Bones: The leg bones of bears were made into skinning knives. One end of the long bone was broken obliquely (slanting - sloping edge). This jagged part was scraped against - between the rawhide and the carcass separating the hide from the carcass.

Other leg bones from caribou, lynx, moose,... were also used. If you can use some flint rock, that will do fine or some other *"sharpened - carved"* flat rock.

f) Shoulder Blade Bones: The shoulder blade bones were formed into spoons and ladles. The spoons and ladles were used as eating utensils including sipping bear soup.

g) Bear Teeth: Bear teeth were used as toggles for fastening. Holes were drilled into the canine teeth (between the incisors-front teeth and the first bicuspids or 1st premolars). The teeth were used like toggles and helped to fasten items together.
Now you don't need to go whoopin on a bear to get some fastners. Carve some pieces of wood and fire em' up in the campfire to harden them. You can either drill a hole in them with your knife or carve-out the center (like a trap & snare trigger) to secure the string.

h) Awls And Needles: Awls (drilling holes for leather and other materials) and sewing needles for making clothes, snowshoes footgear, shelters,... were made from bear bones. The bear bones were cracked and splintered. From the splintered parts, awls and sewing needles were fabricated. You can use just about any animal bones to make awls and sewing needles.

i) Bear Meat: The bear meat of course was eaten. It was cut into square-like sections about the size of a shot glass. These were the portions eaten by those attending the bear meal. I have found no mention of any extra bear meat being dried for future use. Salt (preservative) was also avoided when preparing the bear meat.

j) Bear Hide: The bear hide has many uses like making tee-pee or dome shaped wigwams (shelter). The Naskapi also used other animal hides for wigwams. Birch bark is even used to make wigwam shelters.

Note: The material was probably tanned for long-term use.

k) Bone Food: Bones from various animals are cracked open to retrieve and eat the very nutritious bone marrow.

Beavers: Now let me give a few ways those intelligent beavers were successfully trapped by savvy Indians and fur trappers. Beavers are almost extinct in Europe, they're being re-established in Canada, and are having a comeback in the United States (Castor Canadensis). Beavers can live up 20-years. The beavers eyesight isn't great but it can still pick-up movement (movement always attracts the eyes) backed-up by its keen sense of smell. Its short hears pick-up noise above the surface and below water. Its forepaws and hindpaws claw, dig, grab, and hold to build its dams and beaver lodges. Its webbed hindpaws along with its flat ping pong like tail gives it its after-burner speed in water and steering.

Its hind paws are also used to spread the waterproofing castoreum on its fur during grooming. To evade predators it will dive deep. It has the ability to stay submerged for up to 05-minutes and can swim up to a half mile underwater without coming up for air. But records show beavers trapped underwater have survived for up to 15-minutes underwater.

Kits are trained progressively from learning what foods to eat (shoots, buds,...) to reconning their habitat to sleeping outside the lodge on river banks in a nook or hollow of grass to learn of their habitat especially of their natural predators. The beavers sharp incisors can fall trees that are 02 to 08 inches in diameter but have been known to fall trees that are up to 30-inches in diameter.

The beaver lodge is dome-shaped and about 08-feet wide and 03-feet high. The floor is covered with bark, grass, and wood chips. It has a central chamber and may have adjoining storage rooms. The beaver lodge usually has two entrances.

The dam it builds can be as big as 05-feet high, 10-feet wide and 1,000-feet long. It uses vegetation that grows into all the lumber to strengthen the dam. To build its lodge and dam, it carves out canals that fill with water so it can easily float heavy wooden sections from land to the lodge and dam instead of dragging the heavy weighted wood materials.

Beaver Bank Trap: Beavers had to leave their lodges to get supplies to build their lodges, dams, make repairs, and gather food. And those supplies and food were on land. Trappers placed their traps on the banks where they observed places where beavers exited and entered the water. There they placed their traps. But to insure the beaver entered the trap they placed a few drops of castoreum that compelled the beaver to exit or enter the water where the beaver trap was placed. See *Hypnotizing Castoreum*.

Beaver Blow Holes: During cold winter months, the water turned to ice. The beaver was safe in its lodge but it still ventured out swimming under the ice. And to get air it went to bubbles under the ice or took a quick breath through small holes in the ice. Indians waited patiently at these already formed blow holes or made them to get the beaver to come to them. When they arrived they were speared.

Beaver Dam Traps: Those engineering beavers built dams that protected their lodges. And when their dams leaked too much water and the water level dropped they knew it real quick. Trappers disturbed the dam and placed a trap exactly where the beaver would work to repair the damage but placed the trap a few inches under water. The critter would come along and step in the steel trap holding it in place.

Beaver Deadfall: As you know a deadfall must have specific requirements for it to work. It must have channelization, a trigger, bait, and weight to fall on the critter to trap and/or kill it. And Indians were experts with different deadfalls designed for a specific prey and in this case the beaver deadfall.

The beaver deadfall was placed on top of the beaver dam. The deadfall was U-shaped (channelization) made of 06 stakes with 03 sets of stakes side-to-side and parallel to the other 03 stakes with each set about a foot apart and secured by rawhide. The open end faced the shore.

In the back of the U-shape was a forked-stake with the Y-shape facing up and secured in the dam. At the crook of the Y (trigger), a hefty piece of tasty aspen or cottonwood (bait) was placed which held a tilting heavy log (weight). The beaver would eventually go to the top of his lodge to sunbathe, groom, and lookout. The critter would smell and see the tasty bait and enter the deadfall to take a bite and *"trigger"* the deadfall to fall on it. Even if it tried to escape as quick as it could, backing out isn't one of the beaver's forte. The heavy deadfall would drop on the beaver trapping and/or killing it.

Beaver Drowning Trap: Trappers often had beavers break free of their traps with the beaver leaving part of its leg behind. To prevent this, fur trappers came up with a better idea to quickly drown the beaver after it was trapped. All steel traps were anchored but in this case they were anchored with a 15-foot chain. The beaver would get caught, drag the heavy trap back into the water where it weighed down the beaver who eventually drowned. The fur trappers didn't worry about retrieving the drowned beaver right away for they knew the cold water would preserve the entire beaver and valuable fur for several days.

Beaver Ring Trap: Another beaver trap to trap, drown, and preserve the beaver underwater was the beaver ring trap. It consisted of a thin pole of aspen or cottonwood and a ring of chains that slid down the pole. This is how it worked.

The thin pole or sturdy sapling was anchored upside down in 04 to 05 feet of water. It had a small branch or so of tasty food (wood) that held the ring up. As the beaver gnawed on the small piece of branch that held the ring, the ring dropped. Once this happened the beaver had only one place to go - down (dive dive dive). The ring also dropped down quickly trapping the beaver which drowned and preserved the beaver underwater for days.

Note: The drowning traps not only trapped, drowned, and preserved the beaver under the cold water. It also prevented predators from getting to valuable beaver parts.

Protective Beaver Fur: Beaver furs were valuable especially winter furs that were of a better quality. Between November and April, the beaver fur is denser, softer, and more silky. Beaver furs were exceptional for felting. A single fur particle shows that it overlaps itself like a juniper leaf (conifer) that provides for superior felting. Felting is when a fabric of matted, compressed animal fibers like beaver, wool, are sometimes mixed with vegetable or synthetic fibers to make soft fuzzy fabric. It's done by pressing the fur and other fabrics together with steam and hot water which turns it into felt.

Beaver fur made all types of warm protective clothing like hats, coats, gloves, shoes, robes,.... and proved to be protective during cold winter environments.

Old Bachelor Beavers: The Indians called them 'old bachelor beavers.' These bachelor beavers are different than regular beavers.

They don't build beaver lodges, they don't build beaver dams, and they have no family. They stay to themselves. Their shelter isn't as obvious as a beaver lodge, it's a dug-out hole(s). Fur trappers used deadfalls and steel traps to capture them. For bait they used poplar branches.

I surely hoped you learned some neat survival applications about beavers and have a whole lot more respect for those busy engineers. Remember these applications as well as all others you already learned and will learn can be *"tweaked"* to other survival applications for other critters in totally different environments to save your only life Anytime Anywhere. But we're not done yet. We're not even 1/3rd through this book. Go grab some coffee and come right back.

Bird Pit Trap: Indians wanted those eagle feathers for their war bonnets. Here's a technique the Indians used to capture eagles. But leave the federally protected bird alone. This technique can also be used on other unprotected birds for a quick meal. Heck, you could use it for bigger game.

Ingredients: Shovel, blind, bait (live rabbit or stuffed rabbit).

Step 01: Go to high ground and dig a small pit to accommodate the hunter(s). High ground offers easier detection by small game rather that the concealing low ground. Plus the scent of the bait will carry throughout the area more easily.

Step 02: Make a cover from natural surrounding vegetation for the pit. Insure you're able to see through the this material and at the same time you'll need a small aperture to reach through to grab the bird or small game. This will be both your pit cover and blind.

Step 03: A hide could be dug or you could use the natural terrain without digging. Once inside the hide, secure the rabbit to the top of the blind near the aperture. All one has to do now is wait. Once you hear a raucous outside and the rabbit screaming (squealing) bloody murder, you know the eagle's out there**. They quickly reached out and grabbed the eagle by its legs. Grasping it and pulling it into the hide, they broke its neck real quick or face a repeated attack by the eagles powerful flesh-ripping beak.

Note: ** Other critters might show up before eagles. Dangerous critters like badgers, bobcats, cougars, coyotes, foxes, wolves,...

Black Bag Big Game Pitfall Trap: The following trap & snare is still used today in East Africa and in Australia. The pitfall trap works very well. It contains the fallen critter and immediately incapacitates it till it loses consciousness due to loss of blood followed immediately by death. I like this trap & snare because it's a *"set it up and forget"* trap & snare. The following are step-by-step directions for a Pitfall Trap & Snare. We'll pretend we're using this pitfall for a white-tailed deer which are very common throughout North America and Europe.

Ingredients: Digging tools, knife, 10 sharpened sticks (02-feet by 02-inch), branches, vegetation, dirt, bait, field-expedient ladder, and charcoal.

Step 01: Assess the location of the pitfall. Consider game trails of the species you want to capture, tracks, scat, natural vegetation (growing or moveable) to support channelization, soil (digability), and the habits & migration of the critter, and camouflage & descenting materials. Also consider bait you can use to get that critter to walk into the pitfall. You're hungry, you want that critter walking into your pitfall very soon, NOT next month or next season. Waiting up to a week - max is a reasonable time to wait.

Step 02: Estimate and mark the dimensions of the pitfall. Also consider the depth of the pitfall (at least twice the height of the critter). The long axis (length) of the pitfall should coincide with the game trail. You want that critter walking in lengthwise to the pitfall not the width-wise to prevent escape.

Step 03: Begin digging the pitfall. The dirt from the pitfall can be used as channelization. Dig the dimensions of your pitfall (rectangle) and to the depth that is at least twice the height of the critter the pitfall is designed for. Bring you field-expedient ladder into the pitfall with you.

Step 04: Once the pitfall is excavated to your dimensions the next step is to install sharpened stakes that will incapacitate and eventually kill the critter. Get some thick branches and cut 10 sharpened sticks that are 02-feet long by 02-inches wide. You can char the points over a fire to harden and insure they're penetrating sharp.

Step 05: Now you're going to place 06 sharpened stakes in the bottom of the pitfall and 02 sharpened stakes on each side wall. When that critter falls through the cover blind into the pitfall, its falling weight alone will have it penetrating 1 or more sharpened stakes - all it takes is 01 but you can bet half the sharpened stakes will find their mark.

Now take your knife and dig 06 narrow holes to accommodate the 06 sharpened stakes so their imbedded 01-foot in the ground and 01-foot of each stake is exposed. Next, place 02 stakes on each sidewall. The 01-foot narrow holes should be dug at a 30-degree angle.

Now when that critter falls into the pitfall, it's falling weight will have its body penetrate 01 to several of the stakes. But critters aren't stupid. You have to cover the opening of the pitfall.

Step 06: CAREFULLY climb out of the pitfall using your field-expedient ladder. You don't want to be a victim to your own trap & snare so be careful. Take several thin bare branches and place them across the width of the pitfall so they're a few inches apart. Place flat vegetation over the branches so the entire pitfall is covered.

Step 07: Here's a better cover if you have it. Take a section of plastic (or poncho) or 'black bags - opened up' and smear it with any type of oil - personal care product or even car oil. Stretch the section of plastic over the sticks as above in Step 06 and secure it so it doesn't move.

Now LIGHTLY sprinkle the same dirt as the surrounding dirt in the immediate area (camouflage) on the plastic. That dirt will stick and stay on the section of plastic and blend in real nice. A small branch or so may compliment the covering.

I know what you want to ask: *"Does the pitfall have to have a cover?"* NO. The pitfall will work without a cover. I'd surely use one cause like I've always said *"those critters are smarter than most people think."*

Note: The more traps and snare you have established the higher the odds of your success and dinner vittles! And consider dehydration. Digging is hard work no matter the time of year.

Warning: Mark the area for the pitfall - animals can't read nor identify your warning signs. It will warn & remind you and other survivors of its location cause when your physical attributes deteriorate so will your mental faculties - believe me!

Black Bag Dip Net: Take a sturdy looong branch and cut off all branches so its bare so you have 15-20 foot branch that tapers to a thin point at its end. Take 05 of your cut-off branches and cut-off all their smaller branches so they're bare. What you are going to do is carefully bend back the tip of your 15-20-foot branch. Tieing in the other bare branches with the end portion of the 15-20-foot branch, form a <u>sturdy hoop</u> with a diameter of 01 to 03 1/2-feet. Now take your black bag and cut thirteen 04 1/2-foot strips by 01-inch. Twist 08 strips and tie-in each and to form a CLOSED basketball-type hoop.

Take the other 05 strips and twist them and tie them horizontally at 05 different levels (bottom to top) to complete the net. Make a small incision into the vertical strips weaving the horizontal strips to the vertical strips. This is your *Dip Net*.

Take it to your target site where there are fish and sink it into the water about 03-feet below the surface. When you see any fish above the net, raise the *Dip Net* trapping the fish and bring it to shore. Finish it off by sharply hitting it between the eyes with your weapon or bite off the top of the head (brain). See *Dip Net Fishing*.

Note: Not recommended for fast current rivers. Use in shallow water and slow moving rivers, streams,...

WARNING: Avoid this survival application if you're a non-swimmer, weak swimmer or previously injured.

Black Bag Fish Trap: Them fish just like all critters like shelters for protection from predators, the elements and to use to ambush their prey. Well you can use a black bag to make a quick shelter for fish and may be some other aquatic critters.

Find a slow moving river or stream. You'll need running water to keep the *Fish Trap* inflated. The site must be at least 04-feet deep. Once you've found a spot, lets prepare the black bag first. Open the black bag and begin by cutting approximately 50 01-inch incisions throughout the black bag. The incisions let the black bag *"breathe"* so the water flow pressure isn't great enough to take it downstream. Plus it allows fresh water to flow through the black bag. Secure the very top of the bag and tie a tight overhand in it.

Then secure a line (dental floss) to the overhand knot and secure the other end to the nearside bank. Place the black bag in the water and let it inflate with water. Weigh down the front opening end with a few rocks. To INSURE the black bag stays open at the mouth, you may secure 02 sticks forming a cross at its opening. You may want to add a tumble weed or so to the inside to add to the "shelter effect."

Small fish will seek the shelter and bigger fish will follow. After a day or two, simply pick-up the *Fish Trap* real slow with the opening end skyward and bring it to shore letting the water leak out so the bag doesn't break open with all the water weight. Secure all the big fish for vittles and smaller fish can be set free to attract more big fish once you reset the *Fish Trap*.

WARNING: Avoid this survival application if you're a non-swimmer, weak swimmer or previously injured.

Black Bag Shelter Trap: I'm telling you, critters like dark places of shelter for protection against the elements and predators. Plus depending on the critter, they may use that shelter to attract and ambush their prey.

Before you begin, descent your hands by rubbing them in cold ashes from your firepit or washing them in mud. And have some standing by for later. Find a nook & cranny place in the woods you'd like to go if you were a small to medium sized critter. Look for tracks, scat, rub marks, fur,... Once you found your site, take your bag and place about 15 - 25-pounds of dirt in it. The dirt is to weigh it - anchor it down, plus it provides insulation for the critter.

With the opening downwind, stuff the black bag with non-thorny green vegetation. Go away from your site when gathering the freshly cut vegetation. Place some mud or ashes on all the ends that were cut or pulled away from their source so the critter doesn't smell freshly cut vegetation that will warn them of danger. The vegetation inflates the bag. Next, surgically remove vegetation to make room for a homsteading critter to enter and bed down. Now place more vegetation on and around the shelter to camouflage it. Place FREE bait inside to attract the critter to his new home. Loosen up the dirt near and around the opening so to capture tracks.

After a few days or a week or more, inspect the shelter. If you see evidence of a critter and know its type. You have a wide variety of traps & snares you can use. Or if you have a weapon, you lay in wait and ambush the critter as it enters, lays, or exits the shelter. Once you know it's in the shelter, you can be located just about anywhere and peg it without sighting the actual animal inside the shelter. You already know where it's laying inside the shelter, estimate the location and fire. Odds are high you'll hit its body.

You can also use a *'blocking pole.'* Upon approaching the shelter, quietly and quickly insert the 'blocking pole', thus blocking the animal's escape. You'll have to immediately finish it off especially if it's a predator type animal that will put up a good fight. See *Den Trap*.

Blood Pudding: Blood pudding was made by filling the buffalo's stomach with its own blood and then cooked above the radiating heat of hot coals.

Bola: The bola is another proven weapon used against small game, big game and even man. Below are the details to make your own bola.

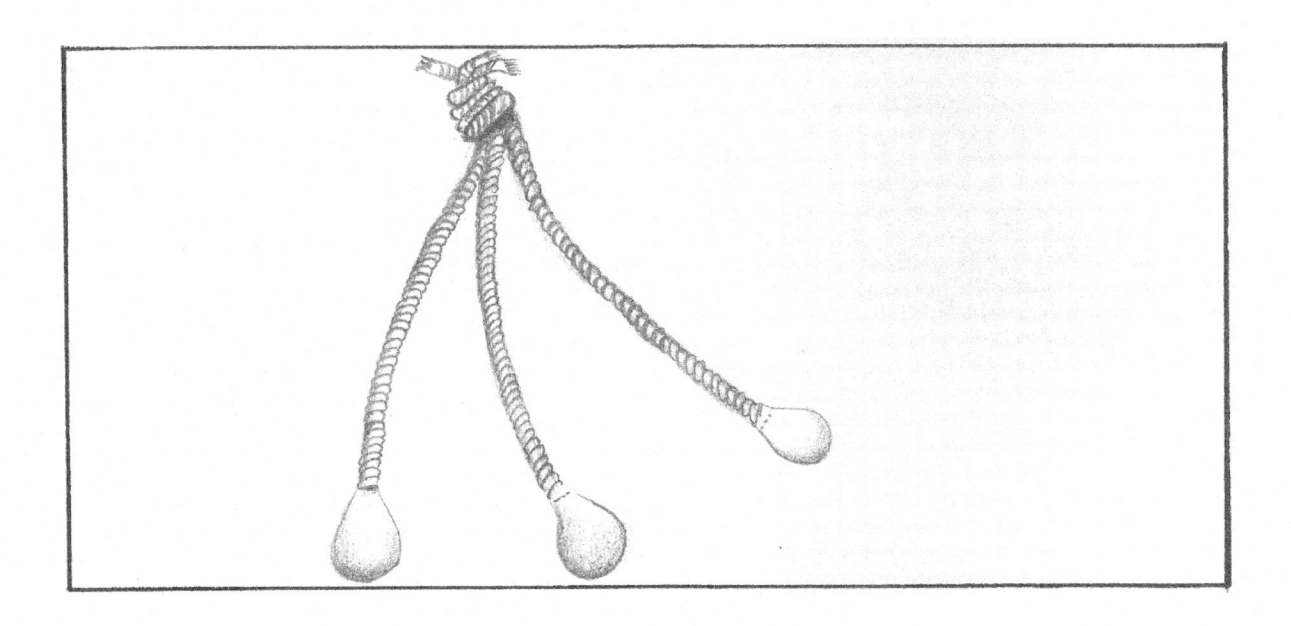

Ingredients Needed to Build a Bola:
The necessary ingredients for a Bola are 03 strands of 1/4 inch cordage or thick string, or rawhide. The length of each strand should be the length of the throwers arm or about 20 inches, 03 01-pound weights (equal in size), 03 pouches (leather, cloth...) to accommodate each weight and a heavy duty sewing needle and nylon thread.

How to build and use the Bola:
Take the 03 strands of cordage, string or rawhide, even them up and securely tie them together at one end.

Next, take your three weights and place them in their respective pouches. Take your sewing needle and thread and sew the weights inside their respective pouches.

Next, securely sew each pouch to one of the strands of 1/4 inch cordage, rawhide...

The Bola is used to *"wrap, tangle & tie-up"* the legs, wings... of wild game. It does this as the Bola thrown toward its intended wild game, the 03 strands are spread in flight. Once the Bola hits its intended target, due to the momentum of each of the three strands, they begin to change direction which causes the strands to *"wrap, tangle & tie"* around the wild games legs, wings...

The Bola is thrown by placing your index and middle-finger of your throwing-hand in between the 03 strands - separating them. They must be separated so that once the Bola is in-flight, the 03 strands are spread (not tangled).

To throw the Bola, swing it above your head in an arc, aim & release it at your target (legs & wings). The three strands of the Bola should spread. The weights will do this. Once the Bola makes contact, it will *"wrap, tangle & tie-up"* around the wild game's legs, wings...

Bottle Trap: A The bottle trap consist of a hole (that is large on the bottom and small on the top), a few rocks and some large deadfall like logs, tree bark, clumps of branches. Dig a hole so that it is approximately two feet deep and is shaped like a upside-down cone.

It must be large at the bottom and small at the top. Place some deadfall over the hole so that it is about two four inches off the ground. Rodents, snakes may caught in this trap once they seek the cover of the deadfall.

The prey will fall or venture into the hole and will be unable to crawl out because of the shape of the hole. Caution must be taken when checking the bottle trap in case of any snakes. Insure to mask the scent of all working pieces of the bottle trap, including your hands. Camouflage, bait, and channelize.

Bottle Trap

Branch Snare: A branch snare is similar to the Simple Snare. It consist of a noose placed over a trail or den hole and attached to a firmly a sturdy branch that has some weight to it.

The snare is anchored to the branch itself. Insure the branch is at least 03-times the weight of the prey you intend to snare so when the prey is caught it is unable to evade too far due to the heavy branch. Insure that the noose is large enough to fit over the intended prey's head. As the prey moves through the noose it will become tighter around its neck. The animal will struggle and the noose becomes tighter - thus secured by the noose and heavy branch. Wire is the best material to use for this type of snare because it will not loosen up like cordage. The bait for this snare is the prey attempting to leave or enter the den and using it's run/game trail.

Branch Snare

Bread Of The Desert: The Bread of the Desert are date fruits from the date palms. One-hundred foot date palm trees grow in the northern half of the Sahara as well as on the Mediterranean coast and offer nutritious oblong date fruits. Dates to the nomads and others in Africa are what maize is to Indians and what rice is to Asians. Dates are also an important food supply to many animals. After 10-years of maturity, the date palm start bearing fruit and continues to bear fruit for approximately 100-years. One date palm bears approximately 40 to 170 pounds of dates each year.

Date palms are often *"tapped"* for palm juice like maple trees are tapped for maple syrup. The palm juice can be drank like it is, it taste like coconut milk. The palm juice is also allowed to ferment which turns into a smelly alcoholic drink. The palm juice is also allowed to evaporate; once evaporated it leaves palm sugar.

The tall date palm provides shade and this shade is used to plant apricots, grapefruit, lemons, oranges, peaches, and pomegranates.

Dates were made into a marmalade by packing them into a goat skin and pressed. Dates were also pressed into bricks which kept long and easily transported.

1st Note: When date palms are tapped for palm juice, it shortens the life of the date palm.

2nd Note: Dates you buy in your local grocery store keep much longer cause they're loaded with preservatives. Date palms grow in North America, but it's unknown if date palm groves exists for annual harvests. If they do exists, they're probably harvested in Florida and California.

3rd Note: There are approximately 1,000 plants in the Sahara. Due to the lack of water, these plants have adapted and aren't clumped together but spread out. Nomads have become experts in which plants can support their lives with respect to the *8 Elements of Survival* (Fire, Water, Shelter, First-Aid, Signal, Food, Weapons, and Navigation).

Buck's Travel Corridor: Also called a *"rub line."* Savvy whitetail bow hunters RECON (pre-season scouting) their specific hunting area a few weeks before hunting season and look for the *"Buck's Travel Corridor."* A travel corridor is where during summer and fall months, whitetail deer travel from bedding sites to feeding sites.

Along these routes, the deer stop and rub against trees and these "rubs" are easily identifiable, the bark of trees big and small are completely rubbed off showing a lighter color that stands out. Once hunters find the *"Buck's Travel Corridor"* or *"rub line"* along this corridor somewhere is where they place their deer stand.

The deer stand is up in a tree cause deer rarely look up as long as your motionless and are downwind (scent) of that four-legged dinner meal. The deer stand is also placed in front of backdrop vegetation so the hunter isn't skylighted against the sky.

Buffalo Waste Not Want Not: The buffalo was the main entre and most used critter for most Indian tribes on the Great Plaines. At their peak, 50,000,000 buffalo were estimated to roam the Great Plaines of North America. Nothing was wasted. The liver was eaten raw, many times right at the kill site. Even the nose, tongue, and hump were eaten raw. The nutritious bone marrow was eaten. Buffalo sausage was made filling the buffalos intestines with chopped buffalo meat. The sausage was then roasted or boiled. Blood pudding was made by filling the buffalo's stomach with its own blood and then cooked above the radiating heat of hot coals. The buffalo hide was made for robes, clothing, moccasins, teepee coverings, shields, bullboats, containers of all sorts (arrows, medicine, jerky, food grain, tobacco, blanket,...).

Bones were used for all sorts of tools (sewing needles, scrapers, awls (pointed tool to drill holes in wood, leather,...), hoes, painting tools,...). The buffalos sinew was used for string for sewing, bow string,... The horns were used for containers to carry water. The horns and hooves were heated to make glue which had many uses. The buffalo's stomach was used as a water container and cooking using the radiating heat of hot coals. The rough buffalo tongue was not only used as a food source, but dried it was a hair brush. Buffalo droppings were gathered, dried, and used as a fuel source. Like cow pies, it didn't put out a lot of light but it did provide heat.

That buffalo critter had many life-saving uses and reflects the many uses of all those other outdoor critters.   Remember *"Waste Not Want Not."*

Note: I added this segment in here to demonstrate the number of uses for most small & big game.

Caged Gill Net (Triple Catch): A The caged gill net consist of twelve sticks of small diameter that are approximately fifteen inches in length; fifty feet of cordage; a thirty foot anchor line; a float large enough to hold the weight of the caged gill net (if a floating device is desired); a short line and a hook; and a gill net large enough to cover the entire cage.

The first step in the construction of the caged gill net is to take the twelve sticks and tie them together at the ends so that you end up with a square cube. Cutting grooves in the sticks so that the cordage doesn't slip may improve the stability of the cage.

Once the cage is complete, test it for stability. Place the gill net around the cage so that it covers all six openings of the cage. Insure that only one layer of the gill net is exposed for each opening.

Tie-in and secure the gill net to the frame of the cage. Any extra portion of the gill net can be bunched-up and secured to the frame without cutting it off.

Next place the short line and hook through the top portion of the gill net and tie it off to the net.

To bait the hook, simply pull up on the line, bait it and drop it back through the gill net.

Next tie-in your floater/anchor line to the top of the cage. The caged gill net lures the fish by the bait. They can approach from any side. Once they swim through one of the apertures of the gill net, they are caught.

In case they completely slip through one of the apertures of the gill net, they may not find their way out of the caged gill net through the same aperture. The fish may also get caught on the way out through one of the apertures! They may also get caught by hook within the caged gill net.

When placing the gill net in the water make sure the top portion (gill net) of it doesn't flip over. If this happens, the bait will float to either side and outside the caged gill net leaving the caged gill net baitless. Once the gill net is in place, you'll need to tie-in the anchor line to the caged gill net which will be anchored at the shore. This is to insure that the oversized fish doesn't swim off with your caged gill net. Insure to mask the scent of all working pieces of the caged gill net, including your hands. Bait and channelize as necessary.

The Caged Gill Net may not be very sturdy and may wobble. As long as it's in one position it will suffice. However, you can make it real sturdy by carving & matching each stick where they join. You can also add cross-members to stabilize it.

Caged Gill Net

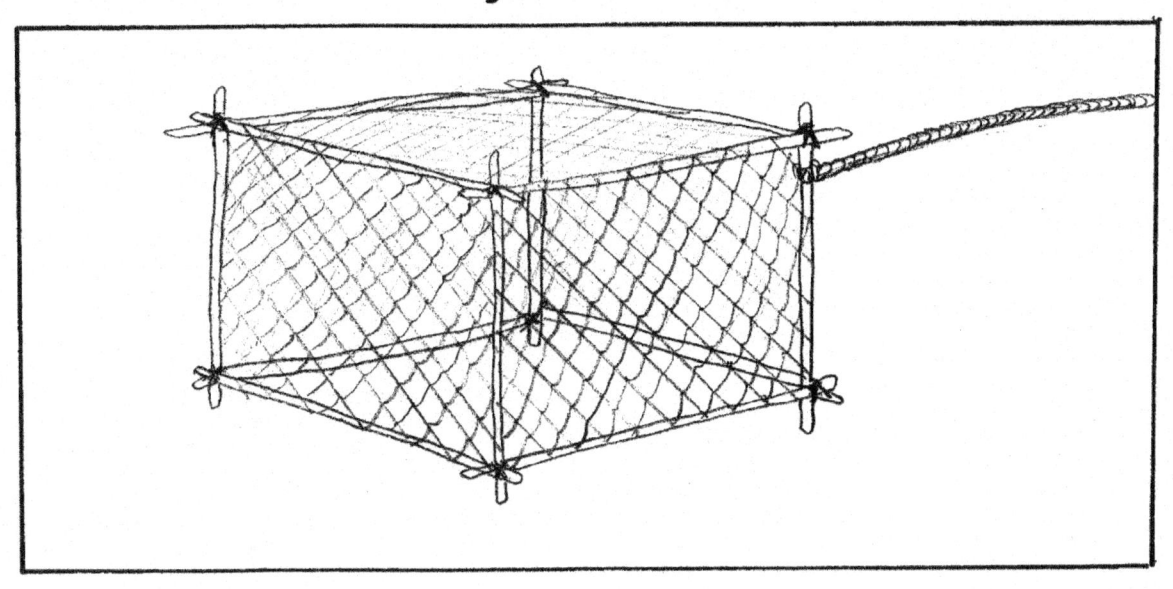

Caribou Hunting: Various tribes in northern North America knew where to hunt caribou. All they had to do was to find moss. Caribou like the moose, provided large amounts of food, fat and natural tools & equipment for the hunters. Hundreds of years ago, massive herds of caribou migrated hundreds of miles northward (where tundra - moss is plentiful), then returning southward, grazing on moss. In forested areas, moss is not as plentiful. Plus moss, like lichen, seaweed,... can be used as an emergency food source. Plus it can be used for insulation (shelters, bedding,...) and tinder for fire-starting.

Catching Scorpions: If you want to hate life, I mean really hate life, get stung by a scorpion (depending on the species.) It will be a painful multi-day 24-hour torture you will remember for the rest of your life!

The STINGING PULSATING pain from the venom is contained in the scorpions 02 venom glands and hollow injector located in its tail. Like I told you about treating all snakes, treat them as if they're all venomous; treat all scorpions like they're VERY VENOMOUS. Now here ARE 02 neat survival tricks to catch those stinging scorpions for food.

a) Whistling While You Work: Scorpions have been around for approximately 440 million years. Scorpions are eaten in Egypt, Morocco,... There are certain people that eat and capture scorpions. And by their passed-down profession & heredity from generations before are immune to the scorpion's very painful sting. Scorpion eaters are called into empty houses taken over by scorpions. The professional sits in the center of the room and begins to softly whistle! Yes, softly whistle, where scorpions would be compelled to leave their hiding places and advance from all directions to the whistling professional. The professional would then pick-up the scorpions placing them in a bag. Neat trick uh! Why whistling attracts scorpions is unknown - RFIR (Requires Further Intensive Research)!

But for you non-whistling, tone-deaf folks, here's a trick to capture scorpions used down in southwest United States!

b) Glowing Scorpions: Scorpions in their dark cold desert environment love the heat given off by the black asphalt from the daylight heat and beaming burning sun. At night, scorpion catchers in Arizona & Texas search the road's dark shoulders using a hand-held black light. The black light magically light-up the scorpion's exoskeleton (frame) having a glow to it you can't miss!

Those glowing critters are carefully secured and held captive in a container. The scorpions range in size from 03 to 07-inches in length! Again, BE CAREFUL of their stinging tail!

WARNING: A small percentage may be allergic to eating insects. If you're allergic to shellfish, this may be an indicator that you're already allergic to insects. Insure you do an *Edibility Test* at the end of this book.

Caw Caw Caw: If you can *"caw caw caw"* like a crow you may get a chance to lure these birds in at point blank range. However another luring trick you might want to consider is to use previous caught crows (dead) as decoys. Simply take some sticks and place the birds on the ground like they're alive. Remember to place some facing into the wind as if they just landed and place others in patches as if they were feeding, watering, resting,... Add some almost authentic *"caw caw caw"* from your concealed position and wait for the critters to get within point blank range.

Chipmunk Call: Before I give you this neat survival trick let me tell you about chipmunks cause the following data ties into how Indians captured these critters for dinner vittles.

There are approximately 25 species of this small rodent that's native to Asia, Europe, and North America. Chipmunks have reddish-brown fur, with white and black stripes on the back and long, furry tails.

Their cheek pouches extend to the back of the head and in some species extend to its shoulders. Chipmunks are distinguished from ground squirrels by their striped faces. They feed on grain, nuts, birds' eggs, and various insects.

During winter months, chipmunks may live in burrows, where it stores food for winter. They remain in their burrow until spring, but it comes out on warm days during winter. Chipmunks mate starting in March and after a gestation of 31 days the female produces a litter of three to five chipmunks. The offspring are mature in only 90-days (by July) and able to breed the following spring.

Chipmunks' sounds are a loud *"chip"* and a rapid trill. Now that you know about these critters here's how those expert Indian hunters captured them for vittles.

Chipmunks were hunted all-year but the best time to hunt them was in March. At this time chipmunks would leave their burrow. Even if there was still snow on the ground, they'd burrow to the surface. Chipmunks liked to socialize at early morning just before sunup and socialize for about 03-04 hours.

The young hunters planned their hunt ahead of time assigning hunting duties and preparing weapons and chipmunk caller devices. Prior to dawn the hunters positioned themselves in their hunting area. A designated chipmunk caller positioned himself in plain sight sitting down but <u>absolutely motionless</u> (remember movement attract the eyes). To call the chipmunks the young Indian boy used an oat straw. Once the caller started calling the chipmunks with the oat straw, those critters came in all directions. Running around they congregated near the caller. They even ran under and over the <u>motionless</u> caller.

On a command shout from the leader, the <u>motionless</u> hunting party emerged. At the sight of the hunting party the confused chipmunks ran up and down trees. Each Indian hunter had an assigned tree and fired their <u>blunt</u> arrows at their target when at the base of the tree. If he missed his target, the blunt arrow just bounced back in the direction of the hunter. However, these young hunters were excellent marksman with their powerful bows and blunt arrows and more times than not stunned or killed their target with their 1st shot.

Note: Blunt arrows were used instead of sharp pointed arrowheads cause blunt arrows can be re-used immediately. The blunt arrows gave the critter a charlie horse paralyzing it. Sharp pointed arrowheads pierced their target or imbedded themselves in the tree which took too much time to retrieve and refire.

Cloth Sling: The Cloth Sling is very simple to make and with practice can be a worthy weapon against all types of small game.

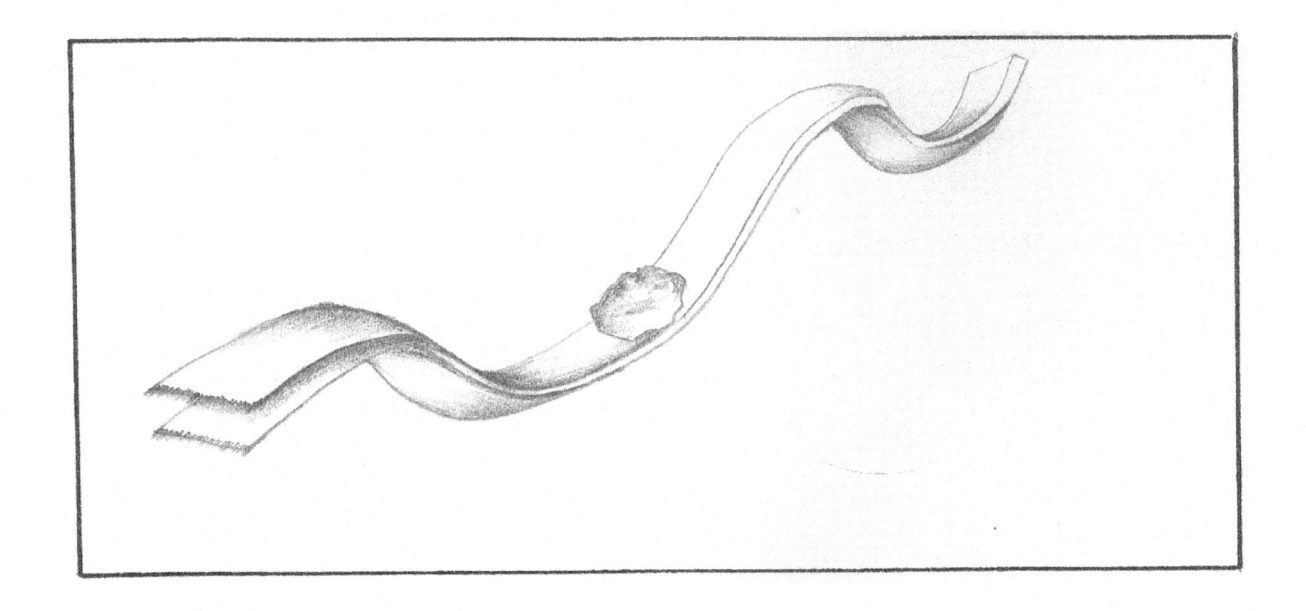

Ingredients Needed to Build a Cloth Sling:
This unique weapon, you'll only need a strip of durable cloth 40-inches long by 03 to 04 inches wide, and a round rock about 03 to 04 pounds.

How to Build and Use the Cloth Sling:
Double-up the strip of cloth. One end of the cloth should be securely wrapped around your throwing hand while the other end is simply grasped by the same hand.

With the Cloth Sling formed and laying vertical, place your weighted round rock inside the cupped sling.

Begin rocking your Cloth Sling back and forth. Begin rotating the cloth Sling in a clock-wise motion (if your right-handed). Increase the rate of rotations till you reach an optimum rate of rotations.

When you estimate that the Cloth Sling is at an almost horizontal position, release one end of the Cloth Sling. The rock should be propelled down range! To obtain accuracy with this survival weapon, practice is recommended.

Civil War Rat Vittles: Elmira Prison, located at Elmira, New York, was a hell hole. As one Confederate POW from Texas put it: *"If there was ever a hell on earth, Elmira prison was that hell."* At Elmira Prison, two observation towers were built just outside the wall to accommodate civilians who paid 15 cents a head to observe the Confederate POWs as they survived at Elmira Prison.

And Elmira Prison had their putrefying Foster's Pond and Andersonville Prison had Andersonville Swamp that was so foul, so squalidly putrid, it aided in growing what seemed like a new species of parasitic maggots that lived up to 18-inches below the putrid, disease-loaded mass of fecal matter. Located inside Andersonville Prison was a stream-fed swamp that collected urine and feces from thousands of POWs on a daily basis. One Union POW related a type of maggot he witnessed: *"The largest crawled out in the hot sand, shed their tail-like appendages; wings would unfold, and an attempt be made to fly; and thousands were clumsily dropping all over the camp. They tumbled into our mush, bedding places, and on the faces of the sick and dying."*

Confederate soldiers held at Elmira POW Prison were starving and turned to capturing rats for food. The rats lived on the banks of Foster's Pond. Confederate POWs lined up along the banks waiting for a rat to leave its burrow. Once sighted the evading rat was pelted with rocks as it ran the gauntlet of screaming POWs. POWs were quoted to state that rat food was: "really very palatable food", "a broiled rat was superb."

According to a diary of a Confederate POW, in September 1864, Confederate POWs at Johnson's Island, Lake Erie, made nightly captures of rats. His diary reads: *"Rats are found to be very good for food, and every night many are captured and slain."*

Coatimundi: I had to add this segment in here to show that critters are very smart. It's beyond instinct. Them critters can contemplate, evaluate, decide,… No, they'll never build a space shuttle but they can THINK!

A relative of the raccoon family, coatimundi are found from the southwestern United States and all the way south to Panama. It looks like a cross between a raccoon and a cat with an extra long furry tail and throw in a long nose. This critter not only taste delicious but it's extremely savvy. While at Fort Gulick, Panama and on the way to the ASP (ammunition supply point), I stopped short of the entrance to the ASP for a family of coatimundis. You know what these critters did? They crossed the road (linear danger area) almost exactly like a combat patrol! Here's what they did:

a) A lone coatimundi (point man) crossed the road alone into the jungle on their farside (right to left).

b) After 20-30 seconds, the main body crossed to the farside with the adults in front and the little coatimundis behind (main body).

c) After about 15 seconds, 02 coatimundis crossed to the farside (rear security).

The coatimundis like a combat patrol treated both the road and the unknown jungle on the farside as danger areas and treated them so with the actions I just described. If I hadn't seen it for myself, I wouldn't believe it. And like I've always said those animal critters are a lot smarter than most people think - even those animal experts. See *Guayaki Coati Hunting*.

Note: During SERE School (SERE Level B), in Panama, our class ate Coatimundi meat and it was super delicious.

Cold Water Diving Reflex: Folks, one of the most unforgiving environments are frigid cold weather environments. Worse yet are **killer cold water environments.** The human body is not designed to hold-up in cold weather environments for any length of time or even short periods. Once the core temperature drops below 98.6 degrees Fahrenheit - problems arise and get worse real quick the lower the body temperature drops. Simple shivering is a sign of hypothermia.

As I said, killer cold water environments are the worst. But there may be a way to **bring back the dead**, it's called *cold water diving reflex*. Let me go back in time and tell you a true story so you can better understand *cold water diving reflex*.

Several years ago during the cold winter months in Fargo, North Dakota, an 11-year old boy with his sled was having fun like any other boy with his sled. The boy and his sled were over frozen water when he fell through the ice. Fargo Rescue and other nearby departments were soon dispatched to the seen. Rescue workers deployed their boats into the water, breaking the ice and probing for the boy's body with grappling poles.

As more and more minutes went by, one would think that there was no hope for the young boy. But the rescue workers knew something most people are unaware of - it's called *cold water diving reflex*. *Cold water diving reflex* not only retards the metabolism but puts the body's main organs in suspended animation to hold-off death! The multiple rescue workers were betting that if they found the boy real soon, *cold water diving reflex* would help them save the boy.

After 45 minutes under water, the boy was finally hooked - they found him. He was brought into the boat where they brought him to shore. His body temperature was only 77-degrees - he was dead dead! Immediate CPR was applied to the boy on the way to the hospital. The paramedics revived the boy! At the hospital, the young boy made a full recovery! He was under the frigid water for 45-minutes and survived! He survived because of *cold water diving reflex*!

Now I'm not sure if *cold water diving reflex* applies only to children only or if it also apples to adults. This subject RFIR. If you know any firemen, paramedics, doctors,... ask them and let me know what they say. Now you understand why I keep telling you "NEVER give-up, there's always a solution." See *Shallow Water Blackout, Hypothermic Water Survival Table* below. And see *Ice Support Measurements Table.*

Hypothermia Water Survival Table!

Water Temperature	Exhaustion & Max Time	Unconscious Survival Time
32.5 F	15-min	15-45 min
32.5-40 F	15-30min	30-90 min
40-50 F	30-60min	01-03 hrs
50-60 F	01-02hrs	01-06 hrs
60-70 F	02-7hrs	02-40 hrs
70-80 F	03-12hrs	03 hours+

1ˢᵗ NOTE: Other considerations are the Survivor's swimming abilities, predators, prior injuries, available flotation equipment or floating debris, weather conditions, soldier's attitude, and other soldiers present and their status (above considerations). See *Ice Support Measurements.*

2ⁿᵈ Note: The night the RMS Titanic sank (14 - 15 April 1912 - Sunday / Monday night) in the North Atlantic Ocean, water temperatures were estimated at 28-degrees Fahrenheit. This would have the Titanic passengers in the water with a survival time of 10-minutes or less. My point to this, is that when submerged in frigid cold water even much less cold water, it could be extremely dangerous. See *Ice Support Measurements Table*.

Comanche Favorite Food: After the 1st day of travel they stopped and the blindfolds taken off. Nelson observed that the Comanches favorite food was horse meat. They cut it in steak size portions and cooked it on a stick over the fire.

I've (author) eaten horse meat and depending how it's prepared it taste real good! With the right condiment - it's very tasty. The Comanches also ate buffalo and venison (deer meat). He noticed with the streams full of fish and all the small ground game and fowl, he never saw them eat it.

The 04 prisoners were tied-up and centered in the camp surrounded by the Comanches. Nelson observed that Martin was silent and kept to himself, Stewart was frightened and in tears, and Aikens in his brave way advised everybody to be courageous to the end. The Indians finished eating their cooked horse meat. They cooked more and when it was burning hot they flingded the hot pieces on the 04 prisoners which had them jerking wildly to escape the burning meat. The Indians laughed crazily - this was their entertainment. The burning horse meat left blisters on the 04 prisoners.

For the night the 04 prisoners were staked spread eagle to the dirt ground, even their head was staked so they couldn't move it. They were frozen in place.

Note: This segment was taken from my book - *"239+ Texas Ranger, Pioneer, Old West,… Survival Tricks And More!"* found at **www.survivalexpertbooks.com**

Critters Big And Small You Gotta Know About: This next subject is not intended to make you a tracker or an expert on any critter, but to make you aware of animals throughout the US & Canada that you'll find in the wilderness environments or even in your own back yard. Certain animal tracks should alert you to danger (depending on the tracks) as well as alert you to possible game that is out there that you can capture, dress, inspect, cook and eat if you're in a survival situation.

It doesn't matter which critter is out there, they all leave their own distinctive tracks, droppings (scat) and marks. Odds are you'll see their tracks before you see the critter if you're moving and aren't static. Once you see these tracks, you should also know basic characteristics of that particular critter. Let's start with *Beavers*.

Beavers: Beavers inhabit all parts of the US except desert regions where water and proper vegetation is lacking. They absolutely need a wet environment to survive. This large rodent weighs-in from 40-60 pounds. An architect by nature, the beaver is known for its *"beaver dams."* There mighty incisor teeth and their self-preservational engineerial instincts have them building dams that not only support their immediate habitat but supports other species as well. Beavers are easily recognized by their large over-grown incisor teeth (buck teeth), back web feet which propels them through water, and their flat tail that resembles a ping pong paddle. This metal-scale like tail acts like a rudder and elevator to steer & navigate them through water. The tail is also used as a warning device when slapped repeatedly in the water to warn other beavers of danger.

Predatorial enemies to the beaver besides man are alligators, bobcats, coyotes, foxes, lynx, otters... Beavers are vegetarians and mostly eat various aquatic vegetation like cattail shoots, and even bark off a tree.

Beavers are very good swimmers. They've been recorded to swim to a depth of 2,500 feet in a single dive and have been clocked as fast as 06 feet & 11 inches per second!

No doubt you'll find beaver tracks near pond and lakes. Their tracks can easily be recognized by a 05-finger hand-shaped appearance. Their front feet are approximately 1/4 the size of their huge hind webbed feet. You might see a 3rd track centered on their front and hind tracks - it's their tail dragging!

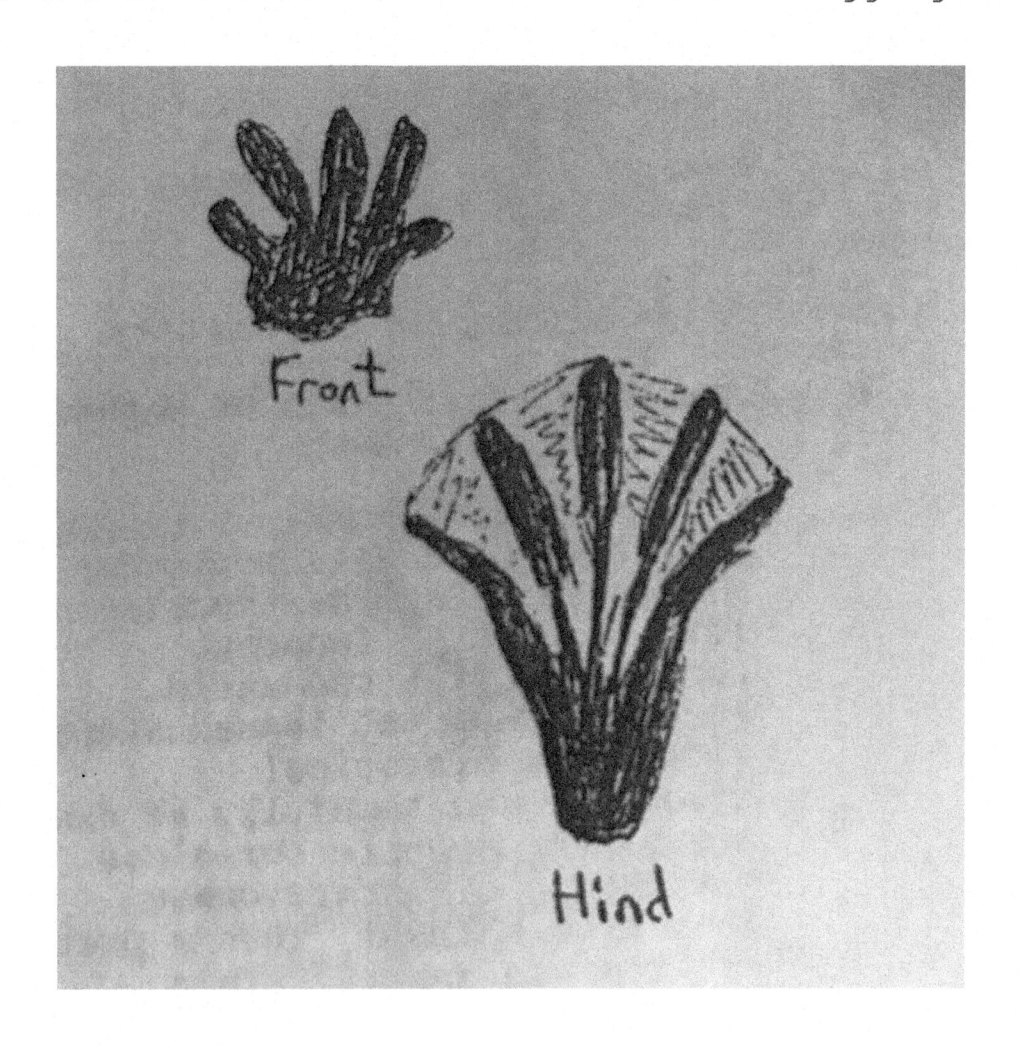

Grizzily Bear: This ferocious near sighted (can't see clearly at a distance) critter will terrify most folks if contact is made in their environment (wilderness). And rightly so. The grizzly is the king. Also called *"humpback bear"* for its pronounced hump on its back, this critter weighs-in at 1,100 pounds but some have weighed as much as 1,500 pounds and stood as tall as 10-feet high! It can also be identified by the frosting silver color on his fur. The grizzly is also known as the *"silvertip bear."*

In the early 1800s, the mighty grizzly roamed the lower 48 (US not including Alaska & Hawaii) in abundant numbers. Today you'll find just a handful of grizzlies where the states of Idaho, Wyoming, & Montana meet. You'll find them in greater numbers in British Columbia (western Canada), the Yukon (northwestern Canada) and most of Alaska.

The grizzly has no known natural enemies. Other species of bears avoid this giant critter all together. Only man is his immediate threat. The grizzly is a omnivore meaning he eats meat as well as vegetable plants, insects, honey, frogs, snakes, lizards, ants, grass, squirrels, berries of all sorts,...

The grizzly has great speed at short distances and could easily outrun & capture any man. It would take a man on a good healthy horse to outrun this short sprinter and tree climber! Yes, this 1,000 pound beast can climb trees with the best of em' (as long as the branches support the weight).

Grizzly tracks can be identified by their foot-shaped front paws with 05 toes and extending claws from each (05 1/4 inches wide by 09 3/4 inches long). Their hind paws are wide but short with its five toe-shaped and claws extending from each of them (05 1/2 inches wide by 04 inches long).

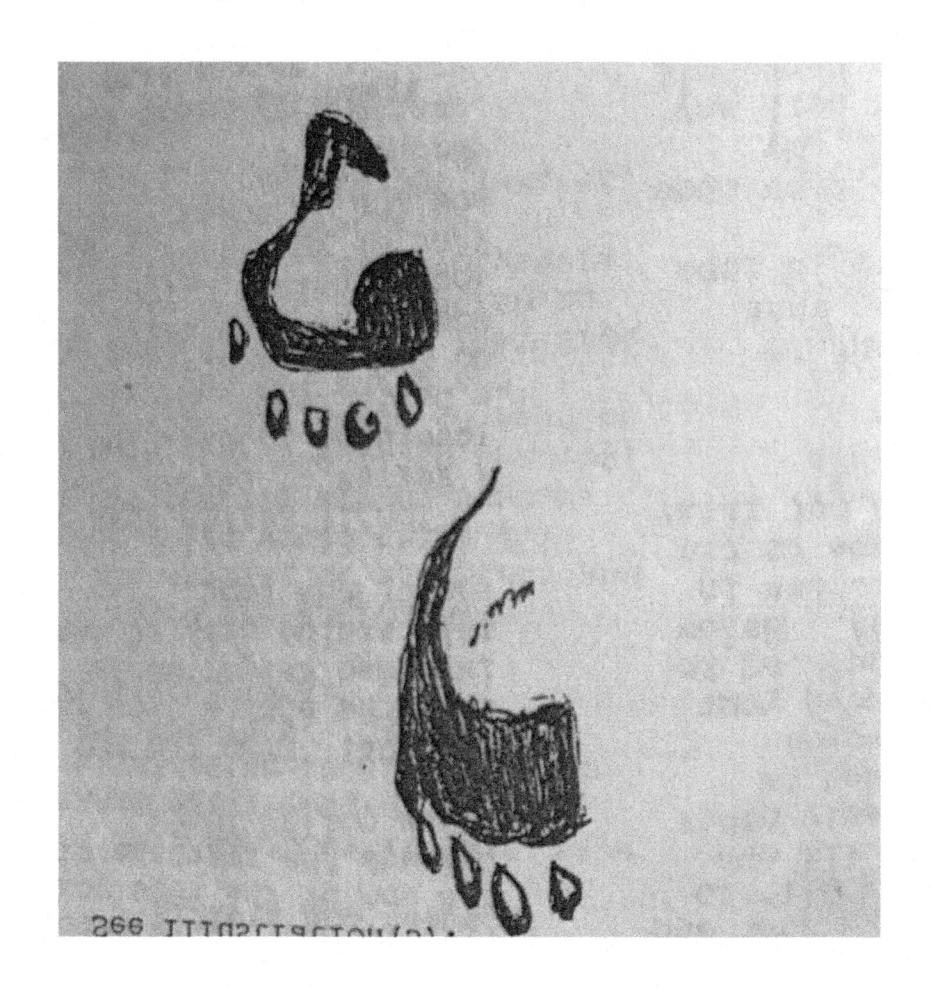

Mountain Lion: Also called cougars, panthers and pumas (depending on the location), mountain lion numbers have increased the last 02 decades but their habitats have shrunken. They're located on the southwestern, western, northwestern US.

These solitary hunters are very secretive, deceptively very strong and weigh-in between 65 to 150 pounds depending on their gender. Male mountain lions weigh-in between 130 to 150 pounds while the female weighs-in between 65 to 90 pounds. This critter is recognized by their long slender bodies, long tail, black-tipped ears, large eyes (superior day & night vision), light brown coat, and they're experts at stalking their prey. Even though human attacks are rare (about 12 since 1900), if you're being stalked, chances are you won't know it till it's too late.

These carnivore critters (meat eaters) are readily able to stalk and bring down a wide variety of small game, large game and even humans, but at the same time have few enemies. Their immediate threat is man. You'll find these critters eating grass (they instinctively do this to clean-out their intestinal tract of parasites and other debris).

Their tracks can be recognized and remembered if you remember the letter *"M"*. Their front and hind paws have *"M-shaped"* pads. This same M-shaped pad is common with many cat critters.

Raccoon Hunting: Indians that hunted raccoon had good success with their techniques and here's one of them. They knew raccoons lived and hunted near water. They'd follow the river and examine the elm trees near the bank. With their keen sense of sight, they'd look for the slightest signs of scratches made on the trunks of trees. These scratch marks were made by the raccoon when they climbed the tree. The Indians would climb the tree after the raccoon.

The raccoons were often hiding in hollows of the tree.
Hollows were also found in the root system of the tree.
Either way, more times than not, Indians got the
raccoon critter for food, fur, bones,...

Front Paw

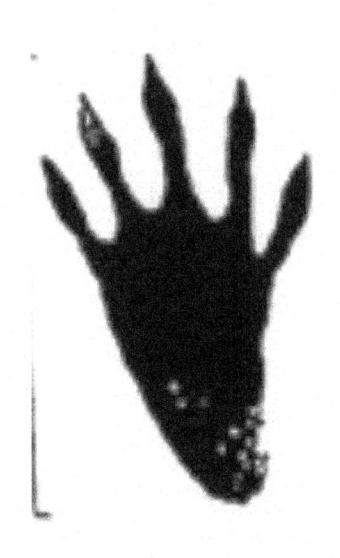

Rear Paw

White-Tailed Deer: White-tailed deer are abundant not only in North America, but also Mexico, Central America and most of South America. And it's been introduced in other parts of the world. It's estimated that there are approximately 30,000,000 white-tailed deer in North America alone. Whether you're legally hunting or you throw all the rules out the window cause your life is on the line - white-tailed deer may be your choice for POUNDS of emergency food. I myself live out in the country and I have deer all over my property all the time. If I wanted, all I have to do is open any of my windows and engage the deer at point blank range. But that's too too easy. Plus I have great respect for them critters. I do not hunt nor do I allow any hunting on my property. OK, let's carry-on.

Today, white-tailed deer are found not only in wilderness areas but right next and in urban areas. There are approximately 30 species of white-tailed deer. As many as 26 million white-tailed deer roam the lower 48 (not including Alaska & Hawaii). Most of these deer are located in the eastern, midwestern and southern US.

This long-neck, meek animal is secretive, shy and is found almost everywhere in the US and the world. It's long large ears - which turn all directions to capture natural and manmade sounds, big eyes and its sense of smell are its major tools to warn it in advance of the many predators wanting to make it its next meal. Its eyes and their location give the deer a 170 degree vision sector while it can detect motion as wide as 310 degree sector coverage.

It's day vision is ok as is its semi-darkness vision. Experts indicate that white-tailed deer can not see color and motionless objects do not seem a threat to them.

They may stomp their feet to warn other deer which not only hear this stomping sound but the vibration may be felt by other deer at greater distances. Deer also learn to hear of warning sounds from other critters in their immediate area. They also alert each other by flashing their *"white tail."* The white tail is also used as a beacon by the doe (female deer) to help guide her fawns (young deer) from danger into darkened areas of the forest. These deer may defend themselves and their fawns by rearing up and striking with their front sharp hooves. A strike which could easily crush the skull of a predator or seriously injure a human. Deer have been sited killing poisonous snakes by this same striking action.

Water is important to deer. They require a minimum of 01 to 05 quarts of water per day. In lieu of water they may eat any available plants rich with water. They've also been seen eating snow. Deer have been sighted in water up to their head to avoid biting insects, predators and to eat aquatic vegetation. They're ok swimmers but would probably drown if molested.

Deer prefer to use game trails and paths leading to their feeding grounds. However they may circle once or twice (checking for predators) before entering the feeding area and that also goes for entering areas to drink, even if it's a puddle of water.

White-tailed deer need 10 to 12 pounds of food a day but could get by on only 02 to 03 pounds of food (vegetation) a day. Deer do not have the capability of storing fat reserves like other critters. They have to eat whatever food is available especially in the winter.

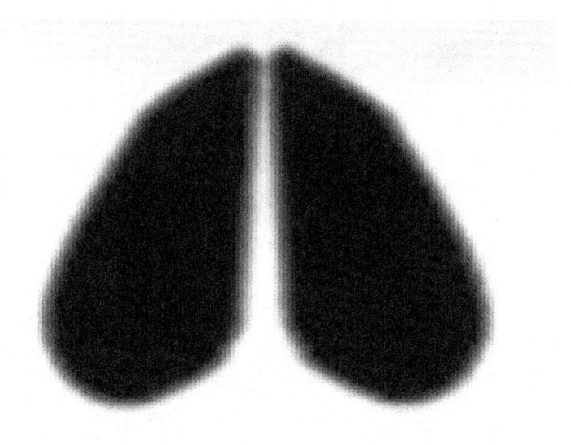

See *White-Tailed Deer Track Size* on the next page.

White-Tailed Deer Track Size

Deer Type	Track Size
Fawn	01 ½ inches
Yearling Doe	02 inches
Adult Doe	02 ½ inches
Yearling Buck	02 ½ inches
02 ½ Year Old Buck	03 inches
03 ½ Year Old Buck	03 ½ - 04 inches
Older Bucks	03 ½ - 04 inches

You must see *Antler Fight, Deer Hunting With A Costume,* and *Pounding Stick*.

White-Tailed Jackrabbit: This long-eared (great hearing) critter is found in the northern US from Washington state to Wisconsin. It's readily identifiable by its white tail no matter it's other colors on its fur. A cousin to the black-tailed jackrabbit, the white-tailed jackrabbit is a tad larger and quicker.

This critter can change its color according to the seasons, but the tips of its ears are always black. And most folks don't know this - this long-eared critter is also a good swimmer! Their wide eyes that are located almost on top of their heads give them almost 360-degree visibility.

Generally, it can run 30-35 miles per hour for a short time and its leaps can be measured at 20-feet each.

The white-tailed jackrabbit has many natural enemies including man but it is still abundant in numbers throughout northern US and Canada. They stay within close range of where they were born - approximately within 1/2 mile.

This critter doesn't require great amounts of water consumption to survive, it can be found eating moist vegetation throughout the year and eat twigs during the winter months. The white-tailed jackrabbit like most other rabbits and hares re-ingest their own fecal matter - this is done to give the rabbit essential vitamins they would get otherwise. The result is pellet droppings.

It's tracks can be identified by its squared-off, stubby foot-shape appearance of both hind and front feet but the hind feet are 02 1/2 times bigger than the front feet and will be located in front of the front feet due to its bounding travel.

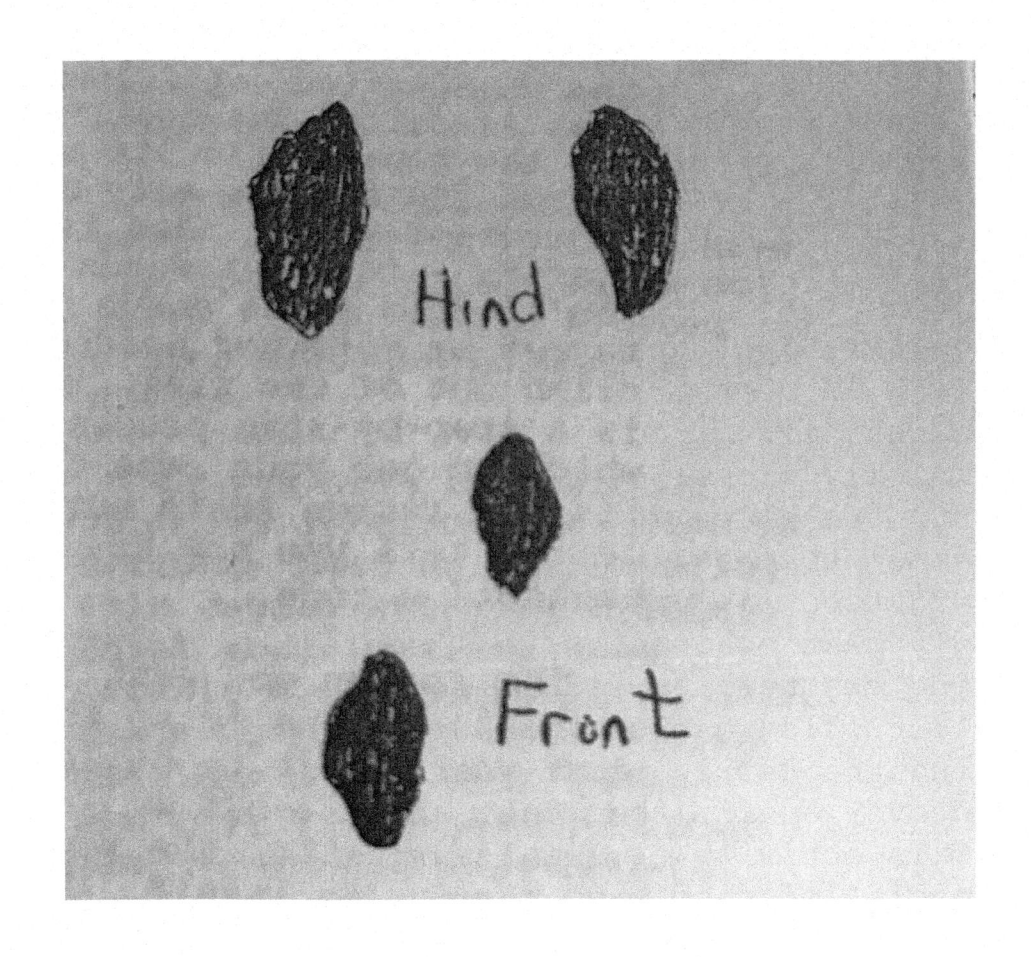

Concussion Fishing: We called it fishing with Dupont Lures. Dupont lures were actually hand grenades used for fishing. Both safeties were pulled, the grenade thrown into the water and the depth charge explosion created a devastating concussion which stunned all fish within close proximity to the underwater explosion. The stunned fish surfaced where they were easily secured. In the Congo a similar technique was employed using dynamite. Double sticks of dynamite exploded underwater in Lake Tanganyika. After 04 or 05 double-charged sticks of dynamite, a bounty of 2,200 pounds of herring-like fish (Stolothrissa tanganicae) were collected. Fishing using Dupont Lures or dynamite are absolutely illegal.

However if you have access to these items during a true life or death survival situation - you be the judge. But here's silent fishing technique used in the Congo to get more fish than you can eat in one sitting.

Congo Dual Fishing Lures: Pygmies used double lures to compel fish to come to them. On a moonless black night floating in their pirogues (dug-out canoes), the pygmies slowly propelled their canoes away from the shore into the black water. Equipped with 15-foot long false bamboo torches, mallets, and nets, the pygmies were guaranteed a bountiful catch. The mallets repeatedly beat against the hulls of the canoes compelling the herring-like fish to come to the sound. And the lit false bamboo torches lit the black night compelling the herring-like fish to come to the light. Over and over again, their nets grabbed hundreds of fish. This activity of light & sound also attracted other species of fish, and crocodiles,...

Congo Fish Baskets: Giant 07-foot conical-shaped fish baskets were set-up off shore in rapids. To hold them in place with the open end facing upstream, a field-expedient scaffold was built. Fisherman on top of scaffolds lowered, raised, and controlled the fish baskets using lianas. Lianas are also used to hold the giant fish basket underwater. It can be raised to checks its contents. The giant fish baskets were made from lianas. The fish baskets had no reverse sticks that prevented fish from escaping, they didn't need any. The super fast rapids help trap the fish till they were retrieved.

Note: I like the *"set em' up and forget em'"* traps and snares like fish baskets. They require no continuous vigilance.

Warning: Any activity near any water obstacle (lake, river, pond, ocean, ice,..) is potentially very dangerous. Precautions must be taken. Think of 12 things that will kill you, hurt you, and cause you loss of equipment and COUNTER THEM - REMEDY THEM before you start the water adventure.

Critters Survive Killer Desert Temperatures: The desert is absolutely unforgiving. The desert critters will kill you dead; the cold temperatures at night will send into hypothermia and the baking heat temperatures literally bake you to death. How can YOU survive this unforgiving environment? First AVOID it (PRSC) but if you can't you a might want to copycat the desert critters who survive baking temperatures day after day.

Temperature studies on US western deserts have revealed some baking information:

06-feet high temperatures can reach 125 degrees Fahrenheit.

12-inches off the ground temperatures can increase to 150 degrees Fahrenheit.

01-inch off the ground temperatures can reach a 160 degrees Fahrenheit.

At ground level, the temperatures still increase to a killer 180-degrees Fahrenheit.

Here's how many desert critters survive baking desert temperatures. They go underground. Look at the following data that could save your life based on the same temperature data above:

06-inches below the surface the temperature drops to 125 degrees Fahrenheit.

12-inches below the surface the temperature drops to 95 degrees Fahrenheit.

18-inches below surface the temperature will drop to 80 degrees Fahrenheit.

36-inches below surface the temperature will drop to a cool room temperature of 70 degrees Fahrenheit!

But wait! Digging should be during hours of limited visibility (after dusk) when temperatures are lower.

Now you know about these killer daytime temperatures and how to counter them by copycatting desert critters that burrow underground to escape the heat!

Crow's Natural Enemy: If crows could talk they'd tell you they hate owls. No one crow could whoop on an owl, but crows will readily gang-up on a single owl. Hunters have used an owl decoy to lure in bunches of angry crows that want to gang-up and beat-up that lone owl. So consider making an owl decoy to lure in them crow critters at point blank range.
See *Crows Can't Count*.

David's Sling: The *David's Sling* is used for ritual games by native Indians high in the Bolivian mountains. Both men and women are well acquainted with using the David's Sling. One thing though, native Indians used not only the underhand rotation but also an overhand rotation with good accuracy. Their David's Slings were made with rawhide and rawhide pouch. With just 02 or 03 rotations, the David's Sling no doubt has far more rock-throwing power than a person's arm & hand (except for maybe an NFL quarterback – Denver Bronco's John Elway). With practice accuracy can be attained. But anyone carrying this or any weapon has a sense of security and with that comes confidence!

Here are the details for the David's Sling.

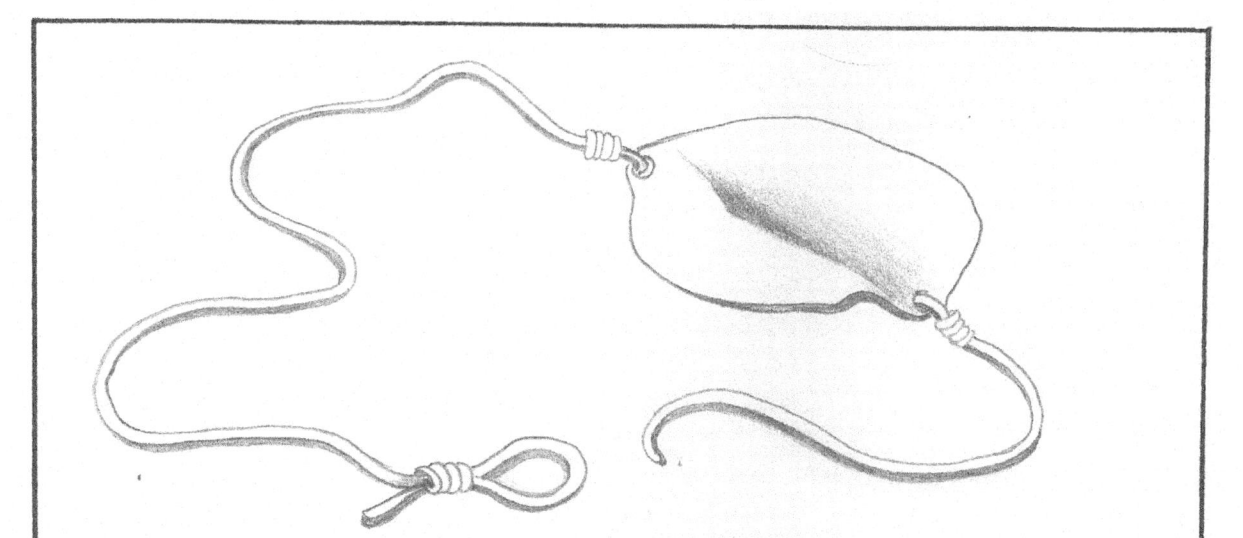

David's Sling

Ingredients Needed to Build a David's Sling:
Similar to the Cloth Sling, but perhaps more effective. To construct the David's Sling, you'll need a leather pouch about 02 1/2 inches wide by 03 1/2 inches long. Insure the leather pouch is pliable. You can also use a piece of canvas, nylon, Levi jean material... - just make sure the pouch material is durable.

The reason I recommend leather material is because of its great durability. Try getting this material from old leather boots (tongue) or go to a shoe repair store, they may have bunches of scraps laying around. You'll also need two pieces of cord or leather strips about 02 feet in length. For ammunition, you'll need small rocks about a couple pounds in weight to insure velocity, sure-flight and effective as a weapon in your survival environment.

How to Build and Use the David's Sling:
Take your pouch and form a 1/8th inch hole at each end (lengthwise) of the pouch. Both apertures should be about 1/4th of an inch from the very edge.

Take each of your cords and tie a round-turn and two half-hitches to each of the holes on the leather pouch.

Next take one end of one of the cords and tie an end-of-rope bowline (big enough to fit around your middle-finger). This loop will be secured around your middle-finger of your throwing hand while the other end is simply grasped by your thumb and index finger of the same hand.

In a safe area place both ends of the cord in your throwing hand (loop secured around your middle-finger and the other cord simply grasped by the thumb and index finger of the same hand). Insure both cords are even and the pouch is level!

Next place a rock in the pouch. Aligned with your target, rock the David's Sling back and forth and as the arc gets wider begin a clockwise rotation (right-handed person). Increase the rate of rotation to an optimum speed.

Once you feel an optimum rotation, just at the horizontal level (or almost pointed at your target), release the cord that is grasped between the thumb and index finger. The rock in the pouch should be propelled to your target at a great speed under the built-up momentum from the centrifugal force of rotations.

The David's Sling requires practice. INSURE you practice in a safe area.

Debilitating Rabbit Sticks: A hunting technique used by the Choinumne Indians (California) was the use of a *Rabbit Sticks*. The rabbit stick was thrown at the legs of the deer. There's no way the rabbit stick would kill any deer but it could break the deer's leg, severely hindering its quick mobility or at least slow it down so the hunter could follow-up with other weapons. See *Rabbit Sticks*.

Deer Encirclement: The Choinumne Indians (California) didn't have powerful bows & arrows to take down deer like their Indian neighbors in the mountains. Even though they had obsidian-tipped arrows (volcanic glass), they still didn't have the powerful punch to take down the big game in their tracks. They had inferior **bows** and arrows (less powerful - range & penetration) so they had to improvise.

As I stated, they knew the habits of the deer. Deer left their game trails, markings on trees, and other overt signs of their presence. They knew their feeding areas and their habits. One technique they used was to surround the deer with many hunters. They'd encircle the deer, close-in from all sides, wound it and disable it with their weapons.

Deer Hunting With A Costume: The Choinumne Indians and Nanticoke Indians hunted deer at point blank range doing a *"deer imitation."* *"Another neat trick used was to imitate their prey so they could get close-in to launch their arrows. They used a hollowed-out deer head, deer fur and sticks to imitate front legs. An Indian would bend over wearing everything and imitating the movements of a deer from its walk to scraping trees, brush,... while very cautiously closing-in on the deer. When in range, he'd use his weapon. DO NOT try this trick during hunting season! You'll feel like Bugs Bunny surrounded by a bunch of trigger happy Elmer Fudds!"*

Deer Snare: The deer snare consist of a log weighing approximately three-hundred fifty pounds or more and about six to ten feet long; 120 foot rope - high tensile strength (2,000 pounds); a forked trigger; a three foot piece of 550-cordage; piece of carpet tape, and a large tree next to the run or game trail.

First find the run or game trail in which to set the deer snare. Insure the game trail has some brush or branches over it in which to hang your slip noose for the deer.

At this time it may be a good idea to mask the scent of all working pieces of the deer snare, including your hands. Camouflage, bait, and channelize as necessary.

Secure the forked trigger firmly in the side of the tree next to the run\game trail. You will have to make a notch in the tree so that the forked-stick is firmly wedged in the tree.

This forked-trigger must be able to withstand the pull of the three-hundred fifty pound log(s). The trigger and the notched-out portion of the tree must match so that tremendous upward pull of the log does not activate the trigger.

The trigger will be activated from the pull of the prey walking into the slip-noose across the trail. Place the trigger into the notched-out portion of the tree and insure it is a good match since they'll be 350 pounds plus pulling on that trigger!

Tie the 550-cordage to the trigger and on the other end tie a double sheet bend knot (tying 02 ropes of unequal diameter) and tie it to the 7/16th 120 foot rope. Vigorously pull on it and test it cause there's going to be a lot of pull on the double sheet bend knot. Your just testing it for now. Insure that the trigger is set properly in the notched portion of side of the tree about four feet high.

Next the rope must be taken over a durable branch at least 30 feet above the ground over the area of the trigger. Secure the rope to the log by tying good knots on both ends of the log so that the log will be horizontally suspended. Hoist the log up. Be careful not to stand under the log at any time.

WARNING: Caution must be taken when working with this trap to insure that the log does not accidently fall on the person setting the trap.

Once the log is to its highest position, estimate where to tie the rope and the 550-cord that secures the trigger. Insure that you have at least twenty feet of rope for the slip-noose that goes over the game trail.

Tie a double sheet-bend (rope and 550-cord) and wrap the double sheet-bend with the carpet tape to insure it secure. Carefully place the forked trigger in the notch in the side of the tree.

At no time do you stand underneath the log. Once the forked trigger is set, carefully take the extra rope and tie a slip-noose.

Place the slip-noose on the brush over the game trail. Insure the slip noose is at least 02-03 feet in diameter. Deer walking on the game trail rarely looking up. Their head will slip through the slip-noose. As they walk further, the noose will tighten around their neck. The rope that is tied to the 550-cord will finally dislodge the trigger from the notched-out portion of the tree. The log will drop and lift-up or at least hold the deer till your arrival.

If you want to incorporate the **Log Drop Trap** with the Deer Snare so that the log actually drops and hits the deer, you may try this additional technique.

Estimate how much extra rope is needed so that the log hits the deer and not land on the ground. You don't want to give the deer any extra slack so to escape.

After you tie-in the entire deer snare, wrap the extra rope in small coils and secure it with any string that has a very low tensile strength. This is to insure that when the deer snare is activated, the coils will easily break free and allow the log to fall on the deer to kill it or at least seriously injure it and at the same time temporarily suspend it.

Hang the tied coils of extra rope in the brush away from the slip-noose. Caution must be taken when working with this trap to insure that the log does not accidently fall on the person setting the snare.

WARNING: Caution must be taken when working with this trap to insure that the log does not accidently fall on the person setting the trap.

Deer Snare

Delicious Peanut Butter Deer Bait: The following was given to me by a Missouri hunter who uses this technique to hunt deer. As you know, peanut butter is very nutritious and gives off a nice aroma even for someone with a stuffy nose could smell.

Once he settles into his hunting site with deer stand setup, he takes peanut butter and smears it on the bark of nearby trees (downrange very near deer stand). The peanut butter is smeared on the bark of trees at head level (06 foot high) and on the nearside of the tree (toward the hunter). This is done so the deer is *reaching* to eat the peanut butter and the tree itself isn't in the line of sight or fire. Deer are attracted to the aroma of the peanut butter and even more-so, the savvy deer want the protein the peanut butter provides.

He also smears peanut butter near his tree stand to mask his human scent. He states this hunting technique works very well. Whether this technique is legal or not - it doesn't matter. This, like the thousands of other survival tricks in this Survival Program are for emergency use only and it's for information use only.

Note: Summer of 2015, I tried this *Deer Bait* just to see if any deer would lick it off the tree trunk (05-foot high) in my back yard. Got up the next morning and the peanut butter was licked clean off the tree. I re-applied peanut butter about 04 more times the following days and each night them deer critters licked all of it off the tree trunk. So here's proof deer like the taste of peanut butter.

Delicious Peanut Butter Emergency Food: I've always said to my subscribers to pack away a jar or two of peanut butter for emergency food. OK, I'm going to go into depth on this one so hang on. Want to insure you get your money's worth. OK here we go –

Nutritious Survival Food Could Save Millions & You Too!

A super nutritious food could save millions of lives cause it's packed with the nutrients the body needs to survive. Millions of starving children and adults could be spared from starvation by a simple and cheap food and that super food is peanut butter. Yes peanut butter. Health experts state 04 - 06 tablespoons of peanut butter is sufficient for normal adults and meets the Recommended Daily Allowance (RDA).

But for those millions of children and adults who suffer from malnutrition, they may be spared from starvation. Dr. Mark Manary, a pediatrician at Washington University Children's Hospital, St. Louis, works in the emergency room, he also works overseas in Malawi, Africa (southeast Africa) with children suffering from malnutrition. According to Dr. Manary, *"We've had 93% of these children fully recover, reach a 100% of weight for height - only 1% of these children died."* The children are put on a 5-week diet eating peanut butter with vitamins and minerals added to it. But peanut butter is a protein-rich, high energy food.

Peanuts are nutritious and high in energy. The seeds contain 40 to 50 percent oil and 20 to 30 percent protein, and an excellent source of B vitamins. About half the peanuts grown in the United States are made into peanut butter, and one-fourth are sold as roasted peanuts.

Peanut oil is also popular as a high-quality salad and cooking oil and is commonly used in margarine. In the United States peanuts are grown primarily for food; in other countries they are used principally for edible oil.

11+ Peanut Butter Facts!

OK, here are the real facts on super nutritious tasty peanut butter:

Fact 01: American consume approximately 700,000,000 pounds of peanut butter each year! That's about a katrillion zillion peanuts!

Fact 02: 02 tablespoons of peanut butter contain 16 grams of fat - the GOOD fat!

Fact 03: 02 tablespoons of peanut butter contain 190 calories!

Fact 04: 02 tablespoons of peanut butter contain sufficient amounts of folate as 05 raw carrots or 01 1/2 cups of raspberries.

Fact 05: 02 tablespoons of peanut butter contain sufficient amounts of Vitamin E as in 20 apricots or 20 bananas or 20 slices of whole wheat bread!

Fact 06: 02 tablespoons of peanut butter contain sufficient amounts of zinc as in 03 cups of cooked broccoli or 40 dried plums.

Fact 07: 02 tablespoons of peanut butter contain sufficient amounts of magnesium as 04 cups of cooked pasta or 20 cooked eggs.

Fact 08: 02 tablespoons of peanut butter contain sufficient amounts of potassium as in 02 cups of cottage cheese or 01 1/2 cups of blackberries.

Fact 09: 02 tablespoons of peanut butter contain sufficient amounts of copper as in 3 cups of cooked white rice or 6 cups of apple juice.

Fact 10: 02 tablespoons of peanut butter contain sufficient amounts of fiber, vitamins, and minerals.

Fact 11:   Experts state women can have 04 tablespoons of peanut butter a day while men can go crazy and eat 06 tablespoons of peanut butter a day to cover the RDA (Recommended Daily Allowance)! Look at all that food you have to eat to get the nutrients your body needs whereas all it takes is 04 to 06 tablespoons of peanut butter a day.   Plus - MMMmmmmmmmmmmmmmmmmmmmmmm!

Fact 12: Peanut butter helps with weight-loss. Last thing you need to do in a survival situation is go on a deliberate diet to lose weight. But according to Richard Mattes Ph.D., R.D. and other researchers, people who ate peanut butter felt satisfied longer than other snacks. They not only felt more satisfied but lost **15-times as much weight** as those that passed on food. A great snack is peanut butter on celery sticks - MMMMMmmmmm!

Fact 13: To get the tasty benefits of peanut butter it doesn't need to be cooked and that tasty peanut butter will be loyally waiting for you cause it doesn't spoil.

Fact 14: Generic brand peanut butter without the fancy name brand label is **cheaper** but still has the same life-saving nutrition. So buy generic peanut butter and save some $$$!

Now what are you going to buy next time you go to your favorite grocery store? Yep, get a couple bottles of that tasty peanut butter! But remember, don't go crazy with it or you may gain a few pounds! So now you know peanut butter RULES! And you have to have some in your backpack and in your bigger static survival kits in your car, boat, trick, plane, home, cabin,... so you're ready Anytime Anywhere. Yes you can make your own peanut butter from regular peanuts if you have a high speed blender.

1st Note: I called Project Peanut Butter and was sent a 01-page note of how peanut butter is helping starving children in Malawi, Africa (southeast Africa). For a donation of only $25 ($25 worth of peanut butter) you can feed 350 children for 3-months and SAVE THEIR LIVES! So consider sending $25 or anything you can to Project Peanut Butter(see POC Section).

2nd Note: Author's Opinion - Here's another super nutritious food that could save starving children cause it's also PACKED with life-saving nutrients. In the February 2001 AASN - Newsletter, I told how - in my humble opinion - **pinon nuts may have saved the entire Donner Party** cause it rejuvenated one of the Forlorn Hope and the ONLY member of the Donner Party to reach help under his own power (with a little help of 02 compassionate Indians). Here's a quote from that AASN (Newsletter):

"The Forlorn Hope weakly continued on. They were so weak, to just step over a downed log, they had to roll over it! The last few days they came across a few Indian tribes and they didn't care if they were hostile or not. Some tribes felt pity for the ragged group and did in fact help them with navigation, and food (raw acorns, prepared acorn meal loafs - November 2000 AASN).

On **17 January,** the chief of one Indian village gave Eddy a handful of **pine nuts!** After eating them, Eddy **"felt wonderfully refreshed!"**

Let's pause again. In your November 2000 AASN I told you about those rat-rich pinyon nuts! Here's a quote from that AASN (Newsletter): "As a matter of fact 01-pound of pinon nuts contains a whopping **3,000 calories!** Pinyon nuts are found in the western United States (Colorado and westward) at elevations of between 4,000 to 7,500 feet. And they're easy to get - just pick em' up off the ground by the handful during the fall and early winter! Different tribes of American Indians gathered the calorie-rich nut. And some tribes like the Navajos traded the fat-rich pinyon nuts for much needed supplies from distant Indian tribes to the east that had no access to them. Pinyon nuts (white in color and almost the size of a kernel of corn), could be eaten as they are or roasted so they last a long time like during the winter months."

Those pine nuts probably saved everyone's life for Eddy had a new strength. Foster and the 05 women couldn't go any further. They stopped dead in their tracks and Eddy went on!

17 January 1847, at about an hour before sundown, in the Sacramento Valley, William Eddy being aided by one then two Indians reached Johnson's Ranch of several make-shift cabins where the Ritchie's cabin was located. The others were several miles (06-10) up the trail. Immediately Eddy was put in a bed and cared for while 04 riders set-off with the 02 Indians following Eddy's blood trail to find the other 06 up the trail. Thee other 06 were found about midnight that night and were finally brought to the settlement on the night of **18 January.**

Other riders set-off to spread the word that the Donner Party were still alive! The Forlorn Hope accomplished their mission! Of the 15 that started their trek to find help on 15 December 1846 only 02 men and 05 women survived their trek to find help.

Maybe pine trees as well as peanuts can be grown in many parts of Africa and help curve the high levels of starvation in that part of the world.

Delicious Peanut Butter Emergency Fire-Starting: I've always You just read some great survival info concerning peanut butter and them very tasty pinon nuts. Now peanut butter can be used to start emergency fires and I demonstrate this in my Survival Videos. But here it is in a 'nut shell.'

First set-up your firepit with handfuls of dry grass, and a form a Tee-pee kindling around it with stacks and stacks of more kindling and sustaining fuel (dry branches, small logs, bigger logs) standing-by. Form a bird nest of tinder (dry grass) and place it in the center of your Tee-pee kindling.

Take a section of your T-shirt (06-inches by 06-inches) and put a good heaping tablespoon of peanut butter in it. Wrap your T-t-shirt around the peanut butter. Immediately the peanut butter oil will start saturating the t-shirt. In several minutes after the t-shirt is wet from the peanut butter it is ready to light.

Now you're turning that 01 match that can stay lit for only 15-seconds into using it on what I call the 'Peanut Butter Torch' that will stay lit for several minutes. Secure your 'Peanut Butter Torch' in the center of your bird nest of tinder. Light the 'Peanut Butter Torch' with your match. Insure you guard the flame from being extinguished by any wind. BAMMM, you got an life-saving fire going. The 'Peanut Butter Torch' should easily lite-up your birdnest of tinder which will lite-up your tee-pee kindling (keep sadding more kindling) which will eventually lite-up your sustaining fuel. See all my *Fire Survival Products* at the end of this book. See *"300,000 Plants On Earth - Edibility Test!"* at the end of this book.

Den Trap: A The den trap consist of a 01' X 01' X 01' square box (untreated lumber or other material); a removable lid for the box; a tunnel that leads to the box that is at least eight inches in diameter and approximately 10-feet long; a blocking pole that is the length of the tunnel. The den itself is constructed so that it is square. The box should be constructed from material that won't readily deteriorate depending on the time period it is being used to trap small game.

Once the den and it's top are constructed, it is buried approximately twelve inches in the ground. You should still be able to lift the top off the den without having to dig or remove any dirt. The aperture or entrance to the den matches the diameter of the tunnel leading to it.

The entrance of the den itself is a couple inches from the bottom of the den box. The tunnel will lead directly to the den entrance. The tunnel can be constructed from #10 cans, large pipe, culverts, wood... Insure that the diameter of the tunnel is large enough to accommodate small game. The entire den trap should be light proof except for the tunnel entrance. The blocking pole will be used to block the escape of the prey. The blocking pole is inserted in the tunnel prior to removing the lid to capture the prey. The blocking pole is nothing more than a long pole that is the length of the tunnel and at one end is material attached to the pole to keep the prey from using the tunnel as an escape route.

The den trap can be used for a wide variety of small game. Insure to mask the scent of all working pieces of the den trap, including your hands. Camouflage, bait, and channelize as necessary.

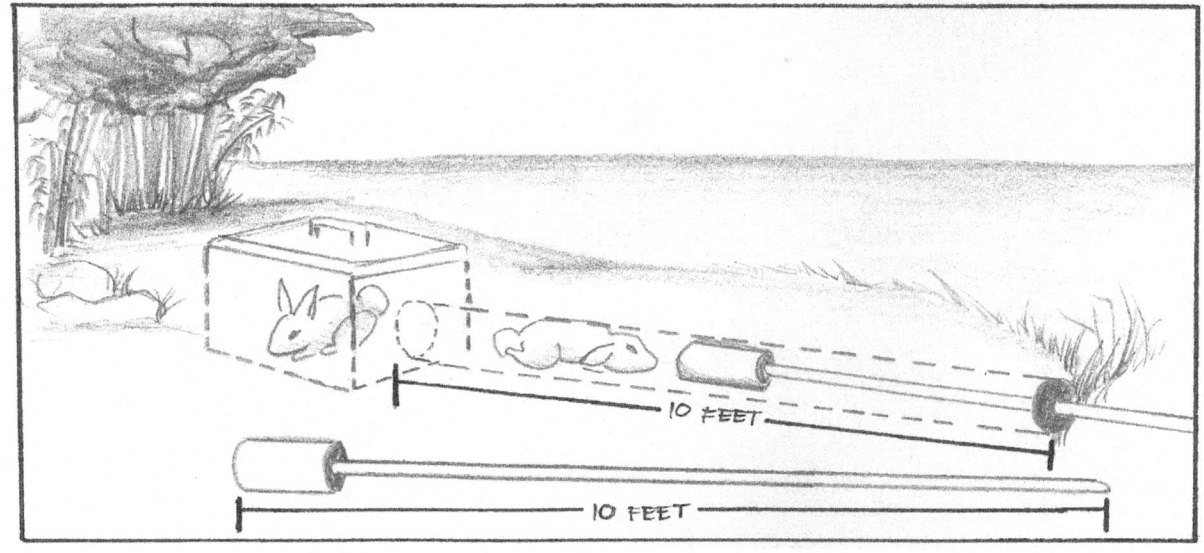

Den Trap

Diaper Decoys: Yep, even white diapers layed-out over a section of ground have been used to lure in snow geese. The diapers look nothing like snow geese but from the air, the snow geese think their buddies are down there so why not join them! Besides diapers, other materials have been used to lure in snow geese. Other materials like newspapers, white paper plates,... and what about white trash bags, white cardboard, large white envelopes,... Insure all decoys are anchored to the ground to prevent being blown away by winds. Also place the decoys in different sections of the field (feeding, watering, resting,...).

Note: Do not look up, NEVER show your face unless you're wearing a white mask or other full-face camouflage. Once a critter sees a human face they're outta there at a full sprint.

Dip Net Fishing: Ahtna Indians are located in southwestern Alaska. They fished using angling methods, fishing weirs, netting, spearing, and a technique called Dip Netting. The Dip Net was primarily used for salmon which could easily be seen swimming upstream just below the surface. A sturdy thin pole that was 10 to 12-foot long is secured to a cone-shaped net with its opening at 02 1/2-feet to 03-feet across with the entire cone-shaped net measuring about 03-feet deep to its point. The easily-built cone-shaped net was made from spruce roots.

The Dip Net was simply *"dipped"* into the water, retrieving and scooping out salmon. Can you use the Dip Net for other species of fish in shallow running water and in deeper water? Sure why not, it may take a bit longer.

Note: Fishing weirs, bag-shaped nets were also used to catch fish.

Djonga Crocodile Call: The crocodile could also be lured from the river to shore where it's speared. *'Crocodile Men'* used what looks like a squash gourde (species unknown) to call male crocodiles. The thinner end (01-inch by 07-inches) was blown into and connected to a section about the size of a 12-ounce soda can. The call from the gourde imitated calls from a female crocodile compelling male crocodiles to seek out the call. What did the crocodile call sound like? Here's good indicator, see *Alligator Defense*.

Djonga Crocodile Trap: Crocodiles were no doubt extremely dangerous. Crocodiles were caught using weighted-down underwater traps. The underwater trap was no more than a cage that baited the crocodile with meat. The crocodile entered the cage to get to the meat. The instant the crocodile went for the bait, it triggered the door to close thus trapping the crocodile. Depending the length of time the crocodile is trapped underwater, it may drown (stay under water for 02-hours at a time). Fresh water crocodiles can hold their breath for almost an hour. Either way, the crocodile was retrieved dead or alive.

Drunk Birds: Those savvy guerrilla fighters had a way to EASILY capture birds, namely bustards (13-pound bird found in plains - grasslands throughout the world). They put out the grain (bait) they knew they would eat but it was saturated with vodka (other alcohol will do just fine). The bustards would eat the grain and get drunk real quick. The drunk birds <u>equilibrium was severely affected</u>. They couldn't run straight, they would fall down, and forget about a flying escape - impossible! Can this survival trick be used for other birds, even other small & big game? Why not!

Dry Land Fishing Pole: The Pawnee were found throughout the Great Plains. Pawnee Indian boys hunted quail and prairie chickens using a long pole like a fishing pole. On the end of the pole was a slip noose that was placed over the critters head. Once the noose was around the neck, the running end of the noose that was secured loosely to the pole was pulled by the Indian boy which tightened the noose securely. Why use a long pole? Cause those quail and prairie chickens critters weren't alarmed by a stick that just looked like vegetation.

And this same technique can be used to capture those fast running lizards. The running lizards will usually seek cover in sage brush, cactus plants, chaparral,... Once they think they're safe in the vegetation, place the noose over their head on their neck and just tighten it up. Those slithering snakes can also be captured at a safe distance using this technique rather than a *Forked Walking Stick*. See *Grouse Are Dumb?*

Note: A great piece of string that works great using this technique is dental floss. I gave you 11-feet of dental floss in each survival kit I sent you.

Dental floss works great because it keeps its loop shape due to the wax. It's easy to put the slip noose around the critter's head and on its neck.

Duck Feeding Call - Splashing Boots: Modern day hunters were wise to Indians using splashing or disturbed water. In conjunction with using a duck call, hiding their body, they exposed their boots in the water and started kicking stirring up the water. This simulated an eating frenzy by a flock of ducks which would lure flying ducks to the water's surface or at least close enough to engage them with ground to air weapons (rifle, slingshot, rocks, nets,...).

Duck Feeding Call - Splashing Fingers: Indians used a neat trick to compel ducks to come to the bank. With home-made duck decoys that put the ducks sense of security to rest, the hidden Indian lured the real ducks to the bank by reaching out to the water and splashing their fingers in the water. This replicated the sound of feeding ducks and compelled ducks to come to the splashing sound. When the ducks came within range they simply grabbed the ducks.

Duck Feeding Underwater Trap: Indians used their home-made duck decoys to put the ducks sense of security to rest, which would have the ducks swimming around the decoys. The Indians were silent and motionless underwater breathing through reeds. But disturbing the water above them made concentric waves in the water which copycatted the same water patterns when ducks are feeding.

When a duck swam above them, they grabbed its web feet and pulled it underwater drowning it immediately. The swift and smooth underwater pull didn't alert the other ducks. Indians simply waited for the next duck to swim above them for another easy kill. As long as the water was an agreeable temperature, an Indian could stay underwater for a long period of time. Most Indians were taught to swim before they could walk and were comfortable in water.

Eagle Vittles: First of all, I'm not telling you to go out and use this neat trick to catch and eat an eagle. That's a federal crime and this Survival Program is solely an informational product. Those savvy Indians patiently caught eagles by taking a long buffalo bone and anchoring it in the ground. They'd take a stuffed rabbit (Indian taxidermy) and secure it on a branch which is secured on the buffalo bone. The hunter hidden within arm's reach of the buffalo bone concealed under vegetation or a manufactured natural blind. The eagle sights the tasty rabbit and dives for it. Once the eagle secures the rabbit, the hidden Indian hunter grabs the eagle. The eagle feathers were used to decorate their ceremonial & war party apparel.

Easy Antelope Vittles: Father Pierre DeSmet (1864 Dakotas explorer) witnessed a neat hunting trick by a white hunter to bring in curious antelope at point blank range. This trick worked so good, bringing down 06 antelope was no problem*.

Antelope would be found. The 1st thing the hunter would do was run at a full gallop at full speed towards the antelope. The antelope would run off at even a greater speed. The hunter stops and dismounts. The antelope at a distance would curiously look back at the hunter. The hunter would fall to the ground and go crazy making all kinds of crazy convulsive-type movements. The curious antelope would turn back and close-in on this strange scene. The hunter would continue these convulsive-type movements and the antelope would continue to close-in. The hunter would pull out a red cloth or handkerchief and wave it around drawing the curious antelope even closer. When the antelope is close enough, the hunter would blend in his movements of grasping his rifle, aiming, and engaging the antelope. Even after the 1st shot, antelope were so close, 05 more could be brought down before they were out of range. For a similar technique and 45+ more; see *"99+ International Pied Piper Tricks To Compel All Types Of Animals To Come To You!"* at **www.survivalexpertbooks.com**

Note: *Back in the mid 1800s, as many as 700 antelope were seen in one herd.

Easy Buffalo Catch: One of the greatest enemies of buffalo was the white man. But another was crusted snow. The buffalo had no problem trekking across fresh snow but when it became crusted it was a trap. The heavy-weight buffalo and its narrow hooves simply couldn't traverse the crusted snow especially the deeper it was. Buffalo were often stuck in place. They were easy pickens for wolves, 9-life critters, and other predators. Indians wearing their snow shoes would often go up to them at point blank range and easily kill them.

To better understand the buffalo's predicament in crusted snow, see *Foot Load Index*.

Note: Other hooved critters like antelope, cows, deer, oxen, sheep,... also have a problem with deep snow and especially deep crusted snow and may be an easy meal in a survival situation.

Easy Seal Vittles: Of the several species of seals, the Weddell Seal may be one of the easiest seal to capture. Like all seals, these critters will satisfy the *8 Elements of Survival* (fire, water, shelter, first-aid, signal, food, weapons, and navigation). The Weddell Seal fears no man. It loves to sleep, and when the blasting freezing snowy winds are too much, it seeks cover in crevasses. At times it may be sealed in the crevasse where it has to chew through the ice to freedom. Anyway, the Weddell Seal fears no man <u>so it may be easy to approach it, capture it, and dress it</u> to satisfy the *8 Elements of Survival* (Fire, Water, Shelter, First-Aid, Signal, Food, Weapons, and Navigation). In the 18th and 19th centuries, seal and whale oils were used for lighting.

Seals have no doubt saved explorers of various expeditions throughout history. Some have favored the meat over the food brought from their home territories. And as you already know, seal blubber is a great alternative fuel source.

Eel Pot Trap: Those tasty eels were caught using an eel pot trap. An eel pot trap was a cylindrical in-shape, almost a 01 1/2-feet long and a diameter of about 07-inches.

It was a cylindrical-shaped basket woven with splints of yellow pine wood or oak splints. To make a nice tight basket, Elwood Wright, a Nanticoke Indian, weaved the eel pot trap around a wooden mold held in a stand. There was an opening at one end and closed-off by bent strips facing to the inside of the eel pot trap. The eel pot was placed on its side in the water near the bank. Rocks were placed in the eel pot trap to sink it to the bottom and to keep it from being carried away by the current.

The eel or fish would enter and like most critters, they like those sheltered environments. The eel pot traps would be secured with the opening-side skyward to prevent the eel from being spilled out or from escaping.

Note: Splints are long thin, flexible wooden strips of wood about 1/2 to 01-inch in width.

Elephant Hunting: Can you imagine 90-pound pygmies hunting a 05 to 07 ton elephant (10,000 to 15,000 pounds) using no modern weapons? Well here's how they did it. A ceremony was conducted prior to the elephant hunt. A 12-pygmy hunting party assembled and off they went using arm & hand signals as they went. Silence was one part of their stalking for the elephant had a keen sense of hearing cause of them big sound-grabbing ears. Searching for signs of elephants, they came across a fresh 15-pound batch of elephant dung. The 12 hunters grabbed the elephant dung and heavily coated their own bodies and helped coat their fellow hunters with it so to cover all parts of the body. No doubt this was done to descent themselves of their human scent so not to alert and give early warning to their prey.

The silent stalking continued. Closing in as close as 100-feet to the elephant, it had not detected the 12 hunters. 02 hunters angled off to the left and 02 to the right and 01 in the center, with the remaining hunters behind the center hunter, they silently and slowly closed on the unaware elephant. This was the beginning of their envelopment formation.

Enveloping the elephant, the 12 pygmies encircled the elephant being 10-feet apart. The elephant was busy eating the leaves, bark, and twigs of a mimosa tree. The center hunter closed in at point blank range to the elephants rear where he launched his spear into the bladder area. The elephant became enraged whipping around to its 1st assaulter. At this, hunters to the elephants rear launched their spears. The elephant went crazy stamping in one direction where more spears were launched into its left & right flanks. Several spears were protruding from all sides of the elephant with more piercing the elephant's hide. Great loss of blood and fatigue were taking its toll on the doomed male elephant. One last spear was launched penetrating the very sensitive upper part of the trunk. It lunged at its last attacker while hunters to its flanks pulled on the innards hanging from the elephants wounds. Soon the elephant dropped to its knees and soon died. The pygmy hunters celebrated, then began dressing the elephant for food and animal parts.

Eskimo Bad To The Bone - Slow Killer: Eskimos also hunted predators like dangerous wolves, plus other game using the following technique. This technique was slow death to the unlucky wolf. Eskimos would take a piece of dry folded whale bone and hide it in a chunk of fat.

The wolf would find the chunk of tasty fat and eat it whole. The fat would melt exposing the whale bone where it would unfold causing serious internal injuries to the wolf where it would eventually die and be retrieved by the Eskimos.

Eskimo Bird In The Hand Trap: Eskimos actually captured live birds with their bare hands and this is how they did it. During winter months when bird food was scarce, Eskimos placed bait on a roof. The birds super keen eyesight spotted the meal and landed on the roof to retrieve the bait. Near the bait was a hole in the roof where the Eskimo suddenly reached out and grabbed the bird, capturing it. As I stated previously, 09 times out of 10, birds land into the wind. So you must place the bait upwind of the hole in the roof so the bird has its back to you for a surprise grab.

Warning: Grab the bird by its legs and insure you quickly finish-off the bird so it doesn't peck you in the hands, eyes,... in a frantic attempt to escape.

Note: Why not incorporate *Eskimo Gull Fishing* (several) on the roof for an easy *"set it up and forget it"* traps & snares.

Eskimo Bird Net: Another technique to hunt birds is using a net. Hunting on high ground, the hunter waits for a flock of low-flying aucks to fly over. The 01 - 02-foot diameter net is secured to a 10-foot pole. Once the aucks are sighted and coming in range the net is raised capturing a bird or two. The hunter humanely kills the auck by pressing his finger on its heart.

Aucks are eaten raw, boiled or stuffed into a seal carcass so it ferments into a delicious delicacy called giviak. See *Eskimo Seabird Sausage*.

Eskimo Blind: Eskimo hunters get within range of seals by using portable blind. The white cloth blind is 05-feet wide and 02-feet high. Its wooden frame supports the blind as the hunter lays in a prone position behind it. In the center of the blind is located an aperture with which the barrel of the weapon is placed and just large enough the hunter can align his front & rear sights on their prey. To put the seal at ease a *seal scratcher* was used to put the seal at ease. See *Eskimo Polar Bear Teacher - item b Polar Bear Scratching*.

Eskimo Caribou Supplies: The caribou (reindeer) was probably the most valuable source of supplies to the Eskimos. Of all the wildlife, the caribou was most bountiful and most readily available. The male bull (400-pounds) and the female provided a bounty of life-saving food, clothing, tools, and weapons for the Eskimo. We'll use the 400-pound bull for this segment. Let's start with *Meat*.

a) Meat: The bull provides a couple hundred pounds of meat to include the organs.

b) Marrow: Its large leg bones provided delicious nutrients.

c) Veggies: There wasn't a bounty of vegetables for the Eskimos. So they got their veggies from the caribou. Their veggies came from the stomach of the caribou. Semi-digested lichens and various mosses were edible providing needed vitamins and minerals.

d) Hide: Its hide is dense with hollow follicles. This mass of dense follicles traps warm providing superior insulation and helping keep the bull and its user warm in their super frigid environment.

e) Sinew: Provides not only strong but very durable thread for binding, sewing, fishing, traps & snares, weapons,...

Eskimo Caribou Weir: In the Spring and during migration, caribou number in the hundreds and Eskimos take advantage of their numbers and use weirs to capture dozens of caribou. A weir is a barrier that channelizes the prey within the weir or to a *"fatal funnel"* where escape was highly improbable. The weir is shaped like a giant arrow. At it's wide open point is where the intended prey entered or was already in it. The wide open point is where the Indians entered forming a line corralling the prey down the weir to the fatal funnel where escape was unlikely. The prey were corralled where they were grabbed or speared (fish); clubbed or rabbit sticked (rabbits); arrowed or speared (deer). The weir is an absolutely incredible GIANT trap & snare! It has that IMPORTANT ingredient you need in all traps & snares - CHANNELIZATION!

Using this technique just about everyone was involved in *"herding"* the caribou to the fatal funnel. One technique is where children and women would be at the base of the weir making noise scaring the caribou in one channelized direction. The caribou were channelized into an area (coral of sod, fences,...) where the hunters would finish them off.

Eskimo Duck Bolas: Eskimo hunters easily captured overhead flying ducks using their duck bolas. Their duck bolas were made of 30-inch strands of braided sinew with 06 or more ivory weights. The bola was twirled to the highest RPM which when released skyward propels the bola into the low-flying ducks which tangles-up the duck(s) or injures it having it fall to the ground. If hunting over water, instead of using ivory-weighted bolas, bolas using weighted driftwood are used. The range of the duck bolas were up to an impressive 40-yards. See *Bola*.

Eskimo Feather Alert: Those World Class survival experts, the Eskimos (meaning *eaters of raw meat*), reigned in Alaska, northern Canada, and Russia. Eskimos (also called Inuit), had a neat survival trick to catch them blubber-rich, oil-rich, meat-rich seals. Now as you already know, seals can't breathe underwater, so they have to come to the surface, grab a big gulp of air and carry-on with their underwater activities. However, if they're swimming under ice, the must find a breathing hole. Well Eskimos don't have x-ray vision and have no idea when a seal will appear at the breathing hole, so to harpoon the unlucky critter. So they used a feather to tell them when to harpoon it. Placing the feather in the calm water of the harpoon hole, the Eskimo waited and the feather floated almost motionless. When the feather moved - the Eskimo propelled his harpoon into the breathe hole down into the frigid water and sure enough he harpooned a seal.

The feather is used because once the seal heads for the breathing hole it moves the water upward which agitates all the surrounding water and the still calm water in the breathing hole. Once the Eskimo saw that the feather was disturbed, he immediately propelled the harpoon through the breathing hole for the seal was quick. If he waited till the seal broke the surface, by the time he propelled his harpoon, odds are it was too late. Can you use this technique for other water game - why not?

Eskimo Flightless Geese Round: What happened to geese when they're molting - shedding their feathers? They're flightless. Geese shed their feathers in the late summer months. And because they're unable to fly, they can't escape. Eskimos waited for geese to moult and descended on them herding them into a corral where they were killed with a stick. Do other birds moult? Sure, you just read about auks that molt and are easily captured. And no doubt there are other species of birds that moult and are temporarily flightless.

Eskimo Gull Fishing: There are approximately 47 species of gulls (common denominator - webbed feet) throughout the world like black-backed gulls, herring gulls,... and Eskimos fished for gulls with great success. Some species of gulls are predators while other species are scavengers. Either way, gulls eat meat. Eskimos baited sharpened bone hooks with a chunk of meat. The hook was attached to an anchored line like fishing.

The keen sighted gull spotted the bait, gulped it down hook and all and you know the rest of the story. See *Hooking Waterfowl Snares*.

Eskimo Hookless Lure: Here's another fishing trick from them World Class survival experts, the Eskimos. Ice fishing was common practice and in this case no hooks were used to catch fish. A 02-foot hole was cut through the ice. A small stick or baton was the fishing pole and attached to it was just a few feet of strong fishing line. Secured to the line, the bait which was a strip of salmon belly skin or a small piece of ivory carved to look like a fish. The bait was lowered several feet into the super cold water below and the Eskimo waited. Sooner or later he eyeballed a salmon closing-on the bait. The Eskimo pulls the bait to the surface towards the ice hole drawing the prey closer and closer to the surface while he draws back on his harpoon. With the salmon within range close to the surface, the harpoon is thrusted through the ice hole to its target. Here's a sketch of the *Eskimo Hookless Lure*.

Note: The two outer prongs of the spear are flexible and made from the horns of a caribou. The collapsing hooked prongs prevent the fish from escaping from the single tine (fork) embedded in the fish.

Eskimo Pitfall Trap: Caribou roam in groups of approximately 20 except in the Spring or during migration where herds of caribou number in the hundreds or more. One trap for a caribou was the pitfall trap which is nothing more than a deep pit with a collapsible blind to cover the top. Some channelization may be required to get the caribou to fall into the pitfall trap. But the bait to compel the caribou to go to the trap was caribou urine. See *Eskimo Caribou Supplies*.

Eskimo Polar Bear Baits: Eskimos hunters baited-in the dangerous polar bears using two (02) baits:

a) Seal Bits: One bait was leaving a trail of seal bits that led to the waiting Eskimos hunters.

b) Seal Impersonation: Another bait was an Eskimo hunter mimicking the movements (raising & lowering the body) of a seal.

Eskimo Polar Bear Teacher: If you want to learn about hunting, study the critter you're hunting or study critters who hunt their prey. Eskimos surely learned valuable hunting tricks from the king of hunters - polar bears. Here are a few techniques used by polar bears to hunt their prey:

a) Polar Bear Camouflage: Polar bears with their white coat blend-in perfectly with the white snow around them. But them savvy polar bears went one step further. Stalking and sneaking up on sleeping seals, polar bears actually put their white paw on their black nose so to better blend-in with their white surroundings while sneaking up on their sleeping prey.

b) Polar Bear Scratching: Eskimo hunters hunted seals using a tool called a *seal scratcher*. The *seal scratcher* is nothing more than a long-armed wooden stick with three (03) seal claws secured to it. The Eskimo hunter uses the *seal scratcher* and scratches against the ice. The seal thinks it's another seal, it's guard is down and isn't none the wiser. And who taught the Eskimos this hunting trick? Polar bears, who do this same exact hunting technique.

c) Polar Bear Walk: Ice is surely slippery slick and walking on it may have you taking some serious falls hitting hard on the concrete-like ice. To walk on it safely, Eskimos copycatted them savvy critters - polar bears. Legs are spread as wide as possible and each foot is slid forward in a quick fashion without stopping.

Eskimo Seabird Sausage: Boy you're going to get hunger pangs after knowing all about *Eskimo Seabird Sausage*. Eskimos living at Thule, Greenland (northwest), complement their diet of fish, seals, walrus,... with a specially made sausage. Eskimos use nets to catch auks which a small black & white seabirds with short wings that nest by the hundreds or thousands on coastal cliffs. At one point, auks shed their feathers needed for flight leaving them temporarily grounded. This may be the time Eskimos capture auks.

Once captured, auks are stuffed - feathers, legs, beaks - everything into a sealskin still lined with all its insulating fat blubber. The sealskin is sewn-up shut with all the auks enclosed and buried under a pile of rocks to prevent scavenging. Six months later, the long fermenting *Eskimo Seabird Sausage* is retrieved revealing a delicacy that taste like oily Camembert cheese - MMMmmmmmmm.

1st Note: Camembert cheese is made in Normandy, France. It's a delicious creamy, mold-ripened cheese that softens inside as it matures. So them savvy Eskimos are on to something.

2nd Note: To give this segment some credibility, I found some Camembert cheese at WalMart - it costs about $5. It wasn't imported from France but was made in Wisconsin, USA. Anyway, all I can say is MMmmm, - the cheese was very tasty so sign me up for some *Eskimo Seabird Sausage*!

Eskimo Seal Imitation: During late Spring, brave Eskimos closed on seals at point blank range to kill them. They'd imitate the movements of seals, all the while stalking closer and closer to their intended prey. The brave Eskimo would slither and crawl in puddles of super cold water just like seals. They'd doze off taking a nap just like seals. They'd scratch for lice just like seals. Drawing closer and closer to the seal they chose for many a dinner vittles, supplies, clothes, tools,... the Eskimo would finally get within range to launch his harpoon (25-meters max), dooming the seal.

Eskimo Snow Pit Ambush: Similar to the Spider Hole Shelter, Eskimos used this type of shelter to ambush caribou. Knowing the routes of caribou, they would dig into the snow which would accommodate and hide the hunter(s). The snow pit would be very close to the path of caribou - but not on top of it. But it would be so close, the hidden Eskimo could launch their spears, use bolas,... into the passing caribou. Eskimos also used blinds to hide their ambush site and no doubt they were downwind of the approaching prey whether they used blinds or snow pits.

Note: Dirt pits to ambush large game were also dug by many tribes far to the south in the warmer climates. Shallow pits were also used to hide from the enemy (white men and other Indian tribes). Apaches were so good at going motionless, they simple threw some dirt over themselves and went motionless. They used this technique to not only evade from their enemy (other Indians and white men) but to also ambush their enemy.

Eskimo Tracking: Eskimos tracked dangerous polar bears simply by following their tracks. But they had a technique to judge the freshness of those tracks. They judged the hardness of the ridgeline between the depression of the sole pad and the five depressions of the toes. If the ridgeline is soft, the track is fresh - minutes old. The harder the ridgeline the older the track. The age of the track gave the Eskimo hunters the probable distance between the trackers and their prey. Can this same technique be used to track other critters to include man not only on the snow but on ground? I don't see why not but it may take practice and trial & error between each type of critter and even humans. Try testing this technique using your own tracks - fresh versus hour & hours old.

Anyway, while tracking polar bears, Eskimo hunters knew the savvy polar bear had a super keen sense of smell and hearing. Hunters avoided talking and used sign language and bird calls for communication so not to alert their evading prey.

Eskimo Waterfowl Snares: Here's a *"set it up and forget it"* snare I think you'll like to know. Eskimos caught plenty of waterfowl by the use of baleen (whale bone) nooses which were placed in shallow water where waterfowl would eventually gather. As the waterfowl ate, socialized, rested,... in the shallow water, they were tangled-up by the baleen nooses which snared them in-place. Like any noose-type knot, the more it's pulled-on, the tighter it gets and like a prussik knot under tension, the baleen noose will NEVER loosen up thus holding its victim in-place, and possibly strangling the prey. I know what you're thinking. You know what a noose is but what the heck is a baleen noose?

A baleen noose is of course a like a slip knot that tightens under pulling, tugging pressure by the prey. I have searched for the actual picture, sketch,... for the baleen noose but have yet to find it. I haven't a sketch of the actual baleen noose - believe me I searched a dozen or so books on knots. But here's a knot that may suffice. Here's a sketch of the Strangle Snare. The strangle snare works by constricting around the prey as it pulls, tuggs on it. While pressure is applied, the strangle snare will close - constrict around the prey and will never open up. Here's a sketch of the strangle snare which can be used as a baleen noose to capture waterfowl and lots of other prey small or big.

Can you use the strangle snare / baleen noose in other parts of the world to capture other species of waterfowl and other prey? Sure you can as long as it's an emergency during a real survival situation.

Eskimo Wolf Lick Killer: Eskimos also had an unforgiving trap that had wolves bleed to death without a shot, harpoon, knife,... being launched. Several sharpened splinters of caribou boner were set into a section of ice and the ice block was smeared with delicious fat and blood. The lone wolf or wolf pack would no doubt smell the blood & fat from a distance and compelled to close on the dinner meal. Reaching the block of ice smeared with fat and blood, it would begin licking-up the meal. Licking-up the fat & blood, its tongue would repeatedly get cut from the embedded sharp splinters of caribou bone and bleed on the small ice block. With its fresh salty blood being spilled on the ice block it would greedily lap-up the blood cutting its tongue again and again causing more bleeding.

The profuse bleeding weakened the animal. If it fled it was easily tracked down. All one had to do was follow the short blood trail. In some cases it bled itself to death there at the *Eskimo Wolf Lick Killer*.

Exploding Mice Concoction: Got problems with them mice, rat,... critters? Here's a concoction that will kill them dead and you can even eat the concoction yourself cause it's safe and tasty too!

Take two bowls where the mice are suspected of roaming around. Place the bowls side-by-side. In one bowl, fill it with instant mash potato flakes. And fill the other bowl with water. Them hungry critters will go for the dried instant mash potatoes and eat till they're full. Thirst from eating all those dried mash potato flakes, they'll drink the water. Water makes contact with the dried mash potato flakes and KABOOM! Those mice, rat,... critters blow-up from the inside killing them. Can you use this concoction for other critters in an emergency survival situation? Sure you can.

Exploding Seagull Concoction: While I'm talking about exploding critters, here's another you might use in an emergency survival situation. This technique is used on seagulls but can also be used on other small game. Take a half or whole Alka-Seltzer tablet and toss it in the direction of a seagull. The seagull will swallow it where the tablet will come in contact with H2O or other digestive chemicals in its stomach causing gas. So much gas that the poor critter is doomed and will explode from the inside out.

Explosive Flavor: Salt (sodium) is an important mineral and required for survival for humans and critters. Plus it provides great flavor. But when salt was absent, hunters used a pinch of gunpowder from their bullets to add a tasty flavor to their meals.

Faceless Hunter: A small team of Army Special Forces (Green Berets) with attached guerillas patrolling in jungles of Central America avoided detection by high-tech Air Force aircraft by imitating animals (herd of cows) around them. And here's a technique you might want to consider. Bending over as far as you can, pretend you're walking on all fours being hunched over. You may want to use your weapon as one of the front legs. Anyway being hunched over acting like an animal you may be able to advance on your prey. Throw in a couple *"moos, grunts or stomps"* to get into character.

But one thing you **NEVER NEVER** do is to show your face. And that goes with any hunting adventure. It's always good to wear a mask that conceals your entire face. Once you're in engagement range for your marksmanship ability & weapon then you can go upright and engage your target once it looks away from you. Again, **NEVER NEVER** show your face to any animal. See *No Weapon Duck Hunting*.

Fat-Laden Termite Trap: Those savvy pygmies had a technique to capture thousands and thousands of fat-laden, protein-rich termites.

First the concrete-like termite mounds were located. The 03-foot high hard conical brown concrete-like mounds were made from earth and the termites saliva. In this case, a scouting party counted 20 termite mounds and the main body of pygmies moved in. The immediate area was cleared of debris around the mounds. Ditches were dug completely around each termite mound.

The ditch was used to capture fallen termites whether crawling or flying. A flat roof of sticks was made and placed over the mound entrance. A smoky fire was set near the base of the mound. Sensing fire, soon flying termites exited the mound entrance flying directly into the flat roof where their wings shattered - and the termites fell into the ditch. Other termites crawled out of the mound falling into the ditch. Pygmies gathered the termites by the hundreds. Some ate as they gathered the crawling food. The thousands and thousands of fat-laden, protein-rich termites provided food for the entire tribe for 04 days. Termites were eaten raw or roasted. Termites tasted between a cross of lobster, snail, and a touch of mushroom.

Figure Four Deadfall: A The figure four deadfall consist of three notched sticks (as shown in the illustration), a log, a large rock, or anything that can be balanced on the figure four deadfall so that once the bait is pulled, the figure four deadfall collapses and kills or incapacitates it's intended prey.

Gather three sticks that are twelve to eighteen inches in length and at least an inch in diameter. Carve the three sticks as shown in the illustration.

You may have to apply weight to them and re-carve them till the sticks form the figure four and hold the weight of the log, large rock or any other object that is being used to fall on the prey.

Once the figure four is constructed; emplace the figure four deadfall near a run or game trail. Insure to mask the scent of all working pieces of the figure four deadfall, including your hands. Camouflage, bait, and channelize as necessary.

Figure-4 Deadfall

Fishing Bonfire: Not only Indians but modern day fisherman use fires and lights to compel fish to come to them for easy fish catching. Another technique is to build a bonfire off shore. This attracts fish to the light where you'll be waiting for them using a variety of fish-catching tricks from this book.

Fishing Hook & Stunner: Indian caught fish by literally hooking them by hand underwater and stunning them. To hook em' they made a large hook and secured it to a handle. Grabbing the handle, they'd feel for underwater rock crevices hooking any fish that sought shelter there. The fish couldn't escape since it was already backed-up into the crevice. Once hooked, they brought the wiggling critter to the surface where it was dressed and cooked (various cooking methods).

To stun fish into total paralysis Indians (namely Cherokee) took a sack of buckeye root, pounded it, and threw it into fishing holes. The pulverized buckeye root stunned all fish in no time. They also used another plant. They took the green hulls from walnuts, pulverized them and threw them into a fishing hole which also stunned fish.

For many more fishing tricks, see *"269+ International Fishing Tricks And More!"* at
www.survivalexpertbooks.com

Fish Spear: The Fish Spear is constructed from a green straight branch about 16-feet long and an inch and a half wide.

You'll also need some lashing, a piece of wood as a spacer, and a knife to form and sharpen two points on the head of the spear. The Fish Spear is used to spear and capture fish in shallow water.

The 16-foot green branch is stripped bare of all branches and smoothed-out by carving out all branch joints.

You'll find that one end of the branch is smaller in width than the other. Go to the smaller end and carefully - carefully split the end of the spear in half about 01-foot lengthwise.

Carefully place the piece of wood (spacer) in between the split ends. Place it about 06-inches from the end of the spear. You should now have two ends of the spear about 1/2 an inch apart.

Take your lashing and securely bind the end of the spear to prevent further splitting and possible breaks.

Take your knife and form and sharpen two points at the end of your spear.

To use the Fish Spear, place it in the water so it barely breaks the surface. Once you spot a fish, slowly align it to the fish. With a quick thrust, impale the fish and hold it at the bottom. Secure the fish with the spear and your free hand and bring to shore.

SAFETY: Insure you use the Fish Spear in shallow water (knee high or less), especially if you're a weak or non-swimmer. You may want to use a safety-line that's tied to a tree near the shore line or simply use the Fish Spear offshore. The Fish Spear can also be constructed from bamboo, metal, willow...

Fish Spear

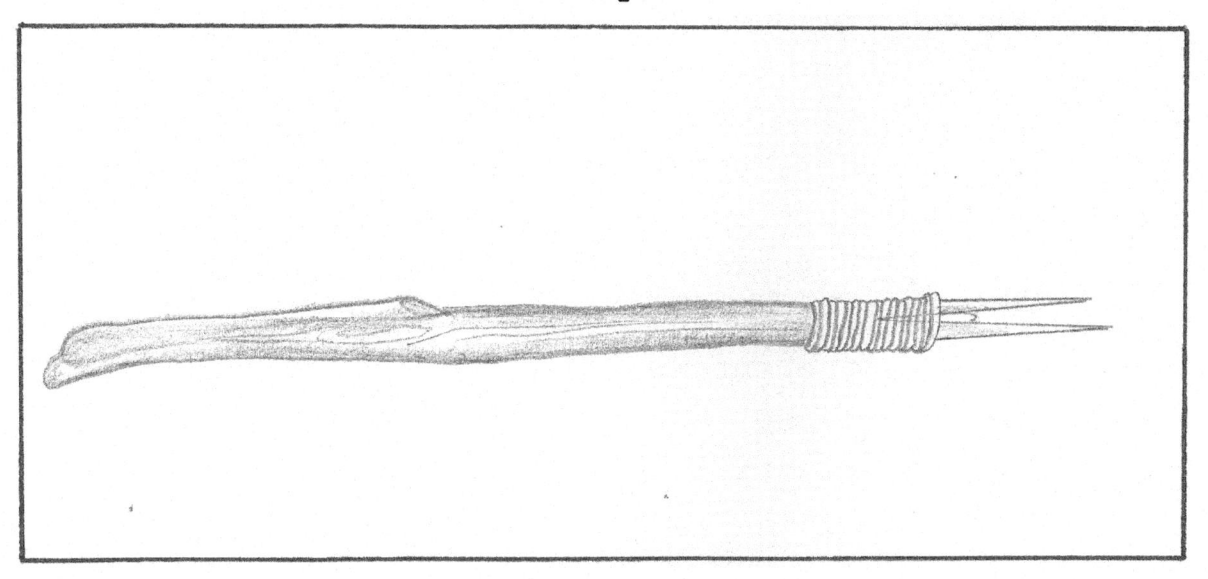

Fish Stake-Out: A The fish stake-out also known as a trout line which consist of a main line (cordage) about ten feet in length; three to four shorter lines less than a foot long; three to four hooks or field expedient hooks; and two poles about five feet by inch in diameter. These poles will secure the fish stake-out under water.

First tie-in the main ten foot line to the top of each pole (six inches from the top).

Next tie-in all the hooks\field expedient hooks to their respective short line. Now tie in the short line to the main line.

Evenly space the short lines on the main line so that no short line can touch or be tangled with any other short line or pole. Insure to mask the scent of all working pieces of the fish stake-out, including your hands. Camouflage and bait, as necessary.

Insure that the fish stake-out is secured with some cordage to the shore to avoid a large fish from uprooting the fish stake-out and swimming off with it. To place the fish stake-out in the water, firmly place each pole in the water and insure the poles are separated using the entire length of the main line. Double check that the short lines are not tangled and that the hooks are still baited.

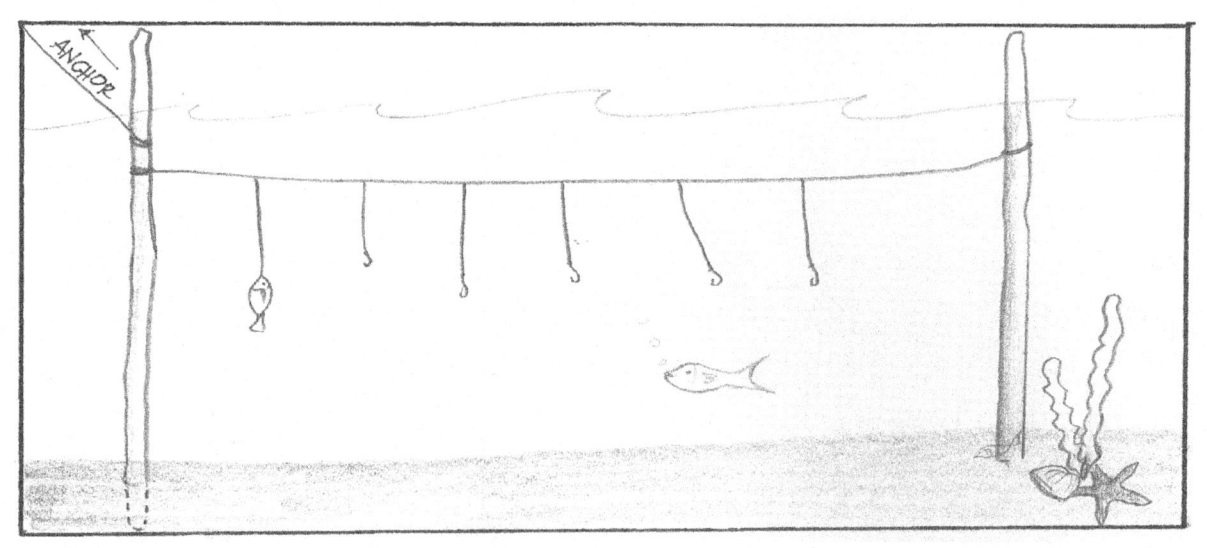

Fish Stake-Out

Floating Platform: A The floating platform consist of several sticks (20) small in diameter and about fourteen inches in length; two, three inch square flags (bright material); fifty feet of cordage; and two hooks\field expedient hooks.

First place about fifteen sticks alongside each other. Theses sticks should be about equal in length. Next place two sticks on each end of the fifteen sticks. These two sticks will secure all the fifteen sticks together that form the platform. Once you have an idea what the platform looks like you can adjust the sticks and add some or take some away.

Now with the cordage, begin tying-in the fifteen sticks with one of the cross-member sticks till it is firmly together. Then tie-in the other cross-member on the opposite end. The platform should be firm.

To give the floating platform more buoyancy, an additional platform can be tied-in; or any debris that floats well can be tied to the underside of the platform. Another floating platform could be a piece of flat wood found at the survival site.

Once the platform is constructed, take one of the remaining sticks and secure it to any corner of the platform. The stick will act as a teeter-totter. The center of the stick will be tied to any corner so that it can teeter-totter and at the same time not slip or break-away from the platform.

You can also drill or carve a hole through the center of the teeter-totter stick and tie it to the platform.

On the part of the stick that is hanging over the platform you'll tie a 01-foot piece of cordage to the end of the stick with a hook\field expedient hook tied to the end of it with bait (to easily get loads of FREE worm bait see *Worm Stick*). On the other end of the stick you'll tie the small bright colored flag or something shiny to attract your attention. This flag will pivot up once the fish is hooked. To insure that the teeter-totter stick and the fishing line are secure, you may want to cut grooves into the teeter-totter sticks.

Next take another stick and prepare it in the same manner as you did on the opposite corner with the first teeter-totter stick. Once the floating platform is complete, you'll need to tie one additional line to the floating platform which will be anchored at the shore. This is to insure that a hooked fish doesn't swim off with your floating platform.

Insure to mask the scent of all working pieces of the floating platform, including your hands. Bait, the hooks with shiny objects (tin foil, shiny hooks, jewelry). See *Worm Stick*.

Floating Platform

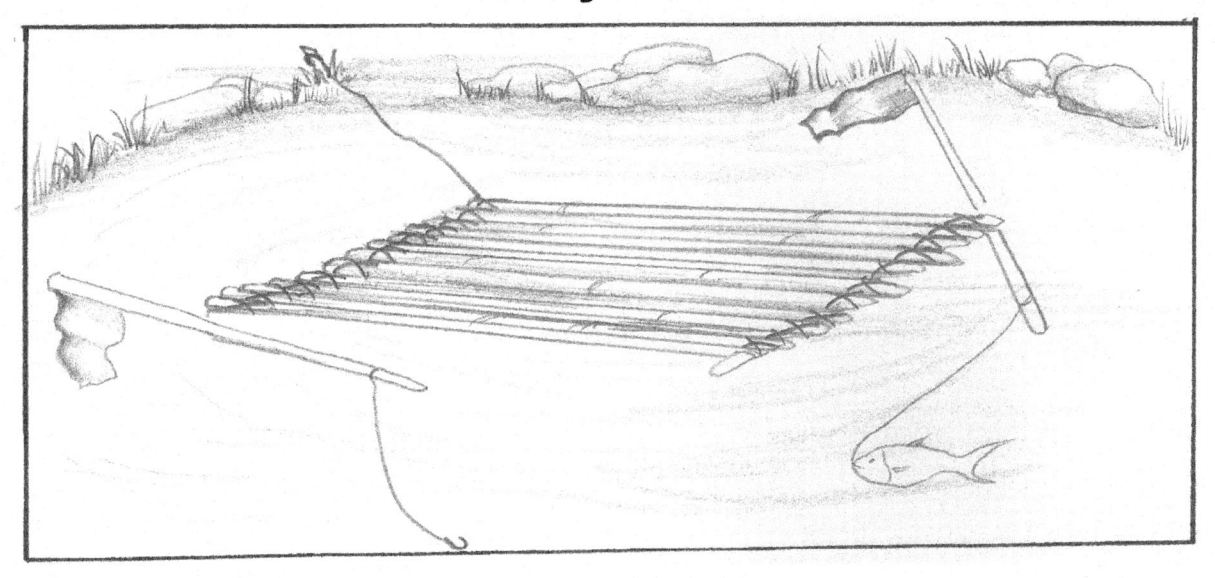

Floating Duck Snare: A The floating duck snare consist of a thirty-two ounce bottle with top; four feet of thin wire; wheat, oats, or barley heads; small rocks; five rubber bands and fifty foot piece of cordage.

First take the bottle and place some rocks in it (replace the top) so that the bottle will stay upright in the water and at the same time not sink to the bottom. Test the ballast of the bottle at the lake or pond prior to completing the construction of the floating duck snare.

Next take a foot long piece of thin wire and secure it to the neck of the bottle. On the other end tie-in a noose approximately five inches in diameter.

Now do the same with three more 01-foot long pieces of the thin wire. Take two rubber-bands and secure the four tie-ins that are around the neck of the bottle to insure that they don't slip off the top of the bottle. Adjust the nooses to insure that they are evenly spaced around the bottle.

Now take plenty of barley, wheat or oat heads and place it all around the bottle and secure it with the remaining rubber-bands. Make sure that the wire nooses aren't bent out of shape. The barley, wheat or oat heads will lure the duck to the snare where eventually it will place it's head through one of the nooses. The duck will struggle and the noose will become tighter and tighter around its neck. The duck will either drown or strangle itself to death. You can also pull-in the snare and neutralize the duck with one of your field-expedient weapons.

Once the duck snare is constructed, tie-in the fifty foot piece of cordage to the floating duck snare and anchor it to the shore to insure a duck doesn't swim off with your floating duck snare.

Floating Duck Snare

Flutter Kicks: Those very curious white-tailed deer have been lured into point blank range by doing flutter kicks! Flutter kicks is an exercise where the hunter is on his back with hands (palms down) placed underneath the buttocks. The knees are locked and the legs are doing a scissor action. Now this is how to use it for luring deer. The hunter is hidden behind vegetation facing the deer with his feet in front. He starts doing flutter kicks with ONLY the legs and feet surfacing above the vegetation so that the deer can easily spot the movement. NEVER show your face.

The deer is curious and closes on the weird unknown site it has never seen before. The hunter may be able to peek through the vegetation to see the advancing progress of the deer. When in range he grabs his rifle, does a half-situp and takes the shot.

Foot Load Index: Canadian biologists John P. Kelsall and Edmund S. Telfer devised what is called the Foot Load Index (FLI). It's a formula addressing the animal's ability to walk on snow. The formula computes the animals weight to area covered by its feet.

The higher the index number the better the animal is better able to traverse deep snow. And the snowshoe hare is a perfect example of a critter that is able to traverse deep snow because its wide feet easily spreads out its weight so the critter doesn't sink in the snow.

The snowshoe hare has a FLI of almost 100 while a heavy elk with its narrow hooves has a FLI of ONLY 33. A pack of hungry wolves could take an elk in deep snow. Wolves have a FLI of 85.

But could a wolf with an FLI of 85 outrun a snowshoe hare with an FLI of almost 100? One on one I'd put my money on the hare, but let me tell you, wolves are more likely to hunt in packs and those critters are smart.

In this case the snowshoe hare is doomed! But then again, those smart wolves would rather hunt much bigger game. And speaking of FLI, what is your FLI?

I figure humans wearing regular shoes in deep snow have an FLI of 33 like an elk or it's probably lower. So have your own snowshoes for a high FLI.

Forked Walking Stick - Staff: How many times have I talked about a Forked Walking Stick in this book? Bottom line when you go outdoors you MUST carry multiple weapons to include this weapon / aid - a Forked Walking Stick - Staff. Below are the details.

Ingredients Needed to Build a Forked Walking Stick: The Forked Stick must be at least as tall as the person using it and at least 01 1/2-inches in diameter! The reason for these dimensions is to keep any wild game at ay at a somewhat safe distance. The width of 1-inch will give your walking stick durability.

Durability to use as a weapon, support while walking, support psychologically, to use as a tool... The forked portion of the walking stick is used as a weapon and to secure or pin snakes while you cut their head off (food).

Unless you're an international snake expert - in a survival situation, treat ALL snakes as if they were poisonous.

How to build and use the Forked Walking Stick:
To build a Forked Walking Stick, try using a hard wood if available (oak, maple, walnut...). Pick a large branch (06 foot by 01 1/2-inches) that is straight as possible!

Strip the Walking Stick of all branches and carefully cut-off all the branch joints so that you have a smooth Walking Stick. There is no need to strip off the bark. Your Walking Stick can also be used as a calendar - just carve the start date of your survival situation and carve small notches for each day thereafter!

Be careful if you're bored and you find yourself carving-up your Forked Walking Stick with designs - it will actually weaken it as a weapon - a weapon that could save your life.

Having weapons in a survival situation is very important! Psychologically it is a must! REMEMBER, the deadliest enemies of survival are FEAR & PANIC! Weapons can no doubt give you that edge to put you in-charge, in-command of your domain! Also there is nothing wrong with carrying more than 02 or more weapons on your person while in a survival situation.

Frostbite Remedy: The Admiral Richard E. Byrd Expedition had their own frostbite remedy. First they'd keep an eye out for each other (prevention). Looking for signs of frostbite on the nose and cheeks, they look for that familiar yellow-white color. The explorers found that vigorous rubbing to the frostbite area injured the tissue at the site. The proper way to remedy the frostbite is to gently rubbing and applying gentle pressure on the afflicted area was found to treat frostbite. This technique must be done with the bare hand using no gloves. The gentle rubbing brings needed blood to the injured area.

Gambel's Quail: Next time you go outdoors and have your children with you. Copycat this survival trick and keep your children safe. Here's another desert critter we can learn from. The Gambel's Quail is about 12-inches long with several colors to it but identified by its black chin. It's located throughout the year in southwestern US. The parents have a unique way to safeguard their young during movement. The male will lead with all the younguns following close behind. The rear security is brought up by the mother. At nightfall before going to sleep, the Gambel's Quail gather in large numbers at a water site to drink.

Georgia Wild Boar Stunner: Several years ago, friends from Georgia invited me to their mountain home north of Atlanta. Extremely cozy, quiet and relaxing, I enjoyed my visit. I remember the owner telling me in case I wanted to wander around, he warned me about wild pigs in the low grounds.

I knew better than to be messing around with any ornery wild boar type critter, especially being unarmed.

Years later a friend told me how, as a novice, he went hunting with experienced friends in Georgia where the area was swampy. The veteran hunters patrolled the swampy areas using pit bulls. They always walked where there was grass for stepping off of it would have them sink up to their waist in water, thus being very vulnerable to attacking wild boars.

To capture the wild boars, the pit bulls were released at the last second. They'd go after the wild boar and go for their neck & throat and hold on. The hunter would arrive and to *hypnotize* the wild boar. They'd flip it on its back. The wild board would no longer fight or move. The hunter would then 100mph-tape its front legs together, rear legs together and 100mph-tape its mouth shut. It would then be hauled off for vittles or sold alive to a buyer.

I believe *'hypnotizing'* the wild boar has the same effect as *'hypnotizing'* sharks. When it's upside down, it causes vertigo which severely disorientates the critter - thus rendering it incapacitated. See *Hypnotizing Sharks*.

Giant Water Weir: Set it up and forget about it! In modern day downtown Boston, MA, a giant weir was found - they named it the Boylston Street Fish Weir. It was discovered in the early 1900s when a building in downtown Boston was being dug up. Archeologist determined the weir was built in 4,500 BP (before the present) and the size of 02-acres.

The same water weir was so successful it would be used year after year for generations. The giant weir was composed of thousands of wooden stakes that were placed side by side in the bay. At high tide, the water covered all the weir stakes and more importantly brought in hundreds and hundreds fish. When the tide went out the water level dropped trapping hundreds of fish and all the Indians had to do was pick em' up! Now it can't get easier than that!

Can you do the same thing? You can do this in a shallow creek, river,... Place the water weir, dam it up downstream, and when you see those tasty vittles swimming around within the water weir, open up the dam to trap the fish! See *"269+ International Fishing Tricks And More!"* at **www.survivalexpertbooks.com**

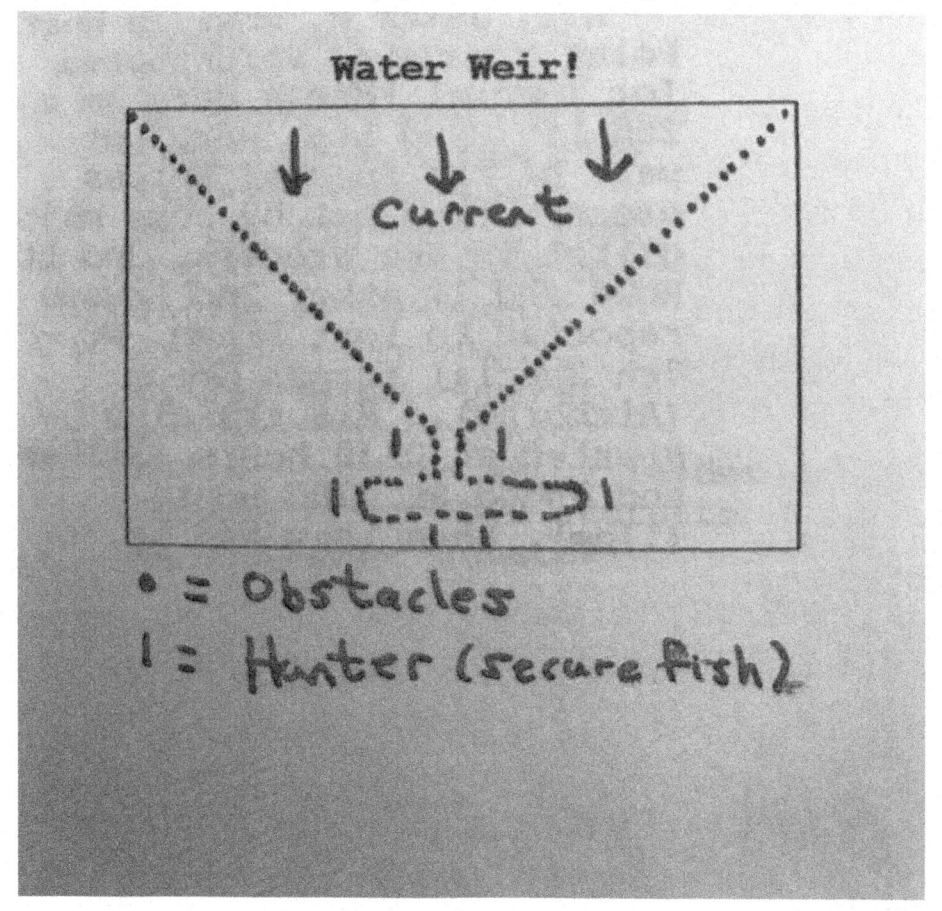

Water Weir!

• = Obstacles
I = Hunter (secure fish)

Gill Net: A The gill net is used to catch fish and is placed in a body of calm water. The gill net consist of four sticks, two that are about five feet in length and the other two are about eight feet in length (these sticks will be used as a frame for the gill net, and to anchor the gill net in the lake, pond, or stream); the outer and inner strands of nylon cord from 550-cord that are about twelve feet in length; and a twenty foot anchor line.

First take the four sticks and time them together at each end in order to construct a five foot square frame. Take the outer portion of the 550-cord, cut it in half and tie one of the halves to the to the top of the frame. This will be called the main line.

Next take one of the twelve foot nylon inner strands and double it up. Tie-in a prussik knot to the far left of the main line. Tie in another inner nylon strand to the main line with a prussik knot two inches to the right of the last one. Continue this till the entire main line is tied-in with the inner strands.

Next take the other six foot outer portion of the 550-cord and tie it two inches below the main line. This outer piece of 550-cord will be used as a guide-cord when tying overhand knots so that they are tied straight across from left to right as you construct the gill net.

To tie the first overhand knot go to the upper left portion of the gill net. Grasp the SECOND and THIRD strand (from the left) of inner nylon cord and tie a overhand knot. **DO NOT** tie an overhand knot with the first and second strand, start with the **second and third strands of string.** Use the guide-cord portion of outer 550-cord to insure the overhand knot is not too high or too low (keep it even and level all the way across the net).

Working from left to right, grasp the next two strands and tie another overhand knot. Continue this till the first row is complete. Drop the guide-cord down two more inches for the second row.

Tie-in the first overhand knot **now using the first and second strand.** After this, and on each new row, you'll alternate between using the first and second strand and the second and third strand. This alteration will give you the diamond-shape of gill net. Continue tying in all the overhand knots on the second row. Drop the guide-cord two inches for the follow-on rows. You'll find that the apertures of the gill net are diamond shape.

The gill net snares the fish as fish swim through one of the apertures of the gill net. The gill net apertures, if they are the right size will tangle in its gills. The shape of the fish and it's gills prevents it from swimming forward or back, - so it caught and you have dinner!

If you find that the fish are quite large, you may want to space the overhand knots farther apart so that the apertures are larger - therefore catching larger fish!

Another technique is to vary the apertures throughout the gill net. This way you have the potential to catch a wide variety of different size fish. Once the gill net is complete, take the guide cord and tie it to the bottom of the frame. Now tie-in all the remaining strands of inner cord with prussik knots. Once the gill net is complete, you'll need to tie one additional line to the gill net which will be anchored at the shore. This is to insure that an over-sized hooked fish doesn't swim off with your gill net. Insure to mask the scent of all working pieces of the gill net, including your hands. Bait and channelize as necessary. See *Metal Gill Net*. And see **"269+ International Fishing Tricks And More!"** at **www.survivalexpertbooks.com**

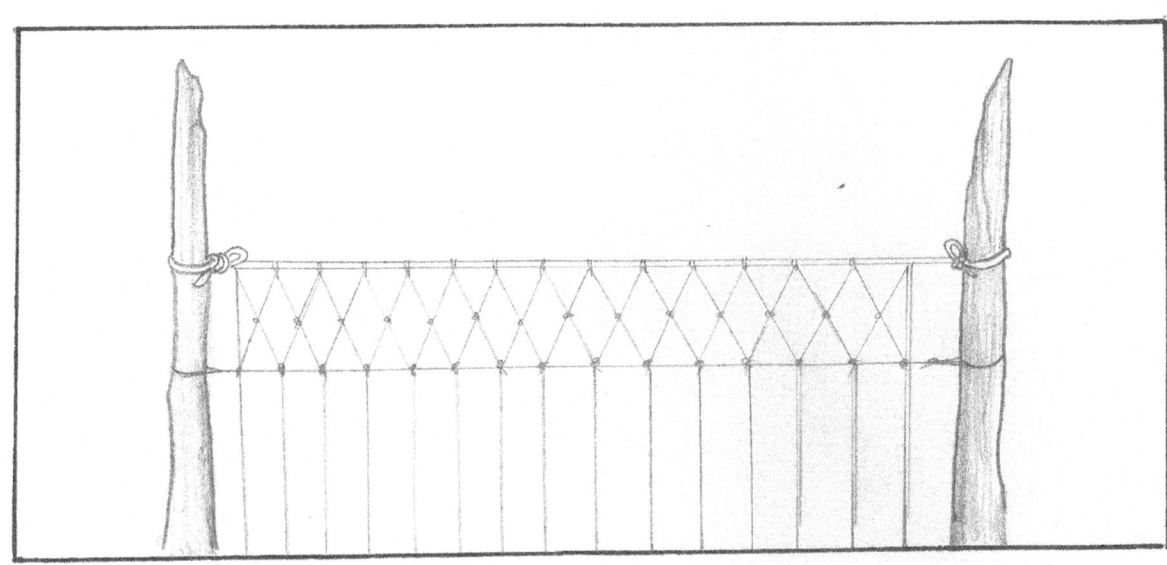

Gill Net

Goose Final Approach: Spring 2011, I was talking to a contract worker about outdoor stuff when the subject turned to hunting. He told me a fascinating story of how EASILY his friend captures geese. He didn't believe it till he saw it for himself. Here's that amazing goose hunting story. His friend lives out in the country and geese fly over his property now and then. Turns out his friend is a talented artist.

One day he painted an outdoor scene on his garage door. The scene was of a patch of land with a small pond on the center. Remember I said this man was a talented painter. He painted that outdoor scene in 3D!! It had depth - dimension to it like it was a real outdoor scene.

Turns out geese thought the painting on his garage door was real too. Guess what happened? Yes, you guessed it. Geese fly right into the painting - their *"final approach"* to the dinner table! I know the contract worker who told me this story. His credentials are backed with a high security clearance so I know he told me the truth. Besides, it does make sense. Other typical methods (decoys) are used to attract ducks and geese to their *"final approach."* Can you imagine having a giant 3D mural on the ground to attract plenty of geese and ducks to their "final approach?"

Great Lakes Ice Fishing: Indians had a sure way to bring fish to the surface over the frozen Lake Superior. First they constructed their shelter on the frozen ice near the shore line. Then they'd cut into the ice for an ice hole. Inside their shelter, the natural light was blocked-out and they could see clearly into the super cold deep water below.

They would place their spears in the water waiting for a target. The trick to this fishing trick was that their pointed spears were up to 40-feet long. The spears were motionless in deep water. Like a waiting motionless snake, the spear waited for a passing target. When a target was within striking distance, it was quickly jabbed into the fish (bass, muskellunge, pickerel, trout, and wall-eyed pike) and brought to the surface. See *"269+ International Fishing Tricks And More!"* at **www.survivalexpertbooks.com**

Ground Squirrels: One thing I haven't had a chance to eat was squirrel meat. Looking at those fur-bearing acrobatic critters (I've seen em' run at a full sprint across a telephone wires), I haven't got the heart to try it just for the heck of it. Besides getting these fur-bearing critters is against the law here in Illinois but in a real life or death situation that's a different story. Here's how those savvy Indians got piles - hundreds of tasty <u>ground</u> squirrels with little effort. This trick worked very well back then and would work extremely well today not only for this burrowed critter but all burrowed critters. No doubt it works so good it's illegal - illegal in non-survival situations.

They would select a large den that housed hundreds of squirrels. They would stuff most of the holes with dry grass and other flammable materials. Just a few mound holes were kept open. They'd light the flammable materials and fan it so the smoke would go down into the tunnels of the den.

Smoke inhalation is absolutely deadly and that's what it did to those trapped ground squirrels. After fanning the smoke into the den, they would let the smoke do its killer work for 02-hours. During the 02-hours they would take a nap, go fishing,... After 02-hours, they unstuff the mounds and find piles of dead ground squirrels. Add this trick to your arsenal of survival tricks so you're ready Anytime Anywhere! See *Pioneer "Bark The Squirrel" Hunting* and see *Squirrel Pole*.

Grouse Are Dumb?: Here's a survival quote from an IRISAP subscriber (WWII Silver Star recipient).

On 09 September 2001, they were located 20-miles south of Eagle, Colorado at an elevation of 10,000-feet. Morning temps at 25-degrees Fahrenheit with 05-inches of snow on the ground. The men were camping, hunting and fishing. Now here's a quote from an IRISAP subscriber: *"Mike and Rod spotted 05 grouse sitting on a pine branch sunning themself late in the afternoon about 3/4 mile from camp.*

One brother took off at right angle heading back to camp. The other **slowly walked backwards** *until he was 10' from their perch. Looking over his L shoulder he took his 22 pistol and shot 2 grouse then shot the center one. One flew off, the last one waited a few seconds then took off. Rod stated when he was a kid he stalked grouse the same way and used a rabbit stick to collect his birds - gun when he was older. Grouse were cooked in a pressure cooker until done. Browned in a steel skillet (10 times better than chicken one hunter stated). Water was saved from pressure cooker and used to make chicken soup and noodles next day."*

Did you see how the grouse were stalked at point blank range? He <u>walked backwards</u>, advancing on them till he was 10-feet away. A neat way to get those grouse critters uh! And the cookn' got me lickn' my chops. Thank you Richard L.H. from Nevada for that real survival trick. See *Rabbit Sticks*.

Guayaki Camoflage Paste: Here's how the Guayaki Indians made a black paste that lasted for several days. They placed equal parts of powdered charcoal, beeswax and resin in an empty armadillo shell and mixed it thoroughly. A small amount was scooped up with a wooden blade and placed near a hot fire where it almost liquified. This heated concoction was then applied to the skin where it was smeared about to their liking and decoration and it lasted several days.

Guayaki Coati Hunting: Before you read the following segment, see *Coatimundi*. Did you read it? OK then. Them coatis are some really smart critters aren't they? And here's how the Guayaki Indians caught them tasty critters. First of all, a cord was made from the woman's hair; this was called a *Pabwe*.

And this long cord was wrapped around the hunters non-grabbing arm. Coatis were sighted in the trees above and surrounded by a band of Guayaki Indians. A lot of racket was made, throwing rocks, launching arrows at the coati, thus forcing the coati into a panic where it would climb down the tree to the ground.

The hunter would force the evading scratching, clawing ornery coati against the trunk of the tree using the *Pabwe* as a shield. The hunter reached around and grabbed the long tail of the coati and swung it around in the air, smashing its head against a hard tree or a large rock, killing it painlessly and instantly. It was dressed, cooked and eaten.

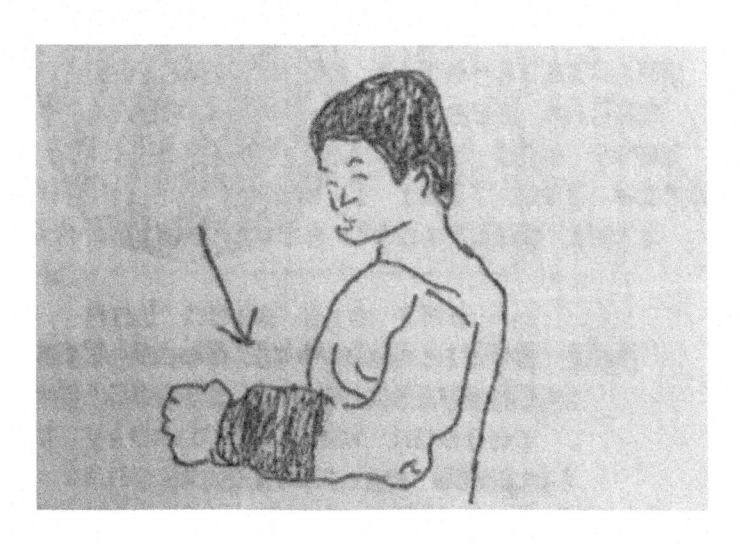

Gulag Blood Food: How many times have I given you real international survival across the globe using blood as an emergency food source? Don't worry about looking them up, I'll give you a listing at the end of this segment. Anyway, here's another way to prepare blood as an emergency food source straight from the Gulag out of freezing Siberia, Russia.

In the infirmary, it was discovered that a large amount of donated blood was too old to use for blood transfusions. The head nurse asked how to dispose of the blood? A doctor responded *"Add some sugar to it for taste and serve it to the patients as a protein supplement."* The head nurse followed orders and issued the sickly patients their rations of sweet blood at the dinner meal.

Since blood is loaded with protein and other nutrients, the head nurse thought nothing of it, especially with the food shortages. The head nurse was fired for *"cannibalism"* but re-hired later.

As it turns out, Janusz Bardach saw blood as a great way to help the malnourished as well as making some money on the side - legally and via the black market. Bardach arranged for Eskimos to draw blood from reindeers. The reindeer blood was collected and transported during the winter months so it remained fresh as possible. The reindeer blood was called Hematogen and sold as a *"high caloric protein supplement"* which is exactly what it was. Prisoners did most of the work and Hematogen turned out to be a great selling product that nourished the malnourished and even benefited already healthy customers.

Gurico Gum: Gurico Gum means ant candy. At night, Kalahari bushmen and women attracted ants and other insects to a lantern. Insects were plentiful and like fish, they were compelled to go to the light source. The bushmen simply grabbed the swarming gurico gum and ate them just like they were - Mmmmmm! See *Ants Follow The Light*.

Hadzabe Leopard Bait: I'm not sure if this was a common practice among the Hazdabe but a young Hazdabe boy was secured to a tree. Hidden at close range, the father would wait in ambush with a rifle. Once the leopard went for the bait (Hazdabe boy), the father shot the leopard.

Hadzabe Night Hunting: Hazdabe hunted small & big game at night. Night time is truly the most dangerous time to hunt for humans even the World Class survivors - the Hazdabe for they surely are in the food-chain. But the Hazdabe used more than their 05 senses to stay alive. Hazdabe knew how-to:
- read the winds
- read the air
- read tracks of any animal
- understand the sounds of different animals
- read the strategy of animal movement
- characteristics of many animals,...
- use plants for medicine
- identify poisonous plants, insects, snakes,...
- identify plants for food, tool-making, containers,...
- forecast weather
- make fire
- make weapons
- make magic
- and more,...

Note: The Hadzabe are World Class hunters who are located around Lake Eyasi (5th largest lake in Tanzania) in Tanzania, Africa, near the Ngorongoro Crater. A hunter-gatherer group, they still make fire with fire sticks (friction), carve their own weapons, hunt their own food and they speak a *"click"* language similar to the Khosian bushmen of the Kalahari Desert. And for medicine, they still use natural medicines to cure ailments, treat wounds,...

Hallet Crocodile Escape Technique: I had to add this in here since this book takes you near and in water obstacles (lakes, ponds, rivers,…).

One dark night on 24 October 1955, Congo explorer Jean-Pierre Hallet lost his arm while *"Concussion Fishing"* and found himself blown out his pirogues (dug out canoe) and in crocodile infested water. This scenario was sure death to 99.999% of most folks but not Hallet. Avoiding FEAR & PANIC, suffering from a missing hand and other multiple bleeding wounds, Hallet had the presence of mind to get out of the water and began swimming for all he was worth to the shore off in the distance.

Wildly scanning his surroundings, he saw multiple crocodiles closing on his bleeding body real quick. Still 100-feet from shore, with crocodiles very close, Hallet changed his horizontal posture in the water and went <u>vertical</u> (straight up & down) using a rapid 01-handed dog paddle. Swimming vertical in the water, crocodiles couldn't bite into Hallet. Their head, jaws, and mouth are positioned to bite down on horizontal or near horizontal objects in the water. A couple savage crocodile bites were attempted but no good, lucky for Hallet. Hallet dog-paddling 01-handed for all he was worth - <u>swimming vertically</u> he felt his feet hit the bottom and he went even faster in the water towards shore. Another crocodile took an attempted BIG BITE at his shoulder but couldn't bite into Hallet. Hallet reached the shore scrambling out of the water. Hallet's swimming technique saved his life.

Hallet was bleeding profusely from his missing hand and multiple wounds. Applying a tourniquet to his arm, Hallet walked a mile to his truck. He drove in reverse for 03-miles to the road and then dog-legged almost 200-miles to the nearest hospital. Arriving at the hospital hours later and near death, Hallet refused aid from nurses and doctors and walked under his own power to the emergency room where he collapsed on a stretcher and woke 02-days later. Hallet survived the impossible of impossible! Now you know a real life-saving technique to survive close contact with them "submarines with teeth." See *Hypnotizing Alligators* in this book for more ways to survive them *"submarines with teeth."*

Here Kitty Kitty Kitty Kitty: Friends of Texas Rangers related how they captured bobcats without getting a single scratch -*"rherrrrrr phut phut phut hiissssss"* - hard to believe cause a regular fighting house cat could tear anybody up with their 04-wheel drive! Anyway, here's how they did it.

Once the critter was treed, they'd lasso it with a rope and pull it down to the ground. A foot would be placed on the cats neck. It would then be pulled up and hung. You see cats will almost always reverse their movement once their secured by the head which was why the lassoed critters can be secured with a rope and a foot. It's like fishing! Regular domesticated house cats will fight the pull like a fish. You ever try to walk a 9-life critter on a leash? It ain't gonna happen folks - it can't be done, not with a regular untrained cat anyway. So now you know how to catch one of those big 9-life bobcat critters like the Texas Rangers without getting a scratch.

Note: DO NOT try this unless all other options are exhausted. Avoid this critter and all giant 9-life critters at all cost.

The following 02 emergency foods comes from a wilderness expert in his own right - George Leonard Herter, author of several self-reliant publications.

Herter Mud Soup: Silt or mud located at the bottoms of lakes, ponds,... provides a wealth of nutrients. The bottoms of lakes, ponds,... have accumulated organic food from plants, insects, clams, crayfish,... over thousands of years. And this mud that's rich in nutrients can be eaten as a valuable food source. And the best way to prepare *Herter Mud Soup* is to make it into a soup. Herter states a compliment of dandelion leaves, juniper berries, wild grape leaves, or wild leeks will add to the flavor of this mud soup.

And to prove *Herter Mud Soup* is a nutritious life-saving food source, a world famous scientist from East African Fisheries Research Organization - named Robert Beauchamp, conducted many scientific tests on mud and silt found at the bottom of Lakes Victoria, Africa. He found the mud and silt rich in food. To prove it, he and his family ate the Lake Victoria mud and everyone gained weight. See *"300,000 Plants On Earth – Edibility Test!"* at the end of this book.

WARNING: Due to disease-causing micro-organisms, parasites,... boil the *Herter Mud Soup* for at least 05-minutes.

Herter Pond Scum Soup: And if you can't get to the bottom of lakes, ponds,... for emergency *Herter Mud Soup*, then just go to the surface. On the surface of the water you'll see a green layer floating at the water's edge and on the water itself. This is green algae and it's rich in nutrients. It's been around for 02.5 billion years. And it has the unique ability to reproduce itself. A single cell can reproduce itself into 04 new cells in 20 to 24-hours. So green algae is practically an inexhaustible food source. Gather the green algae, cook it up in some fresh pure water and you have raw pumpkin-like tasting *Herter Pond Scum Soup* and it's healthily rich in:

- Amino Acids
- Minerals
- Protein
- Vitamins

And if you want green algae at your next water hole, take some green algae in a water-laden container and start the mass producing green algae all over again. You'll have green algae vittles ready in no time. See "*300,000 Plants On Earth - Edibility Test!*" at the end of this book.

WARNING: Due to disease-causing micro-organisms, parasites,... boil the *Herter Pond Scum Soup* for at least 05-minutes.

Hippopotamus Traps: Any hippopotamus (called *Momos*) was extremely dangerous and very difficult to capture. Mainly an aquatic animal, on the ground, the 6,000+ pound hippo can outrun any man on foot and kill with their powerful jaws with tusk-like teeth, and don't forget about its tremendous weight.

Just stepping on you, you're done for. Knowing the difficulty in capturing any hippo, *Crocodile Men* went after only the young hippos and old sickly hippos. To capture them they picked the kill zone - dry land. To capture an adult hippo (healthy or sick) in their aquatic environment was impossible. So they waited for the dry season when the water receded. During this time they might have a chance capturing a young hippo in shallow water or on land. To capture an old sickly hippo, they waited for it to come on land and ambushed it from all sides throwing large spears into it.

Hogging: Hogging is a term to catch big fat catfish and also them dangerous snapping turtles. As I stated before, critters like to homestead in places for shelter from the elements and from predators. And here's a fishing and turtling technique to take advantage catfish and snapping turtles that find shelter in shallow water.

a) Hogging For Catfish: This technique is done in Illinois, Arkansas,... The fisherman has a rope tied to the waist to retrieve him. This is done to pull the fisherman out of the water while he holds on to the catfish that can weigh up to 80-pounds! The bare-footed fisherman wades in the shallow water. Feeling with his feet, he feels for a log, a hollow log. Catfish hole-up in hollow logs and just sit there taking it easy all day long. Smaller fish enter the log and the catfish's mouth where they're eaten. Anyway, once the fisherman identifies an empty log. He carefully reaches down feeling with his hand inside the hollow log.

Once he feels the catfish, he thrusts his hand into the catfish's mouth and retracts it grabbing and holding on to one of the catfish's gills. He pulls on the rope giving the que to his buddies to carefully pull into shore with the catfish in tow.

b) Hogging For Snapping Turtles: This technique is done in Illinois, Arkansas,... The fisherman has a rope tied to the waist to retrieve him. This is done to pull the fisherman out of the water while he holds on to the snapping turtle's short tail. The bare-footed fisherman wades in the shallow water. Feeling with his feet, he feels for a log, a hollow log. Snapping turtles hole-up in hollow logs. Once the fisherman identifies an empty log. He carefully reaches down feeling with his hand inside the hollow log. Once he feels the turtles tail, he grabs it and pulls on the rope giving the que to his buddies to carefully pull him into shore with the dangerous snapping turtle. See *"269+ International Fishing Tricks And More!"* at **www.survivalexpertbooks.com**

WARNING: Snapping turtles with their extremely painful bites are extremely dangerous, especially in water where the survivor could drown while the snapping turtle inflicts its painful bite.

Hooking Eyes Trap & Snare: If there's one video I'd love to do would be a video on *Traps & Snares* but my current address prevents this. For years I've wanted to publish a few traps in the past Newsletters using fish hooks. But I figured most of you would call them too cruel to its prey. So I decided to keep them to myself for now.

However, you already have an idea of one of these types of traps & snares that works by hooking and entangling the critter and causes more pain each time it moves so it kinda paralyzes it in place. See *Rabbit Stopper*.

Hooking Eyes Trap & Snare!

Ingredients: Enemy avenue of approach, 02 sturdy trees, 50-feet of string, ten (10) #2 (preferably) or #4 hooks, natural debris for channelization, and vines for camouflage.

Step 01: A sight of probable avenue of approach of enemy personnel is chosen. A sight of 02 sturdy trees with which to secure the Hooking Eyes is located.

Step 02: Channelize the sight with vegetation, deadfall,... so the approaching enemy personnel are channelized between the 02 chosen trees.

Step 03: A line of thin but strong string is tightly secured horizontally between two trees at face level.

Step 04: Several #2 (preferred) or #4 hooks tied to a string about 02 to 03 inches long. These lines with their hooks are secured evenly-spaced to the tight horizontal line. All knots are secured so that the hooks are facing into the path of the approaching enemy. The horizontal line and hooks can be camouflaged by carefully rubbing wood ashes (black) on them. Minimum use of vines can also be used.

Step 05: A larger horizontal line is strung across the same tree at ankle level. This uncamouflaged line is meant to catch the eyes of its victim and <u>misdirect</u> the victim so the Hooking Eyes catches the victim in the eyes and face.

1st Note: Camouflaging the Hooking Eyes with wood ash really works to hide this or any trap & snare in plain sight. Plus it masks the human scent.

2nd Note: Once the victim or victims become casualties to the Hooking Eyes, this should slow down the enemy pursuers. Since they already have your general direction of travel, it is highly advisable to alter course and employ several anti-tracking tactics and more non-lethal human boobytraps during the evasion if time permittable.

Hooking Traps & Snares: Throughout this book, you learned about 99+ international traps and snares. Can any of these traps and snares be complimented with small to big hooks to insure the prey is crushed, choked, hanged, entangled, trapped, and snared? Sure, and here's a partial list of those traps and snares that may work better when small and/or big hooks are incorporated to capture that small, medium, or big game.
- Bear Deadfall
- Beaver Bank Trap
- Beaver Deadfall
- Beaver Ring Trap
- Beaver Dam Trap
- Beaver Deadfall
- Beaver Drowning Trap
- Bird Pit Trap
- Bottle Trap
- Branch Snare
- Coyote Deadfall
- Deer Snare

- Den Trap
- Figure-Four Dead Fall
- Fish, Eel Pot Trap
- Floating Platform
- Floating Duck Snare
- Kalahari Antelope Snare
- Kalahari Bird Snare
- Kalahari Glue Snare
- Kalahari Smoke-Out
- Kalahari Tsama Trap & Snare (mice)
- Log Drop Trap
- Ojibwa Bird Pole
- Onoda Wild Cat Trap
- Onoda Sock Rat Trap
- Onoda Jungle Fowl Trap
- Onoda Rat Trap
- Prairie Dog Deadfall
- Punji Trap & Snare
- Rabbit Deadfall
- Rat Vittles (Box Trap)
- Salt Lick Ambush
- Simple Snare
- Snow Drift Traps
- Squirrel Pole
- Treadle Spring Snare
- Twitch-Up Snare
- Waiting Snake Trap & Snare

Got the idea? Now there are various sizes of fish hooks designed for fish. And fish hooks can be used to compliment just about any trap & snare. Fresh water fish hooks range in size from tiny #18 treble hooks (03 hooks) to #4/0 catfish hooks. And hooks designed for giant marine life are much bigger.

You already have #6 or #4 fish hooks in the *75+ Use Survival Kits* I sent you, but a #1 fishing hook or larger may work better to easier hook into any burrowing critter with little effort compared to smaller fishing hooks. See *Laydon Static Bola Snare* and *Hooking Waterfowl Snares*.

Hooking Waterfowl Snares: You might think the following snare is vicious because it incorporates fishing hooks. But it's really not a vicious trap & snare when your life and those under your care are on the line. The *Hooking Water Fowl Snares* are kinda like an upside down *Fish Stake-Out (Trout Line)* as you read previously.

Ingredients: Spool of fishing line; knife, 24 #6 hooks; 24 10-pound rocks; and 24 small pieces of wood.

Step 01: Locate a shallow water site where waterfowl are known to congregate. Water should be no deeper than 04-feet deep. Consider cold water temperature.

Step 02: Located just off shore to your snare site, so you don't get tangled-up in your own snares, form your weights in a line parallel to the shore line with each weight being about 03-feet apart. Each snare will be built on shore and placed in the water one at a time.

Step 03: Secure 06-feet of fishing line and tie-off to the 1st rock. Secure your hook to the fishing line using a fisherman's knot (see Note). Then take your small piece of floatable wood and place it on your hook and drive through the hook and about an inch or so down the line. Carefully secure the rock (weight), line, & hook and secure it in 03 to 04 feet of water.

The line should be vertical with the hook floating just inches from the surface. Adjust location as necessary so the hook is floating a few inches from the surface.

Note: Here's how to tie a **fisherman's knot** - well this is how I tie one. Place you fishing line through the eye of the hook and loop the line back on itself so you have a loop about 02-inches long. Now holding the loop, twist the hook in circles about 12-times so the line is twisted on itself. Take the free short-end of the loop and place it through the top of the loop of the line just below the eye of the hook. Now carefully hold the hook and PULL on the end of the 06-foot line. The twisted line will dress itself towards the eye of the hook, looking like a noose, and voila (vwa lah - 'there it is' - French) you have a fisherman's knot.

Step 04: Repeat *Step 03* for all the other 23 snares but insure each snare is about 03-feet apart forming a line parallel to the shoreline. This separation is so when you retrieve any snared bird, you don't entangle yourself with another snare.

The hooks will catch and snag on any part of the bird (feathers, head, body, webbed feet,...) and the harder it pulls the more embedded the hook will be. Once you're aware of a snared bird, go to the snare, pull the bird underwater for a silent drowning kill and secure it back to the campsite. Or you may use the live bird as a decoy to lure in more birds.
For another snare using hooks, see *Laydon's Static Bola Snare*.

Hopi Snake Catching: The Hopi Indians are located in northeastern Arizona. One of the more important Hopi ceremonies was the Snake Dance using real snakes. Priests would go north, then west, then south, then east to collect snakes (counter clockwise - Why? - RFIR). The priests had an unusual technique to collect rattlesnakes, bull snakes, and other species of snakes.

a) Tracking: First the snakes were tracked by the thin trail they left in the dry dust. Yes, I bet them Hopi could track them crawling critters over rocks too.

b) Corn Meal: Once located, if the snakes is uncoiled, some corn meal is thrown towards it where the priest secured it by its neck, stroked it gently to calm it down, and placed it in the rawhide bag.

c) Smoke: If the snake coiled, a quick prayer was said and tobacco smoke was blown toward it till it uncoiled, then it was secured and placed in the rawhide bag.

d) Digging Stick: If the snake's trail led to a hole, a digging stick is used to excavate and retrieve the snake - securing it in the rawhide bag.

These techniques are interesting. Why corn meal calms the snake is unknown. But smoke may have the same effect on snakes as it has on bees - it dulls their senses, makes them drowsy,... thus incapacitates them, disables them from striking or the desire to strike.

My best advice is to ALWAYS ALWAYS have a forked walking stick (weapon) when outdoors and another back-up weapon according to the type of the most deadliest critter(s) in your area.

Hot Gear: Hot gear is a military slang term for warm clothing against cold temperatures. Our northern friends braved bitterly cold winter storms that would kill the ignorant in seconds. They routinely braved 30-degree below zero temperatures on their days of routine hunting. How do they survive bitterly cold temperatures? For underwear they wore feathered duck skins. Over this they wore a snug suit of caribou hide with the fur to the inside against the skin. Over this they wore another but looser suit with the fur facing out. The gap between both suits provided insulation. The hood was made of wolverine fur - the only fur that doesn't frost from moisture from breathing. The boots are made of double hide and lined with moss for insulation and to keep the boots dry.

Hotter Gear: This is probably the warmest fur on Earth and it's called qiviut wool and it comes from a far north critter called musk oxen. Musk oxen can withstand temperatures that go down as much as 100-degrees below zero because of its qiviut wool which is 08-times warmer than wool! This very warm and soft fur is harvested during the summer months to make warm coats. To harvest it, it's simply combed off the gentle critter. Many garments are made from this warm wool. If you can find it, get some garments for yourself. At the time of this writing, the only POC is from Alaska and their exact address is unknown. If you have a POC here in the continental US let me know so I can pass the word. I'd love to have some qiviut socks and gloves! See *Musk Oxen*.

Human Traps: To insure you don't miss the 'human traps' listed in this book, I thought I'd list all of them here for you. Other traps & snares in this book can be used for human too (war time evasion). Here's the list:
- Hooking Eyes Trap & Snare
- Man Trap
- Punji Traps
- Waiting Snake Trap & Snare

Hunting The King Of The Jungle: Pygmies employed military-type tactics to track down, close with and kill lions using no modern weapons. First scouts were deployed to reconnoiter the surrounding area. On this occasion, 01 scout returned while the others kept *"eyes on target."* The lone scout informed the main body of the current situation. There were 03 lions, but the group of pygmy hunters were only after one lone lion. To close on a pack of lions was asking for disaster. Later, the other 02 scouts returned and soon after the hunters trotted to their objective 01-hour away.

Arriving at their objective they found the lions in a clump of bushes. Forming a circle around the lions, they let the 02 smaller ones escape, concentrating on the large male lion. But the large 400-pound male lion escaped too. Immediately forming in 02 parallel files, 19 pygmy hunters trotted chasing the lion. An hour later, the hunters formed a circle surrounding the lion. Armed with spears and shields, the circle tightened. The lion attacked one pygmy and broke through the encirclement. Again 02 parallel files were formed and the chase was on. 02-hours later, the expert trackers encircled the lion again.

The 400-pound male lion was tired. The hunters closed the circle tighter and tighter all while yelling at the top of their lungs. Again the lion leaped at one of the hunters. This time a spear was launched and met the lion in mid-air. As the lion hit the ground so did the spear which penetrated the lion even more. The lion crawled for 30-feet attempting to kill the hunter but died. The lion was skinned, claws taken and the rest left to scavengers.

If need be, all the other hunters would have propelled their spears into the lion causing a quick death. The 19 pygmy warriors was nothing more than <u>safety in numbers</u>. As far as their self-protecting travelling formations of 02 parallel files, this was used in case of chance contacts with other animals while enroute. Enroute back to their village, instead of using 02 parallel files, they used a single file formation. See *1st, 2nd, 3rd, 4th Lion Repeller*. And see *Massai Lion Hunting* and *Lions Hunt For You*.

1st Note: Pygmies used small <u>mute dogs</u> to aid in their hunting. The barkless dog didn't give an early warning to the prey (animal and human) like most hunting dogs do.

2nd Note: Pygmies also used a network of undervegetation tunnels to travel while staying hidden.

Hunters Harvest: Also called harvest moon, it's the use of the moon to time the best possible times to hunt white-tailed deer. Historians give credit to savvy Iroquois for understanding and employing the harvest moon for successful hunts.

The Iroquois studied how the moon affected deer movements especially during breeding season and this greatly enhanced their hunting success. According to one hunting expert, more deer will be seen from dawn to high noon on the *day with a full moon than any other day in the entire hunting season. This subject RFIR. But to get a great book on this subject see *Hunting Whitetails by the Moon* in the POC Section.

Hypnotize Venomous Snakes To Avoid Their Deadly Bite: Since you can remember your parents, teachers, elders... have warned you to never look directly into the sun. Well the sun is exactly what we're going to use to temporarily distract that poisonous snake so you can carefully & safely withdraw and leave that critters local habitat.

But first before you venture out, know what kind of critters good or bad are in the area. If you find that venomous snakes are in your area of interest, plan to AVOID them from the start and also plan for trouble too.

Here's one neat trick to distract that venomous critter while you carefully & safely withdraw from its habitat.

You'll need a mirror and the sun - a bright sun. Simply take your mirror and angle it so the blinding bright rays of the sun are beamed directly into the eyes of the snake.

The blinding bright beam is overpowering to any creature that has eyes. The bright beam will give you that opportunity to safely withdraw cause the snake is now occupied with the troublesome blinding bright beam.

It may want to turn away from it. If it does that, it can't possibly strike at you since its head is pointing away from you. The blinding bright beam affects the snakes eyesight. If it affects its other senses of heat seeking (facial pits) and smell (forked tongues) is unknown at this time (RFIR - Requires Further Intensive Research).

So next time you go outdoors, take a small mirror with you to distract that venomous critter so you're safe Anytime Anywhere! See *Forked Walking Stick - Staff.*

Hypnotizing Alligators: Before I tell you how to hypnotize an alligator, let me give you some data on these **"submarines with teeth"** so you have a better respect for those ornery critter. There are 02 species of alligators, the American alligator (Alligator mississipiensis) and the Chinese alligator (Alligator sinensis). The Chinese alligator dominates the Yangtze River Basin of China. The American alligator reigns in southeastern United States from the Carolina costal swamps to southern Florida and as far west to the western Gulf Coast to the Rio Grande in Texas. Its habitats are found in freshwater swamps, lakes, and bayous.

Alligators are identified by their broad, flat, rounded snout compared to their cousins (crocodiles, caymans,...) that have pointed, longer snouts. When their mouths are closed, alligators lower teeth can't be seen as compared to their cousins (crocodiles, caymans,...).

It eats birds, fish, frogs, snakes, turtles, birds, mammals, carrion (animal carcass), and known to attack and eat humans.

Alligators can grow to monstrous sizes. An alligator captured in the Florida Everglades was recorded at 11-feet 06-inches long and weighing 591 pounds. However, other captured alligators were even bigger. Another alligator captured in the Florida Everglades clocked-in at 17-feet 05-inches long (estimated weight - 880-lbs). An alligator captured in the swamps of Louisiana clocked-in at 19-feet 02-inches long (estimated weight - 970-lbs). Alligators have a bursting speed and can go from 0mph to 20mph in a blink of an eye. They can also travel as fast as 30mph in their *"high walk"* mode for a very short distance.

Its breeding season usually occurs during the Spring. The males are very territorial at this time and make bellowing sounds to attract females while at the same time warning male alligators to stay away. Intruders will be warned with a gaping mouth, hissing and lunging. The female will lay between 30 and 60 eggs and build a nest of mud and vegetation (above flood level). The fresh but decaying vegetation actually increases in temperature and incubates the eggs.

Since the incursion of the white man in the 1800s, like the buffalo, the American alligator was hunted for food, its hide, and just for the sport of it. It's numbers were dangerously low till in 1967, the American alligator was declared an endangered species. At that time it was federally protected by law and over the last few decades, it has made a comeback.

With that comeback, there are a lot more ornery alligators than ever. The best defense against alligators is to STAY OUT OF THEIR ENVIRONMENT. But if you find yourself in close contact with this ornery critter there are a couple ways to defend yourself. You have to do something or face a terrible death.

Like an RI (US Army Ranger Instructor) I remember screaming at a Ranger student who was paralyzed during an enemy contact while on patrol: *"Ranger do something. Even if it's wrong, do something. Doing nothing is the worst thing you can do!"* Yes, there was some cussing in there but I left it out.

And doing nothing in this case is sure death so you have to do something and here are 03 courses of action. Remember, the best course of action is to STAY OUT of their environment. If in an urban environment, call 911.

Walking Staff Defense!

The 1st technique is to take your sturdy Walking Staff (forked stick) and shove it into the alligators mouth and shove it in deep so it stays there. Don't cut that ornery critters any slack cause he won't cut you any slack when he gets a hold of you. This prevents the ornery critter from chomping away at you. If available, shove an additional sturdy long branch in with the walking staff and RETREAT RETREAT RETREAT - (away from water)! Get the hell out of there before his *"submarine with teeth"* buddies arrive.

Headlocking An Alligator!

Remember the alligators mouth is easily held shut - put it in a headlock so it can't open it to start chomping on you. However, to hold an open mouth from shutting on you is impossible. They may not have much power opening their mouth, but they have substantial power when it comes to closing their mouth.

Hypnotizing Alligators!

In this book, you already know how to put chickens, scorpions, sharks, snakes,... in a hypnosis-like condition so YOU'RE IN CONTROL! And here's how to *"hypnotize"* an alligator when you're in close "hand to claw contact." You have to do something to SAVE YOUR LIFE so why not try this trick that really works!

Reach under the alligator's long chin and grab - "*pinch*" some skin with the index and thumb and hold on. Hold on to this piece of skin and push or pull, forward, back, right or left in the direction you want the alligator to go. Maneuver the alligator so you put it in a direction favorable for your quick escape and evasion. And watch-out for that whipping tail.

Now you know how to control an alligator when you're in close contact to SAVE YOUR LIFE. Remember, doing nothing may mean a terrible death. But the best defense is to STAY OUT OF THEIR ENVIRONMENT. See *Hallet Crocodile Escape Technique*. And see ***"269+ International Fishing Tricks And More!"*** at **www.survivalexpertbooks.com**

WAIT! WAIT! I'm not done yet. Let me tell you this TRUE story about them **"submarines with teeth"** so you have a better respect for those ornery critter. OK are you ready? Let's get ready to RUUUMMMMBBLLEEE! In this corner - 900 armed Japanese soldiers. And in this corner - a bunch of hungry and very smart crocodiles with their own plan of attack - AMBUSH!!!!

900+ Japanese Soldiers Mass Slaughtered And They Never Saw Em' Comin'!

Here's a TRUE and fascinating story about these man-eating critters. During WWII when the British were recapturing Burma, approximately 1,000 withdrawing Japanese soldiers entered a mangrove swamp between Burma and Ramree Island. They were expecting Japanese ships to evacuate them! Well the ships never showed and it was turning dark.

Darkness came and let me tell you this real quick from experience - in the jungle at night its *"char cloth dark!"* I mean you can't see your hand in front of your face if your life depended on it - due to the triple canopy and such plus being in a swamp - it's a real BAD situation to be in!

The Japanese ships never showed to evacuate the stranded 1,000 battle-tested, battle-hardened Japanese soldiers because of a Royal Navy blockade. Well those tail-wagging all-mouth critters moved-in. Not 02 or 03, but every crocodile around!

Them crocs moved in underwater and WAITED. They WAITED till it got 'can't see a dang thing dark.' Once it was stone black dark, them all teeth ornery critters attacked - AMBUSHED their prey from all sides simultaneously like a military operation.

Throughout the terrifying night, most of the 1,000 Japanese soldiers were mass slaughtered by the night-stalking critters. Some Japanese may have drowned and some shot & killed by friendly fire (I know how that goes) but most were mass slaughtered by the unseen attacking crocodiles.

Only 20, only 20 Japanese soldiers survived that terrifying continuous night slaughter. Only 20 lived to tell about this unknown mass slaughter of already battle-tested, battle-hardened armed soldiers of the Japanese Empire who were NO MATCH for Mother Nature and her **smart** & hungry gators!

Most Important Note: I keep telling anybody that will listen to me. Them critters go far beyond instinct. Them critters (all species) can think, they can evaluate, they can decide, they can contemplate, they can plan,… They are a lot smarter than most people think to include them scientists and experts with their fancy Ph.D.s. Them critters may not be able to build a space shuttle but they can think for themselves, so give them the respect they deserve. And I just gave you another great example above.

Hypnotizing Castoreum: Before the invasion of the white man, beginning in the 1700s, millions of beavers habitated North America. The only threat to beavers were predators like bears, bobcats, cougars, coyotes, eagles, fox, hawks, lynxes, otters, wolverines, and wolves.

Indians throughout North America hunted beaver but only took what they needed to survive and never hunted the beaver into extinction. With all these threats against the beaver, they still numbered in the millions.

Beavers had their own defenses. Upon any sign of danger, beavers slapped their tail in the water to alert other beavers. Beavers would dive into the safety of deep water at high speed using their flat muscled-tail. If cornered, the 40 to 60 pound beaver would fight back with its powerful slashing hind claws and sharp biting teeth.

But the beavers were no match to the hunting tactics of swarms of white fur trappers. Using several hunting tricks, trappers used a concoction that beavers could not resist to bring them to various beaver traps. And this concoction was from the beaver itself. It's called castoreum or castor oil.

A waterproofing oil from the castoreum sac - 02 large glands located in front of the rectum. The beaver grooms itself for hours with this waterproofing castor oil. This foul scented oil was used in various trapping techniques like placing a drop or two on a stick, or scenting a trap (natural or manmade). It was even used on open-water.

Castoreum scent is so compelling, beavers already trapped have been known to pull their injured bodies - trap and all to another trap scented with castoreum. Castoreum scent is so compelling, predators like bears, lynx, martins, mink, otters, wolverines with their super keen sense of smell have ventured to waiting beaver traps in hopes of finding an injured or dead beaver.

Hypnotizing Lobsters: Throughout this book, you learned how to hypnotize - stun various critters. And here's technique you can use to hypnotize lobsters. This technique can be done underwater.

Step 01: Insure the lobster's left and right claws are secured with heavy-duty rubberbands, so you don't get severely pinched by that ornery critter.

Step 02: Secure the lobster with your non-dominant hand (left ?) with the lobster facing right-side up and facing your dominant hand (right ?).

Step 03: Stand the lobster on its head facing down.

Step 04: Take your index finger of your dominant hand (right ?) and gently stroke the lobster up & down between the carapace (head portion) insuring your rubbing between its two beady eyes.

Step 05: After a dozen or so gentle strokes, the lobster should stand on its head supported by its claws that form a triangle foundation. It may stay in this position for a surprisingly long time. Why it can be hypnotized by the gently rubbing between its eyes is unknown.

Hypnotizing the lobster puts you in control for handling and dressing it. See Sketches below.

Can other crustaceans (crayfish, crawdads, crabs, shrimp,...) be hypnotized using this same technique? It's unknown but I figure it's a high possibility. See *Lobster Trap & Snare* and see **"269+ International Fishing Tricks And More!"** at **www.survivalexpertbooks.com**

Imitating Duck Call: Are you ready to talk to some ducks? You're going to quack-up over this duck calling technique. The best part is, you don't need to purchase any manmade or natural devices to call ducks.

Take the tip of your tongue and place it at the roof of your mouth near your upper teeth. Now at the same time without removing your tongue from this spot, <u>try to say as loud as you can</u> *"quack"* for ducks and to call geese say *"ah-hunk."* You'll be surprised with a little practice how real they sound and even more surprised when them quacking and honking critters come landing near your blind. OK, go ahead and <u>try it</u> - place your tongue at the roof of your mouth near your upper teeth say real loud *"quack"* for ducks and
"ah-hunk" to call geese. Good - excellent!

Note: Ducks, geese,... tend to migrate at the <u>west side</u> of streams, lakes ponds,... when breeding.

Ice Support Measurements!

You & Equipment Weigh ???	Ice Should Be:
One survivor - no equipment	02-inches thick
Group of Survivors in a file	03-inches thick
Car or snowmobile (02 tons)	07.5-inches thick
Light truck (02.5 tons)	08-inches thick
Medium truck (03.5 tons)	10-inches thick
Heavy truck (09 tons)	12-inches thick
10 tons of weight	15-inches thick
25 tons of weight	20-inches thick

NOTE: Before you venture on frozen ice (lakes or ponds), ensure you see the local Forest Ranger for best and up-to-date safe ice-thickness measurements. If you're in a survival environment, walk around the frozen water obstacle.

Indian Appetite Suppressant: Tahltan Indians are located in British Columbia, Canada. A Tahltan girl is isolated during her menstruation period - only girls are allowed to be with her. During her isolation, she wears a bag which contains animal grease (fat). She applies this fat to her lips which suppresses her appetite. This may be an option if you find yourself without adequate food but have some fat available (fat candles, fat reflectors, fat heaters,...).

Indian Bad To The Bone - Slow Killer: Previously in this book, I gave you *Eskimo Bad To The Bone - Slow Killer*. It was a technique they used to slowly kill predators like wolves,... And Indians had a similar technique but they used it to kill all sorts of game for food, tools, clothing, weapons,... Indians took a piece of flexible steel or whalebone and bent into the smallest circle possible secured by deer sinew. This compressed steel or whalebone would be inserted in a piece of tasty meat, flesh, or fat complimented with blood and allowed to freeze. Once frozen, a number of these would be placed at the intended game's area of stalking. The animal would eat the coiled killer. Lodged in its stomach, it would melt and the stomach acids would eat away the sinew and the coiled killer would spring open causing serious internal injuries which would lead to a painful quick death. During this time, the animal was tracked and eventually be found *"dead in its tracks."*

In the late 1930s, as a teenager, Joachim (Jim) Dierlich was drafted into the German military. Fighting at the Russian Front, he was returned to Germany and released from military service in 1942. In May 1945, as the Russians advanced from the east and the Americans from the west, Joachim evaded to the Austrian forest. Joachim had a limited supplies to support his survival in the Austrian forest. But one most important factor in his survival in the wilderness was the survival training he received as a boy when he first entered German military service. The survival training was real & serious because the threat of war in the near future was real.

The survival training was real and was noted to turn boys into men. The American Boy Scout training was noted as *"ridiculous"* compared to the German survival training. The following is just 01 of several of Joachim's survival tricks that kept him alive in the dense Austrian forest.

Joachim's Traps & Snares: Joachim constructed traps & snares from the wire and cord he brought with him to catch rabbits. However, he knew the more traps & snares he had, the better chances of dinner vittles. So Joachim made additional cordage from the inner bark of locust limbs. He'd shredded it by rubbing it between 02 rocks. Then he'd weave it into cordage. Joachim used the last portions of his food supply as bait.

In quick succession, he captured 03 rabbits. What rabbit meat he didn't eat, he smoked for future use. He also used rabbit meat as bait and captured foxes, weasels, and more rabbits. He also used other bait to capture more rabbits like wild greens and roots of plants.

Now it doesn't state exactly which traps & snares Joachim used but you have many in this book that can be used in just about any environment.

Note: Let me repeat a portion of this segment which I think is important: *"The survival training was real and was noted to turn boys into men. The American Boy Scout training was noted as 'ridiculous\' compared to the German survival training."*

This book gives YOU far more survival training with respect to hunting alone than most survival books or survival courses. I annotated several 'fishing tricks' in this book. I'm sure you're interested in plenty of fishing tricks so go to **www.survivalexpertbooks.com** and see *"269+ International Fishing Tricks And More!"*

Jacking: Jacking is a survival trick using a light to catch fish at night. It's illegal in most US states. Jacking is done by placing a flashlight in a waterproof jar that's horizontally suspended below the water's surface.

Or you can horizontally suspend a flashlight designed for underwater use. The light attracts fish. And this is a great opportunity to spear, net, or fish using a variety of baits. See *"269+ International Fishing Tricks And More!"* at **www.survivalexpertbooks.com**

Jigging Pole: A The jigging pole is made-up of a durable sapling about eight feet in length and a one inch width at the base which tapers off to half an inch at its point. Twenty feet of cordage, one foot of cordage, a hook, light weight and bait are tied together.

Make a small groove one inch from the tip of the sapling. This will be used to tie-off the twenty-foot line and prevents the knot from slipping off the pole. Wrap one end of the line in the groove at least three times. Insure the wraps are very tight. Secure the wraps with a square knot. Pine sap may be used to secure the knot.

Tie-off the weight/sinker to the end of the line. Tie-off the one foot of cordage about two feet from the weight/sinker.

Secure the bait (insects) or something shiny to the hook. Believe it or not, **a straw has been noted to be an excellent bait** and it really works!!!

As you face the water obstacle (pond. lake...) lay-out the line behind you. Secure the jigging pole and hold it straight over your head.

Vigorously swing the jigging pole to your front. This motion of the jigging pole will propel the fishing line into the water.

While the line is in the water, gently slap the water with the tip of the pole. This will hopefully attract any fish. Take the pole and jerk/jig it so to give movement to your bait and attract it to any fish. Jig the pole in towards the shore till the bait is out of the water. Recast the line, slap the water with the pole (arouse attention), and jig the bait. See **"269+ *International Fishing Tricks And More!"* at www.survivalexpertbooks.com**

Jigging Pole

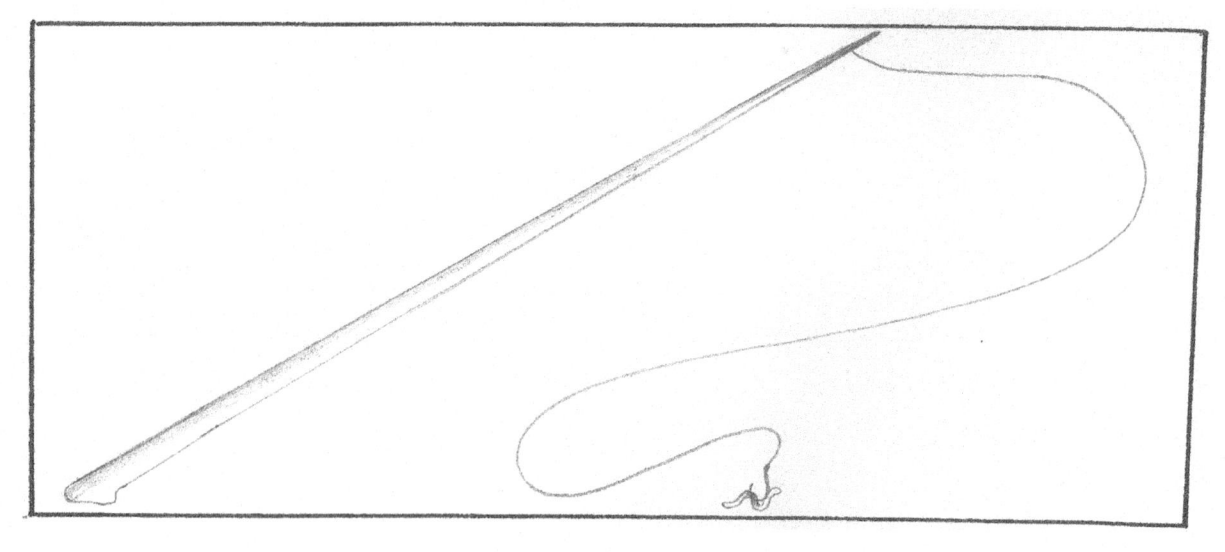

Juicy Cooking: One of the most favorite ways of cooking fish and birds was not over an open fire but below the fire. Indians got a good fire going then buried the fresh fish under the fire. The same technique was used for birds but before the bird was buried feathers and all, its feathers were saturated with water prior to cooking. Using this technique, the meat was cooked and very juicy.

Note: I've used this same technique. I double-wrapped vegetables and meat in aluminum foil. Dug a hole, placed the package in the hole and covered it with dirt. Had a fire over it and cooked the package for 02-03 hours. It was delicious. You can do the same thing in your oven!

Kalahari Antelope Snare: In the Kalahari, there are different species of antelope like the duiker, eland (*Advancing Crouch*), gemsbok, impala, kongoni, pronghorn, springbok, steinbok, wildebeest,... The snare used by the bushmen is very similar to the Kalahari Bird Snare (see below), except the Kalahari Antelope Snare is much larger and incorporates a couple different items. It incorporates a hole 05-inches across by 05-inches deep that holds the trigger that secures the slip noose. The trigger is only a stick wedged securely across the hole that holds the slip noose and the constant pulling cordage in place.

The constant tension is from a large branch secured in the ground - acts like a twitch-up like the Twitch-Up Snare and Kalahari Bird Snare. The small hole is covered with a piece of bark and the entire slip noose that's laid-out in wait is covered with dirt.

The curious antelope is channelled into the corral of sticks 12-inches high and eventually steps into the hole setting off the trigger which snares the antelope's leg with a tightening slip noose around its leg holding it in place. What baits the antelope into the corral? Its curiosity! However, for teasing bait, just observe what they like eating and use that as bait. See sketch below.

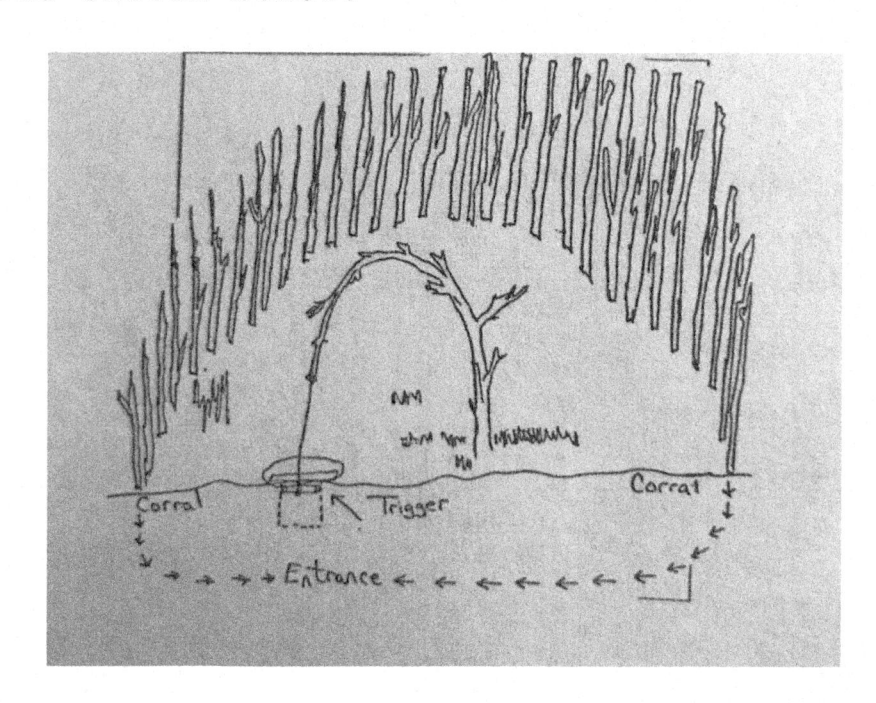

Kalahari Bird Snare: The savvy bushmen used a variety of traps and snares to catch a variety of small and big game. One trap and snare was a bird snare that incorporated the important principles of most or all traps and snares - bait, channelization, tension, and a trigger. Remember, small and big game don't know a bird snare from a deer snare but rely on their super acute senses to alert them to warn them of danger. So all parts of the snare must be descented from the human scent.

Anyway, the Kalahari Bird Snare baited the bird (tasty Lesser Bustard) with acacia gum, tsama seeds or other seeds and nuts. The bait was placed inside a small corral-like 06-inch diameter perimeter made-up of several sticks placed in the ground but leveled evenly on the top. Now we got the bird to go for the bait - acacia gum. Now to snare the bird, a deep hole is dug a couple feet from the corral. A sturdy 06-foot long pliable green branch is placed in the hole and the dirt is securely replaced and packed around the pliable yet stiff stick - this is the tension for the trigger.

Home-made cordage is tied to the end of the branch and a trigger tied to it a couple feet down the cordage. To hold the trigger, a smaller deep hole is dug and a small arch-shaped branch inserted in the hole. Dirt is securely packed around it. The trigger is placed in the upper portion of the arch with an additional small stick holding it in place.

The remaining cordage is formed into a slip noose which goes on top of the small corral. The bird goes for the bait of acacia gum inside the center of the small corral and sets-off the sensitive trigger. The nearby bent branch springs back whipping the cordage up which wraps the noose tightly around the neck or body of the bird snaring it - trapping it in mid-air. See sketch below and to better understand the concepts and engineering of all traps and snares see *Traps and Snares* in the A-Z Index.

1st Note: You have to fine tune the <u>triggers</u> and adjust the tension, adjust cordage,... to get that trap and snare so sensitive that it will trap even the most savvy and cautious critter. And remember to re-descent (charcoal, dirt, mud,...) all parts you touched.

2nd Note: Once the small or big game is captured, predators may move-in quickly to steal your meal. So you must periodically check all traps and snares.

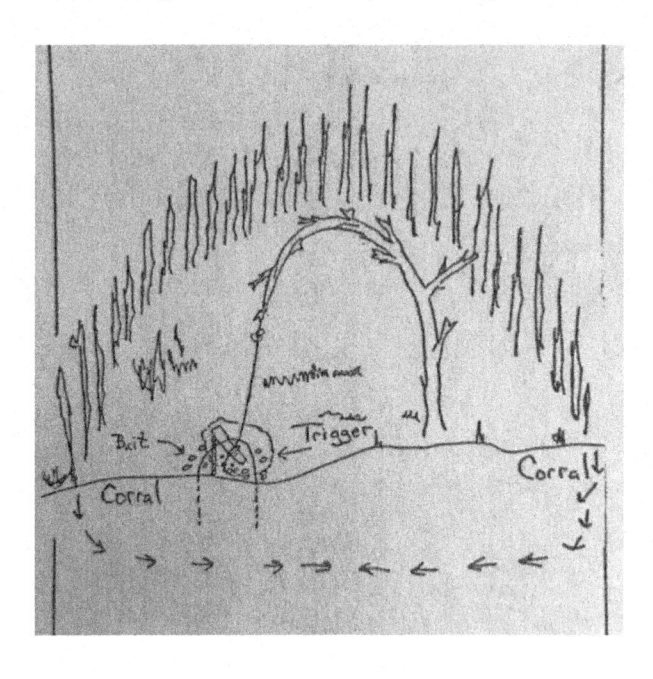

Kalahari Glue Snares: The Kalahari bushmen made a Glue Snare that baited and held on to its victims. The glue was made from a plant that was shaped like an elephant's ear and as tough as a hippopotamus hide. This plant excreted a milky white liquid. The bushmen made a paste from this liquid and placed it on traps to capture fowl. The traps were baited with grain, the fowl landed next to the bait and became stuck.

Birds have superior eyesight. So good, by comparison to humans, we're half-way blind compared to birds. And birds can spot a meal a long ways away. Did you know that there are glues, contact paper, 02-sided tape,... that can capture and hold-on to fowl and other small game (rodents, rabbits,...)? Just thought I'd give you something to think about.

Kalahari Smoke-Out: Kalahari trapped small game in their own underground dens. Building a fire near the den of a burrowing animal, the fire and smoke either forced the animal to the surface or killed it in its own den. See *Kalahari Underground Fishing* below on how bushmen retrieved underground animals dead or alive.

Kalahari Tsama Trap And Snare: Tsama melons are a very important water and food source, plus the tsama shell had several uses. One creature that was hated by the African bushmen were mice for they burrowed into the valuable tsama melons and made them worthless. So bushboys made traps and snares capturing the mice. The traps and snares were made from:
- Sinew
- A bending branch from a bush
- Noose
- Tsama seeds for bait
- Several twigs pushed into the ground forming a circle.
- One twig used as a trigger
- Ground swept clean

This trap and snare looks like a cross between the *Twitch-Up Snare* and the *Onoda Jungle Fowl Trap*. So here's a sketch of what I think it looks like.

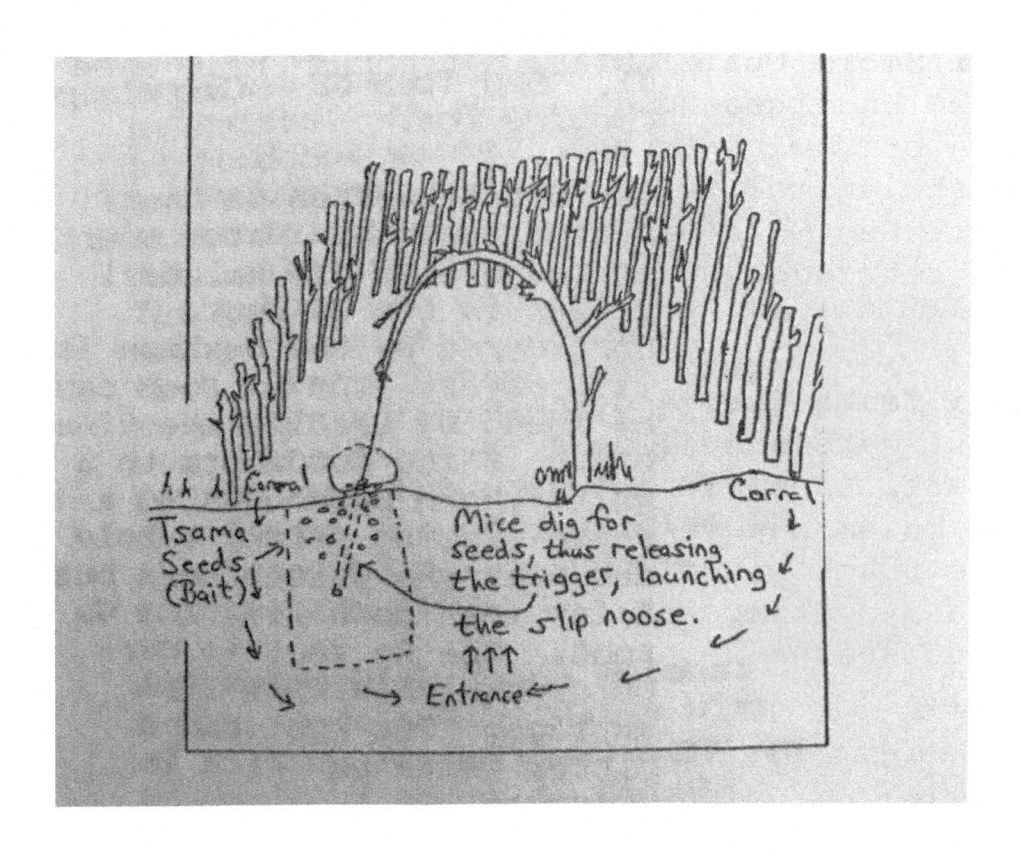

Kalahari Underground Fishing: Kalahari also went fishing for game that burrowed underground. Taking a sturdy sapling, they tied a hook to the end of it. The probing sapling with hook searched the burrow for small game. The invading searching sapling with its hook found its prey. Hooking the prey, it was forcibly dragged out of the burrow where it was finished-off at the surface.

Note: If you decide to use this technique in a real life or death survival situation, my recommendation is to secure a barbed fishing hook to your durable sapling. You already have #6 or #4 hooks in the *75+ Use Survival Kits* I sent you, but a #1 fishing hook or larger may work better to easier hook into any burrowing critter with little effort compared to smaller fishing hooks.

Kephart – 'The Dean Of Camping': Horace Kephart was born 08 September 1862 when the American Civil War was already several months old. A very avid outdoorsman, Kephart wrote volumes on camping. So much so and evident was his expertise, Kephart is known as the *"Dean of American Campers."* One of his most complete writings is his combined 02-Volume, 405-page & 479-page book is *Camping And Woodcraft* which is rich in camping tricks of the trade.

But another of Kephart's claim to fame' was his instrumental work to establish the mountainous 2,050-mile Appalachian Trail that runs from Newfoundland, Canada to Alabama, United States.

Here are a few dozen of Kephart's survival tricks that are worthy of your attention so you're ready Anytime Anywhere.

Kephart's Baited Snare: The good thing about the *Kephart Baited Snare (KBS)* is that it can be constructed for small game and bigger game. For small game use small parts and for big game use bigger sturdier parts. OK, let's get started.

The 1st step is to find a game path and attempt to identify the type of game by the size of the game path (width and wear & tear), tracks, fur, scat,... Your hands and any items used to construct the *KBS* should be descented using mud or cold ashes (dry or wet) from your cold firepit,...

The main part of the *KBS* is the arched loop that goes over the game trail. The arched loop supports the trigger and baited stick. Find a thin 06-foot green stick and soak it in warm water or soak it in fresh water for a day or so.

This will make the stick pliable and bendable. Sharpen both ends. Carefully bend the green stick to form a U-shape the width of the game trail. Insert both pointed ends into the edges of the game trail. This will be the entrance to the *KBS*.

Now take two 01-foot straight thin sticks and carve one end of both ends so they form a sharp pointed angle so they slip off each other. The other ends of the sticks are flat and blunt. These 02 sticks will form your trigger.

On the vertical stick, you'll secure your bait by simply hooking the bait halfway down the stick. The vertical stick is also resting on a rock instead of into the dirt so it's more sensitive to any movement from the animal biting into the bait. The horizontal stick is receiving tension from the green sapling with its upward pull.

A green sturdy sapling is pulled down just above the arch. A wire or string is secured to the tail-end of the green sapling and also tied to the horizontal stick. From there the wire (brass, copper,...) or string (550-cord) forms a slip noose smaller than the arched loop and this loop should accommodate your intended prey.

Channelization should be used to <u>insure the prey comes into the noose to get to the bait</u> and NOT go for the bait on the other side of the *KBS*. Without channelization, it could easily grab the bait and evade scott free. Anyway, once the prey enters the noose, it goes further in and bites into the bait on the vertical bait stick.

The vertical stick is agitated and no longer supports the downward pull of the horizontal stick. This triggers the upward pull from the sapling which tightens the noose around the prey lifting it into the air, suspending it. The suspended prey strangles under its own suspended weight.

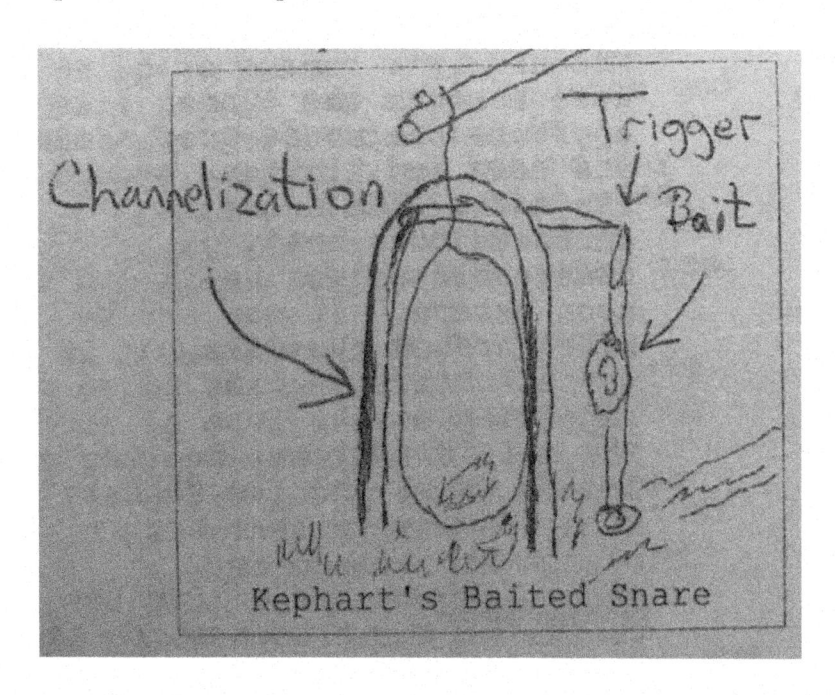

Kephart's Baited Snare

Note: I've told you before what I think of traps & snares using saplings for tension. They're great initially but will NEVER last - will NEVER have the required tension after a day or so. I like using weighted objects because the tension will still be there days later. Weighted objects will always have that potential energy ready-to-go when required.

Kephart's Branch Snare: I already gave you my version of the Branch Snare, now here's how Kephart does it. Obviously you should place the branch trap & snare on a known small game path used by birds or other small game. A small branch or 02 but thick smaller branches, leaves,... is placed over the path so its laying about a foot or more above the chosen path.

Then surgically remove smaller branches, leaves,... in the center of the path so you have a tunnel-like aperture through the branches that block the path. A branch or 02 act as channelization and your tunnel-like aperture gives access to the small game through the thicket of branches. A wire slip noose is placed over the tunnel-like aperture.

When the small game, whether it's coming or going - goes through the tunnel-like aperture the noose goes around its head and tightens around its neck. The noose is anchored to a heavy or immoveable object so it can't soon escape.

It may try to bite through the wire but it may take it some time to do so depending on the type of wire. The main difference between my Branch Snare and the Kephart's Branch Snare is that his branch(s) is used to <u>channelize</u> the prey into the center of the branch which is cut away for access through the blocked vegetation.

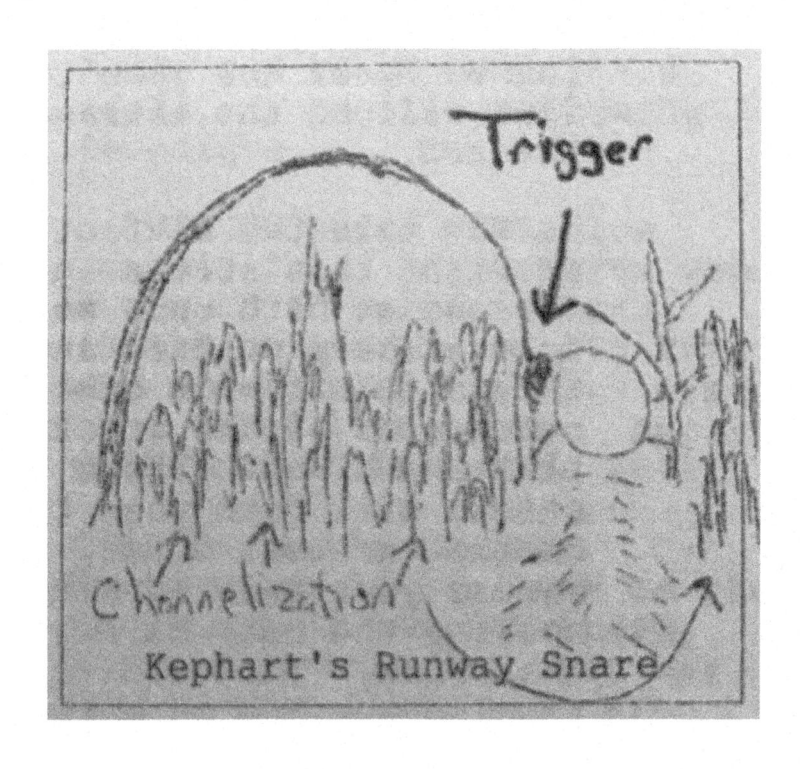

Kephart's Runway Snare

Kephart's Deer Drag: The deer is never near the truck when it's down for the final count. Some laws prohibit dressing the deer where it lay and the whole deer must be recovered and brought to a site for a required tag.

Then again hunters hunting on private land, bleed and dress the deer and immediately put it on ice where the deer lay. But if you have to drag that heavy critter, here's a technique you ought to consider. Dragging the deer over leaves and snow decreases the friction between the deer's fur and the ground.

The deer's head should lead the way for dragging the deer from the tail-end forward, has the lay of the deer's fur going against the grain causing more friction. To get a handle on the deer, tie the front legs to the deer's lower jaw. Attach a small sturdy sapling or bush to the deer's head and start dragging away. While we're dragging them deer vittles to the camp, now we have to dress the deer.

Kephart's Deer Dressing: Different deer hunters across the globe and throughout history have different and common techniques to dress deer. And here's Kephart's step-by-step technique to dress and store valuable deer meat.

a) Verify Kill: The last thing you want to do is come up unarmed on a downed deer, elk, moose,... that's playing opossum and surprisingly find yourself in hand-to-hoof & horn combat. Odds are you'll lose and that ornery critter will surely kill you dead before it dies. So stand at a safe distance with your weapon at the ready and VERIFY the critter is dead. If necessary, put another bullet, arrow,... through its head and/or heart.

b) Bleed: Game both small & big should be hung to bleed and cool off. The meat will be tenderer. The deer can also be bled and dressed where it lay. Just insure its belly is facing downhill so when its bled and dressed, the fluids, intestines, debris,... flow downhill away from the deer.

To bleed the deer, cut into the side of the throat. You can also cut 02 or 03-inches into the breast in front of the sternum or breastbone and move the knife around so to sever major blood vessels.

c) Skinning: Place your knife at the hide where the neck meets the back and cut a circular pattern below the head. This is done if you want the use the head for mounting. Insert the knife at the paunch and cut upwards following the chest line to the cut at the neck. Reverse the cut following the same cut downward all the way to the tail. Do not cut deep into the belly. Cut off the two front legs at the knee of the forelegs and the 01 1/2-inches below the hocks on the hind legs.

Now pull off the skin using both hands a apply any cutting if necessary. Remove the top-half of skin then do the bottom half by rolling the deer over. If you plan on keeping the hide, stretch it out fur-side down to dry. Then scrape any fat, debris,... from it before tanning. See *Leather And Hides* and *Tanning* in the A-Z Index.

Note: Kephart also notes that one of the fastest ways to skin a deer is to hang it up by 01 of its hind legs and begin skinning at the hocks. Peeling the skin down from the hind legs to the body, to the neck and removing the head.

d) Gralloching: Gralloching is a term meaning to remove all offal (viscera[internal organs] and trimmings of a butchered animal often considered inedible by humans). Now that the deer is skinned, take your knife and insert it at the breastbone and cut through the false ribs to the sternum. Cut open the abdominal cavity but DO NOT cut into any organs. Prop open the chest using a stick. Cut the diaphragm away which is between the chest organs and the abdomen.

All the internal organs are now free to remove except the neck vessels and the anus. Reach into the neck and cut away all the vessels. Cut around the rectum and urinary organs cutting close to the bone as possible. Flush with plenty of fresh water so other organs are not tainted.

Remove and SAVE the:

01) Antlers (tools, weapons,...

02) Backbone ligaments (sinew thread)

03) Bladder (pouch, catgut, bait,...)

04) Blood (emergency food, plus blood has several other uses. See *Blood* in the A-Z Index.)

05) Brain (food, tanning, bait,...)

06) Caul fat (fuel for fire, food, cooking, body insulation, waterproofing, bait,...)

07) Heart (food, bait,...)

08) Hide (emergency food, clothing, containers, foot gear, gloves, tools, weapons, bait,...)

09) Hoofs (glue)

10) Kidneys (food, bait,...)

11) Large intestine (pouch, catgut, bait,...)

12) Liver (food, bait,...)

13) Marrow bones (food, tools, bait,...)

14) Pericardium (pouch, catgut, bait...)

15) Scrotum (tobacco pouch, catgut, container,...)

16) Spleen (food, bait,...)

Note: The <u>Pericardium</u> is the outer skin covering the heart. <u>Catgut</u> is not from them 9-life critters but a thin cord made from dried intestines of animals. Catgut has many field uses and is used to strings tennis rackets, musical instruments, surgical ligatures,... And <u>Caul Fat</u> is a folded membrane loaded with fat and located at the intestines.

e) Cooking And Jerkying: Deer meat, organs, fat and marrow are all foods that can be easily cooked for immediate consumption or jerkied to preserve for future food. The fat can be eaten and used to fry the meat and organs. The food can be baked, fried, jerkied, parboiled, stewed,...

f) Hide Tanning: Here's a couple techniques in which Kephart prepared the rawhide so to use it for clothing, containers, footgear, gloves, shelter cover,...

01) Soaking: The deer hide is soaked in water for 03-05 days. Hides of bigger game animals like elk and buffalo are soaked in a concoction of lye of wood ashes and water. Another technique is to roll-up the hide in moist wood ashes for a few days.

02) Depilating & Fleshing: The deer hide is depilitated (removing hair) and fleshed (removing fat, debris,...). This is done by securing the hide to a log and using a smooth fleshing tool of sorts. The hair, fat, debris are removed. This may be a hard workout depending on the technique, tools and experience.

03) Hide Stretching & Tanning: The hide is stretched in all directions within a framework. The brains of the deer are slow cooked. A paste is the end result. The paste is applied and worked into the hairside of the hide. Multiple applications may be required.

04) Smoking: Smoking closes the pores of the hide, toughens the hide, acts as a water repellent and gives a color to the hide. One of the best smoking fuels is rotted wood that's spongy. The rotted spongy wood will give off a blue smoke but will not ignite. The hide is placed over the small smudge firepit like a tee-pee and smoked for several hours.

Deer parts have many uses like food, shelter, clothing, tools, concoctions, insulation, preserving food, weapons,...

Kephart's Mosquito Trap And Drowner: Now a days we have to collectively KILL the mosquito, preferably the female mosquito. Wars are won on attrition and I think the best fighter to prevent West Nile Virus (WNV) is to kill the mosquito. The more we kill, the better.

And because of the progressively growing threat of WNV in the United States, companies are coming out with plenty of mosquito traps. Some are ingenious and expensive while others are worthless and still expensive. But here's a mosquito trap that's real cheap. Kephart states that female mosquitos (may be males too) love the sweet nectar of wine. So why not get the sweetest tasting wine you can find, pour a healthy portion in a jar and place it outside. Let mosquitoes and other nagging, biting insects have at the wine and let them drunkenly drown in it too. See *Drunk Birds*.

Note: I wonder if sodas will compel the female mosquito for a drink or two followed by a drowning. Non-diet sodas are LOADED with sugar. Or how about plain ol' tap water with plenty of sugar stirred into it till it's saturated for some super sweet sugar water. Worth some future R&D - we'll see.

Kephart's Runway Snare: The *Kephart Runway Snare (KRS)* is designed and set-up to catch small game travelling in either direction on their game paths. The 1st step is to find a game path and attempt to identify the type of game by the size of the game path (width and wear & tear), tracks, fur, scat,... Your hands and any items used to construct the *KRS* should be <u>descented</u> using <u>mud</u> or cold ashes (dry or wet) from your cold firepit,...

Also a good site on the game path that provides a good green sapling that can be used as tension and anchors for the *KRS*. This green sapling should be about 05-feet off the game trail. On the edges of each side of the game trail and in-line with the sturdy green sapling, there should be some smaller saplings to anchor the noose.

Secure a 01-foot stake and carve a sharp pointed end to it and a notch near the top of the stake to anchor the trigger. Emplace and drive the stake firmly into the ground with the notch facing the game trail.

Secure some thin & pliable wire (brass, copper,...) - yet strong or high tensile string (550-cord) and form a slip noose with a diameter of about 09-inches. This noose is anchored and held to form a noose by the smaller saplings on the edges of the game trail. The tail-end if the noose is secured to the trigger itself. And the trigger is carved to match the notch in the 01-foot stake on the edge of the game trail.

The tail-end of the noose is not only tied to the trigger but also to the tail-end of the springy green sapling. The green sapling and trigger are carefully bent towards the stake at the edge of the game trail where the trigger now under tension is *"hooked"* into notch on the stake.

The noose is redressed so it's round and can accommodate the critter. Once the critter attempts to walk through the KRS it will set off the trigger which will have the green sapling immediately tighten the noose around its neck and pull the prey above the ground - suspending it. The weight of the prey will strangle it. See Sketch below.

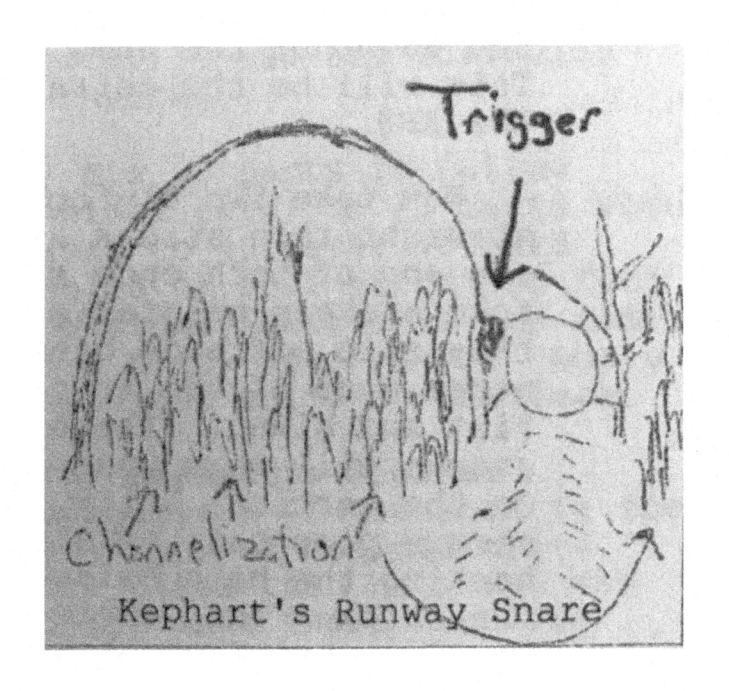

Kephart's Runway Snare (Channelization, Trigger)

Kissing For Blue Quail: There are many species of quail but here's one for blue quail found in Kansas, Colorado, Oklahoma, Arizona, New Mexico, and Mexico. Here's a neat trick to call blue quail that requires no fancy calling devices. Take the palm of your right-hand and place it horizontally against your lips.

Kiss your hand loudly and at the same time pull your hand away starting at the fingers - pulling your kissing lips away from your *"peeling"* hand. Immediately repeat this kissing sound. Also do it with your back to the quail critters so the sound is muffled and any foreign sounds are not heard by them - alerting them to danger. See *Gambel's Quail*.

Lakota Rattlesnake Hunt: The Sioux called themselves the Dakota and Lakota meaning 'allies.' The Lakota went to the bluffs and hunted those deadly rattlesnakes for food and tool parts and this is how they did it. They took a long sturdy stick that had short forks at the end. They'd find the rattlesnakes, pin them down with the forks right behind the head and chop off its head. They'd CAREFULLY put the parts in a bag that was secured to their side and carried-on to the next rattlesnake. See *"Forked Walking Stick / Staff."*

WARNING: When in close proximity with a dead venomous snake, DO NOT TOUCH the head or fangs of the snake.

Laydon Static Bola Snare: Here are the details on the *Laydon Static Bola Snare* (LSBS), and yes I named it after myself. Folks I don't even have to test the LSBS cause I already know it works. Have you ever hooked your clothing or skin with a barbed fishing hook? Difficult and painful to un-hook isn't it? Well how about several barbed hooks simultaneously, that will painfully paralyze you in place? That's what this trap & snare is all about. OK, are you ready? Here it goes.

Ingredients: Shovel, a dozen or so #16 treble hooks - very small to #4/0 hooks - large (depending the size of the prey), 50+ yards of fishing line (02 pound to 36-pound depending on the prey), 05 anchor points or heavy anchors (logs, rocks,...), cayenne pepper (minimum 95,000+ SHU), charcoal, mud, and alarm system (bells, electric mercury alarms).

Step 01 - Emplacement of LSBS: The LSBS is designed for small game to medium game from squirrels, rabbits,... to fox, coyotes, wild dogs, cougars,... that have a low silhouette (unlike tall-legged deer). Find a location to emplace the LSBS. Look for game trails, tracks, scat, fur, bones,...

Step 02 - Descenting LSBS: I'm telling you, them critters can smell and hear you long before they see you and that includes anything you touch. Them smart critters don't know a LSBS from a Lobster Trap, but they can sure smell and hear you which alerts them of DANGER thus detouring them from your trap & snare. So first thing is to wash your hands and arms with mud or charcoal to get rid of your human scent.

Second, wash all the materials you're going to use to construct the LSBS and especially all trap & snare parts. Scrub that mud or charcoal into all materials especially trap & snare parts cause it will rain, snow, wind on them and you need the descenting process to last.

Step 03 - Emplace Cayenne Pepper: Take your shovel and dig a 03-foot wide shallow concave depression about 12-inches deep. Place the excavated dirt at least 100-meters downwind from the LSBS. Place a good handful of cayenne pepper at the bottom center of the shallow depression and cover it with a light sprinkle of dirt (keep reading).

Warning: When taking the cayenne pepper out of the bag or pouring it from the bag, INSURE you're positioned UPWIND so the cayenne particles don't fly in your eyes. Once just one speck of cayenne pepper gets in your eyes - you'll know it in a New York second and may spazz out!! So be careful!

Step 04 - Emplace Bait: Place your bait in the bottom center of this shallow depression above where you placed the handful of cayenne pepper. The bait could be several drops of your own blood on a piece of bark or guts from any critter or sections of carrion,... The prey will go for that bait. INSURE you choose your bait according to your prey. Depending on the species, rabbits may be more apt to go for a few or all rabbit vittles like bark, berries, buds, fecal pellets, fungi, grass, leaves, plant stems, shoots, roots, and twigs than guts of a critter whereas scavengers will go for just about anything they could put their sharp teeth into.

Once the bait is placed in the center of the shallow depression, place some natural debris over the depression. If it's freshly cut, INSURE you cut it at least 100-meters downwind of the LSBS and INSURE you rub mud or charcoal on all the fresh cut ends of the freshly cut vegetation for them critters can smell freshly cut vegetation and take it as a warning of danger.

Step 05 - Emplacing Hooks: Here's the hardest but easy part of the LSBS. Take 03 hooks with their eyes and tie them into the 1st part of a 12-foot fishing line. The hooks with lines should be tied-in about 01-foot apart with the remaining fishing line secured to a heavy anchor like a log, stake, rock.

Step 06 - Emplacing Remaining Hooks: Carry-on repeating Step 05 and emplace the remaining 4/0 hooks within and on the vegetation concealing the baited depression. Start at one section and go around and work in a clockwise or counter-clockwise circle so you don't' get tangled in the LSBS.

Step 07 - Burying Fish Lines: If there are any exposed fish lines leading away from the LSBS, you may want to place some mud over them just to cover them up initially. You want the prey to get hooked on the interior hooks first.

Step 08 - Channelization: With the LSBS, there is no need for channelization. That critter can come from any direction and get tangled-up, move around trying to escape and get tangled up some more and may be hooked be several different hooks on several parts of its body.

Step 09 - Alarm System: You may attach an alarm system that goes off when prey is snared by the LSBS.

Step 10 - Descent & Camouflage Again: Once the LSBS is completed, double check and descent and camouflage as necessary.

This is how the *Laydon Static Bola Snare* works. The prey will be compelled to the bait by the scent it gives off. Once it enters the shallow depression to get to the bait, odds are it may already be "hooked" in its fur by 01 or more of the hooks within the vegetation.

Like a real bola, the LSBS tangles-up the prey, except the LSBS is static (stationary). Once it reaches the bait and disturbs the dirt, it disturbs the highly irritating cayenne pepper which enters the eyes and respiratory tract of the prey.

At this point the prey is blind, has trouble breathing and goes wild, thus entangling itself more and more by the multiple hooks that are hooking into its fur, paws, legs, belly, ears, face.

The more the prey pulls one way the more the multiple hooks on the opposite side embed themselves in the prey causing pain. The prey goes in that direction to relieve the pain thus embedding more hooks that are pulling & embedding themselves from the opposite direction. The prey is soon embedded with hooks pulling in all directions and its now static by the hooks but also by all anchors.

The LSBS is a vicious trap & snare and should be used only in emergency situations.

Step 11 - Kill And Dress The Prey: Once you're alert to a capture, insure you finish off the very ornery prey with one of your natural or manmade weapons as soon as possible. Because of the stinging painful cayenne pepper and several hooks in its body, it has a *"kill or be killed"* attitude so be very careful when finishing off the prey, and be alert for any in-coming curious & hungry predators who hear the prey's cries or predators downwind smelling its blood.

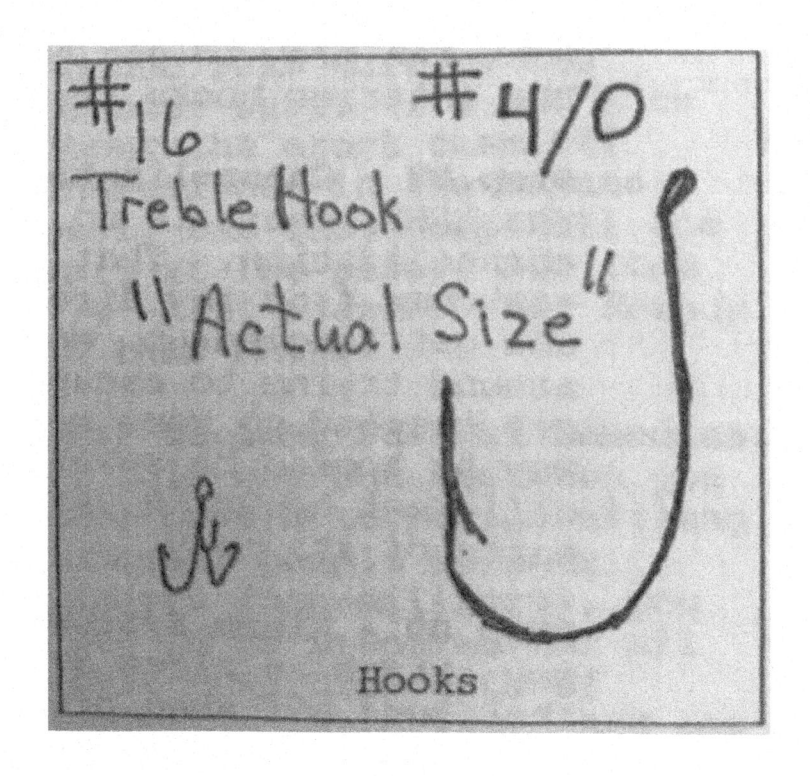

Hooks

Laydon Static Bola Snare

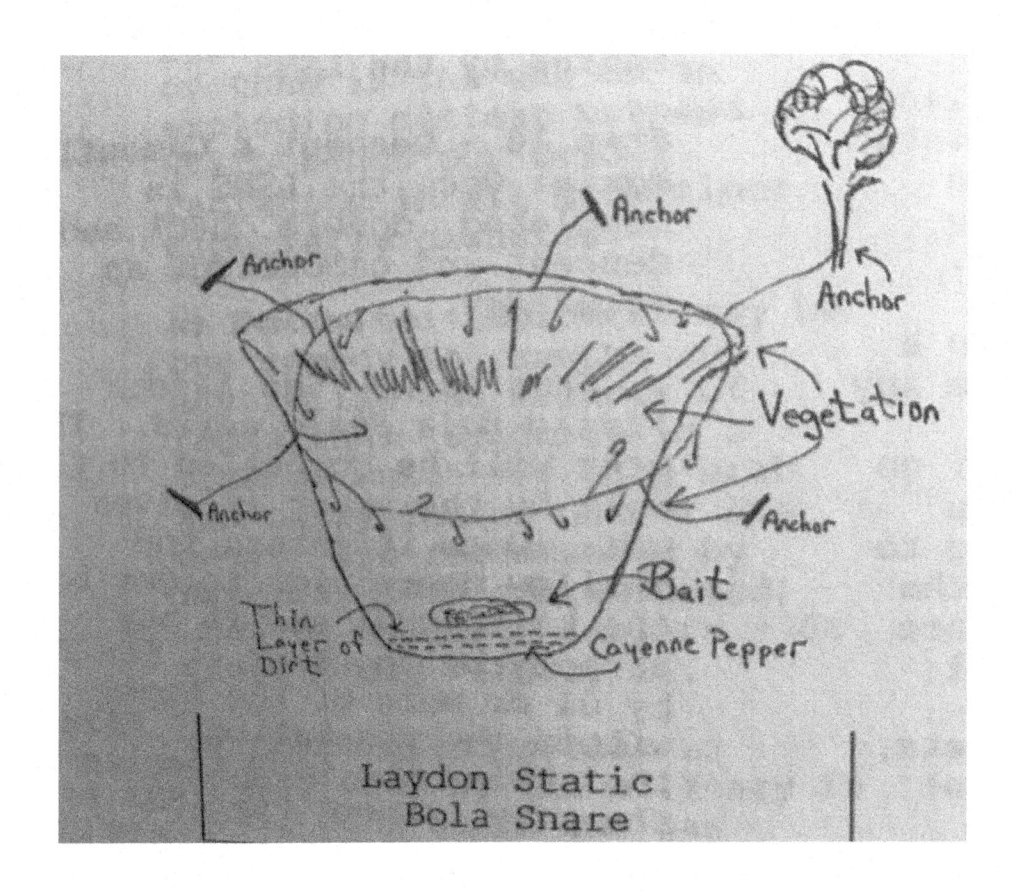

Lichen Emergency Food: Numerous plants consisting of a fungus,... grow on rocks, tree trunks,... Lichen is a **very available food source** for many arctic critters and even human critters - you! Ishi (extinct Yahi tribe - Northern California) and fellow Indians scraped lichen off rocks and added it to their meals to enhance taste. Besides, lichen is loaded with nutrients.

There are approximately 3,600 species of lichens in North America (US, Canada & their northern Territories). And I know you've seen lichens of some type growing on roof shingles, abandoned cars, street signs,...

Lichens are neither plant nor animal but are a fungus with a colony of algae or cyanobacteria or both. Lichens have long been used as emergency foods for man & beast and also used for medicines, dyes, perfumes, tinders, decorations, pollution detectors, shelters, clothing,... Lichens are composed of approximately 600 chemicals which aid the lichens to survive marginal life support environments. Lichens can fight-off bacteria, other fungi, and even seem attractive to roaming herbivores. Here's a small list of common lichens and their normal and <u>emergency uses</u>. Let's start with *Coyote's Long Hair*.

a) Coyote's Long Hair: Coyote's Long Hair lichens (*Bryoria fremontii*) was a delicacy for some indian tribes. Some tribes made clothes from this lichen. Interior Salish (northwestern US and B.C. Canada tribes) mixed this lichen with mud for chinking (fill small openings) cabins. Smart northern flying squirrels gathered this lichen to build their cozy warm nests. And in emergency times, their lichen nest was eaten.

b) Crustose: Crustose lichens (*Pleopidium oxytonum*) are used by Northern Paiute for medicinal uses.

c) Pine Gauze: Pine Gauze *(Usnea longissima)* located in the Pacific Northwest has been used by the Chinese for medicinal purposes since the 6th century.

d) Reindeer: Reindeer lichen(*Cladina stellaris*) is eaten by both North American caribou and their Eurasian counterpart - reindeer. Animals will dig down into the snow to get to the lichen. Arctic natives eat reindeer lichen after boiling it in water. And it's even eaten by the natives when the fermented lichen is retrieved from the stomachs of caribous.

e) Witch's Hair: Witch's Hair (*Alectoria sarmentosa*) is an emergency nourishing food for black-tail deer of the Pacific Northwest. See *"300,000 Plants On Earth – Edibility Test!"* at the end of this book.

Lift Pole Snare: A The Lift Pole Snare is made-up of 10 to 20 pound weight, 05-foot pole, a green sturdy forked stick (each fork at least 09-inches long) about 03-feet in height, 03-foot snare wire or string, a trigger - hooked-stick, and a few feet of string. Smear all parts with mud or charcoal to help mask your scent.

The Lift Pole Snare works by snaring the prey as it goes through the snare loop. Once the prey pulls on the snare loop, it triggers the weighted stick which tightens the loop around the prey and suspends it.

To make the Lift Pole Snare, first find a small game trail. Take your forked stick and place it - bury it about 02 feet from the game trail. Take the hooked-stick and place it - bury it about 6-inches from game trail.

Tie a 10 to 20 pound rock at the end of your lift pole and place it on the forked stick. The other end should be placed underneath the hooked portion of the hooked-stick.

Make a slip loop (end-of-rope bowline and loop it on itself) and tie it to your 5-foot lift pole - about 06-inches from the end of the lift pole so that it is aligned with the game trail. It may help to place the loop around some available vegetation on the game trail to form and stabilize the loop.

Readjust the lift pole so that is barely held by the hooked-stick.

To insure your Lift Pole Snare works, trip it. It shouldn't take much to trip the snare. The lift pole should immediately lift without it jumping out of the forked stick. The forked stick should be sturdy and stable in the ground.

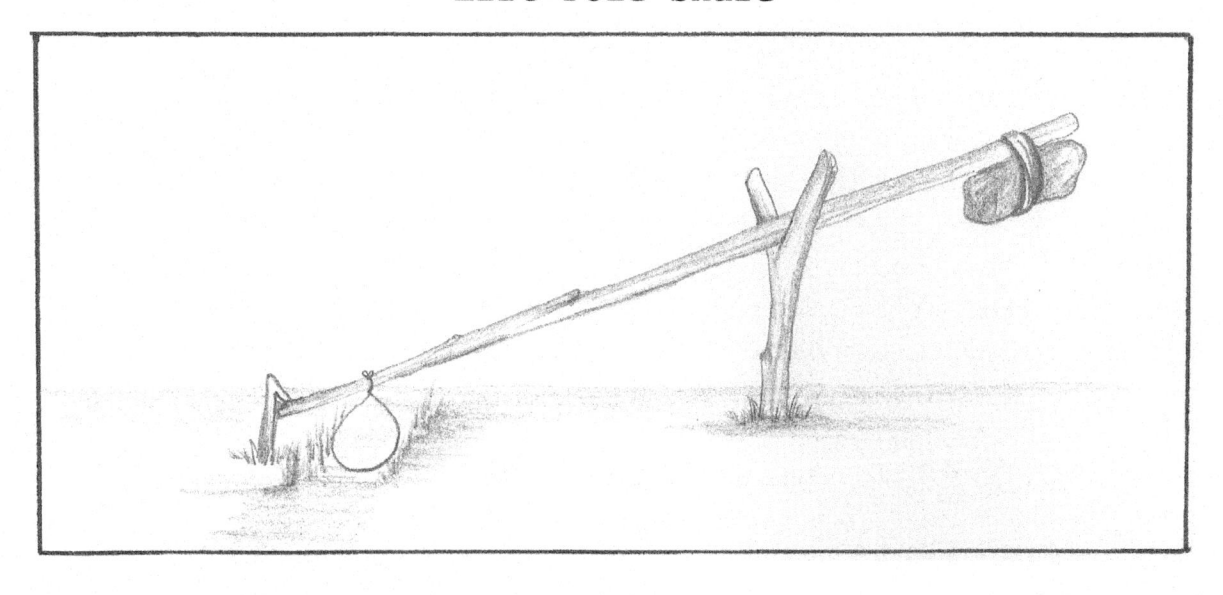

Lift Pole Snare

Lions Hunt For You: African bushmen had a technique to gather game without hunting for it. These World Class hunters would track lions. Following their tracks, they kept their distance. Eventually the lions would capture and eat their big game prey. The wise hunters kept their distance till the lion(s) had just the right amount of food to fill their bellies and make them lazy. That's when the bushmen attacked scaring-off the lions. The lions would not protect their prey for their hunger was already satisfied and they were lazy from their meal and not wanting to put up a fight. The bushmen would capture the half-eaten carcass and retrieve as much food as possible. For a half-eaten big game carcass, it still provided plenty of food.

Note: Often strategically located smoke-producing fires were used to force the lion to move from its meal. Most small & big game want nothing to do with smoke and fires.

Lobster Trap & Snare: I'm proud to say that I actually own 02 real ready-to-go lobster traps actually used at one time to catch plenty of them tasty lobster critters, and the traps are still in good shape. I acquired them back in 1999, cause I knew some day I'd need them as a training aids (this AASN and Trap & Snare Video). So here's how the lobster trap is constructed and why it works.

Lobster Trap Stats!

Name: Maine Lobster Trap, also called a Lobster Pot was initially used off the coast of Maine in 1850. New England states are the top lobster producers in the United States.

Prey: Maine Lobsters. Also called spiders or bugs because lobsters belong to the Arthropod Family.

Bait: Lobsters eat redfish, herring, fish bait, fish eggs, animal hide, bovine (cow) parts,... Lobsters are also known to be cannibalistic.

Trigger: None

Tension: None

Channelization: Open at one end leading to the lounge room that leads to a funnel-shaped nylon net, that leads into the dining room where the bait is located.

Weight: 07-pounds

Shape: <u>Rectangular</u> or Half-Round.

Length: 36-inches

Width: 18-inches

Construction: Slatted oak wood and steamed oak wood is bent to curve the wood (half-round traps), small 3/4-inch nails, and nylon netting. Wood may be treated to resist salt water corrosion.

The lobster trap is composed of a wooden rectangular box or half-round box made of 01-inch oak wood slats (straight & curved) spaced about 02-inches apart. The lobster trap has two sections called the *lounge room* and the *dining room*. One side of the *Lobster Trap* is closed off while the other end is open. The hungry lobster enters the open end of the lobster trap entering the *lounge room*.

The lobster maneuvers through the funnelled nylon net entering the *dining room* where the bait is located. Eating the bait, it's unable to leave the dining room because it can't negotiate the reverse side of the nylon-funneled net. In some cases the bait is encased in a mesh nylon netting so it can't be eaten so it can be used again and again.

Note: Researchers have found that lobsters actually came and went throughout the Lobster Trap and weren't really totally trapped at all.

The *Lobster Trap* is retrieved and the lobster(s) is removed and processed for markets and restaurants (dead or alive) throughout North America and abroad.

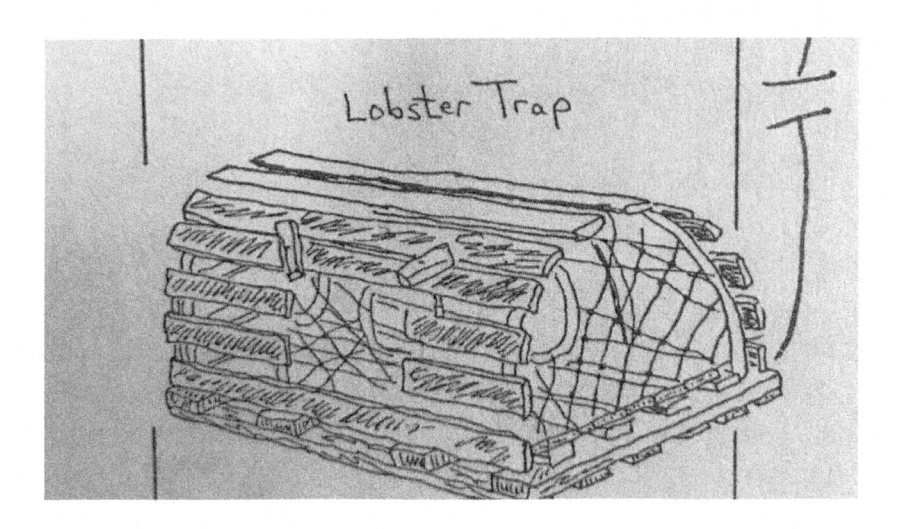

Can you replicate the *Lobster Trap* for other salt and fresh water fish, crustaceans,...? YES, why not. Depending on your prey, the trap may have to be a lot smaller or larger. I like the *Lobster Trap* because it's a *"set it up and forget it"* type trap & snare. See ***"269+ International Fishing Tricks And More!"*** at **www.survivalexpertbooks.com**

Log Drop Trap: A The Log Drop Trap consist of a log weighing approximately one-hundred eighty pounds and about six feet long; a 60-feet of high tensile strength cordage (550-cord); a one foot stake; a notched trigger; and a sizeable tree next to the run or game trail.

First find the run or game trail in which to set the trap. At this time it may be a good idea to mask the scent of all working pieces of the Log Drop Trap, including your hands. Camouflage, bait, and channelize as necessary. Secure the one foot steak firmly in the ground next to the run\game trail. This steak is across the run\game trail from the tree.

Next step is to find a point in the bottom portion of the tree in which to carve out a notched portion for the trigger. The trigger and this notched-out portion of the tree must match so that tremendous upward pull of a one-hundred eighty pound log does not accidently activate the trigger. The trigger will be activated from the sideways pull from the prey travelling across the game trail and tripping the cordage across the run\game trail as shown in the illustration.

Place the trigger into the notched-out portion of the tree and insure it's a good match. Tie the cordage to the trigger and vigorously pull up on it to test it. Insure that the trigger is set properly in the notched portion of the bottom of the tree. Now tie the forty foot cordage to the log as shown in the illustration.

Take an estimation of where to tie the trigger and secure the trigger to the cordage. You may have to notch-out the trigger so that the cordage doesn't slip off it. I highly recommend that you do notch the trigger.

Throw the cordage over the branch and hoist up the log. Try to hoist it up at least twelve feet from the ground. Maintaining pull on the cordage, place the trigger in the notched-out portion of the tree. If there is too much slack or not enough of it, you'll have to lower the log and retie the trigger in a better position.

Once the trigger is in place, carefully take the cordage across the run\game trail and measure the required amount of cordage needed. The cordage will go across the run\game trail, and is anchored on the one foot stake with a loop (end of rope bowline - see Section 21) at least twice the size of the stake.

The reason for this is so the log will freely drop on the prey. Once the prey trips the Log Drop Trap (because of the sideways pull of the cordage), this will pull the trigger from the tree which then allows the log to fall downward. The loop will insure the free downward fall of the log because the cordage is not tied into the anchor stake but is simply looped around it.

WARNING: Caution must be taken when working with this trap to insure that the log does not accidently fall on the person setting the trap.

Log Drop Trap

Long-Range Boomerang: Indians throughout southern California made a rabbit stick called *"macana"* that looked like a boomerang. It's length was 24-inches long. A skilled hunter could cripple an evading running rabbit at a long-range of 50-yards!

The flat-shaped macana was carved from a hardwood and carved with sharp edges. Its winged aerodynamics were so good, it's range was farther than thrown rocks. The macana was also used kill venomous snakes (thrown or used as a hatchet). Its flight was so fast and edges so sharp it easily cut the venomous snake in-half. See *Rabbit Sticks*.

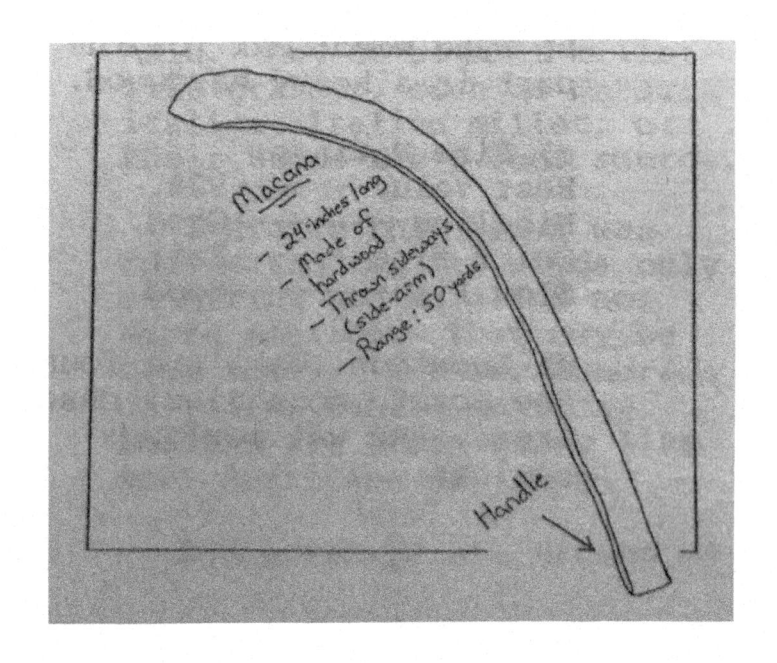

[Sketch of a Macana: 24 inches long, made of hardwood, thrown sideways (side-arm), Range: 50 yards. Handle labeled at bottom.]

Man Against Anaconda: Anacondas are located in the wet jungles of the Americas. They're non-venomous and kill their prey by constriction. These silent stalkers coil their powerful body around their prey and it's already too late for their doomed prey. One way (there might be more) to fight-off the anaconda is to submerge its head in mud. This will immediately calm down the snake and may eventually kill it through suffocation. You see, when the anaconda finally kills its prey, it swallows it whole. But in order to breathe, it has a gland the size of a giant hollowed out pencil in its mouth that allows it to breathe while it's swallowing its prey. Block this vital gland and you cut-off its vital oxygen supply. Force the anaconda's head in the mud and you place mud in its mouth and that gland, thus suffocating it. Again the best thing to do is 1st do your homework, 2nd never go alone (hire an expert guide), 3rd carry lethal weapons, and 4th AVOID these silent stalkers from the get go.

Man Against Python: There probably isn't a man (non-bushman) walking this Earth that could wrestle an adult python and live to talk about it. African bushmen and women folk are World Class survival experts in their specific wilderness environment. The hunters with their **superior** sense of smell could recognize different animals by smelling their scent at a distance. With their **superior** hearing they'd get an early warning by hearing the pads of an approaching leopard or the hiss of a python,... They knew which tracks and scat (dung) belonged to which animal big or small. They knew which trace of fur, hair, feather,... belonged to which animal big or small. They knew which animal had recently or days ago, passed through the jungle by the hidden signs only their experienced eyes could see.

But one of the most fascinating survival feats of these bushman is killing an adult python with their bare hands. Selected hunters battled and killed pythons that are well known to literally squeeze the life out of their prey to include humans. They called pythons *"samba."* So there's nothing lost in the translation, here's a direct quote from the book The Pitless Jungle, by John L. Brom:

"There was a faint rustling, the crackling of twigs, a slight hissing, and a python came slowly out of the bushes. Mahagi (bushman) gave a lightning leap, and hurled himself upon the reptile; in a flash two hands held its neck in a grip of steel. But the snake reacted with equal speed and in a second or two had twined itself round Mahagi. He did not defend himself against the terrible embrace, but held the snake in the same grip, twisting the head to one side, slowly strangling it. Fighting hard, the snake could not deploy its full strength to break its assailant's bones, which it would have snapped like dry twigs had

Mahagi relaxed for a moment the iron grip of his fingers. But it could not tighten its coils, although it was shaking Mahagi furiously; he lay there on the ground, tightening his own grip on its neck still further with his right hand while he continued to twist the neck with his left. He kept on twisting, twisting, and now, straining with the effort, he felt the snake quivering feebly and slightly loosening its grasp. At last there was a sharp crack, and the snake's neck snapped like a green branch. Its coiled loosened completely, and Mahagi-still holding the head, now impotent forever-climbed out of the ring of its body, then threw the head to the ground." This fascinating battle lasted only 02-minutes.

Note: There are far better ways to capture and kill a python or any giant snake using several hunters with lethal weapons. As for the python, Mahgi just didn't have a fight to the death with the python to show his manliness, the python made a great meal for many bushmen and family members.

And while I'm at it, let me give you another tactic to fight-off one of them killer constricting snakes like anacondas, boa constrictors, pythons,... - all of which fall under the family Boidae. All are non-poisonous snakes but just as lethal once they wrap themselves around their prey. Anacondas are found in the jungles of the Americas, boa constrictors are also found in jungles of the Americas, and those killer pythons are located in the wet jungles of Africa.

You already know about whoopin' on a constricting killer python and I gotta tell you, once that python initially grabs you (more than likely with a bite first, then coiling), odds are real super high you're a gonner. So why not try this technique?

But the best thing to do is do is 1st do your homework, 2nd never go alone (hire an expert guide), 3rd carry lethal weapons, and 4th AVOID these silent stalkers from the get go. Now here's a different technique to fight-off an anaconda.

Man Trap: Cpt. Wohlfeld evaded (American WWII evader - Philippines) using a game trail.

Note: Let me interrupt real quick. As an ex-infantryman I was taught from the very beginning to stay the hell off trails and never use the same route twice. This not only applies to combat but <u>also applies to ornery big game critters</u> - keep reading.

Anyway, using a game trail, just a few meters down the game trail, the ground went out from underneath him. He fell into a trap 04-feet deep and 02 1/3 feet wide & 03 feet long that's designed to capture big game like wild pigs. As luck would have it, Cpt. Wohlfeld missed all the sharpened stakes embedded at an upward angle on all walls of the pit.

None of the sharp stakes impaled him but he did take a slight cut. I added this segment to tell you to STAY OFF game trails. If you go to Alaska and want to get a whoopin by a bear, then walk on game trails. If you're a soldier and want to get killed, walk on roads, trails, ridges,... Plus now you know how to make a wild pig trap. Make it bigger for bears. But one thing though, several <u>sharpened stakes should be emplaced on the floor</u> of the trap too.

Marten Vittles: Martens (*Martes americana*) are found in forest and woodland in the United States, Canada, Europe and Central Asia. Its identified by its soft & durable reddish brown fur on top and lighter color undercoat. It's 20 to 25-inches long to include its very bush 07 to 09-inch tail. It's an acrobatic animal. A carnivore (meat eater), it also eats small animals, carrion (carcass), insects, honey, fruits and nuts.

The marten spends time in trees where it preys on squirrels. The marten is one of the very few animals that prey on American porcupines. Martens make their dens in hollow trees and about April, produce a litter of 02 to 04 young.

Now that we RECONNED a bit about this critter which should be done prior to all hunting activities, here are a few techniques to capture martens:
a) Deadfall (various)
b) Den Trap
c) Simple Snare
d) Squirrel Pole
e) Treaddle Snare
f) many more...

Remember to use bait that compels martens into the trap & snare (small animals, carrion (carcass), insects, honey, fruits, nuts, and squirrels). Indians have tied down live birds to attract marten into their traps & snares. And don't forget *1st, 2nd, 3rd & 4th Super Baits*.

Massai Blood Food: Masai located in northern Tanzania and southern Kenya (southeastern Africa) are a nomadic people and their population number approximately 250,000. Cattle are their lives. Cattle provide their food (blood, meat, milk), their materials for shelter (skin for clothing and dung to seal their houses), and the number of cattle each family possesses relates to their status and wealth. The Masai use a special hollow arrow to pierce the vein of cattle and sheep. The arrow has a stop on it so it doesn't pierce deep into the neck. Blood is drawn from the vein and consumed on the spot. The special arrow is plugged at the opening so it can be used for a future quick meal.

Massai Lion Hunting: Massai herdsmen of Kenya Africa, had a technique to hunt and kill lions.

1st - the Massai were EXPERT trackers.

2nd - the Massai hunted in groups of 20 to 30 hunters.

3rd - they'd separate the lion from the lioness and went after the lion.

The 02 weapons each hunter carried was a hand-made 08-foot spear with a sharpened arrowhead and a sword. The Massai hunters closed within point blank range of the lion. The lion assaulted a hunter but the other hunters counter-assaulted and threw their piecing spears into the lion's body with more and more spears on the way.

With the lion succumbing to it wounds, staggering and falling, more hunters assaulted with more spears, finishing-off the king of the jungle.

Metal Gill Net: Did you learn how to make a gill net at Gill Net? Here's an easier gill net. The storm of September of 2008 – *Hurricane Ike* hit the great state of Texas. When water levels dropped, dozens of fish were found trapped in a chain link fence. Yes, a chain link fence is diamond-shaped like a home-made gill net. Some fish were measured as big as 10-inches long. Now you know another neat trick to catch fish. (Ripley's Believe It Or Not - 2009).

Minnow Trap: Minnows are great bait for the bigger fish you want to catch for dinner vittles. But have you ever tried to catch minnows? Extremely difficult I gotta tell you. Even in SERE School at my isolated site in the Panamanian jungle, I tried catching minnows for hours and couldn't do it. And I remember distinctly that if I did catch any, I was going to eat them raw right then and there. Thoroughly wash & cook the meat\fish before eating.

Anyway, here's an old angler's trick to catch plenty of minnows that takes hardly any effort at all. Old timer anglers were very savvy decades ago. They used a hand-made jar with a closeable top. The large jar was approximately 14-inches high with a 10-inch diameter. And the secret trick to this unique jar was that it had 05 funnels forming to the inside of the jar at different levels and at different positions around the jar.

The aperture of the 05 funnels was the size for minnows only. The jar was submerged underwater and them minnows went into the jar but couldn't find their way out! Kinda like a *Basket Fish Trap* uh! I'll give you a POC to get an exact replica *Minnow Trap* as described above, but for right now, let me show you how you can easily make your own *Minnow Trap* for just about nuthin'.

Ingredients: Large clear plastic container, utility knife, gloves, a 25-cent piece, thin-point magic marker, and a miniature chem stick (optional).

Step 01: My plastic container holds about 03-quarts of water. You can get bigger ones and even use a plastic soda bottle (small and large). Take the plastic container and draw 05 circles with your magic marker, using the 25-cent piece as a guide. If your plastic container is small, only draw 01 or 02 circles. Now in all the circles, place a dot in all the centers.

Warning: When cutting into the container - <u>cut away from your body</u> in case the knife slips.

Step 02: Put on the work gloves for safety reasons. Take your carpet knife and place the pointed tip at the dot in the center. Slowly cut into the dot and cut outward to the perimeter of the circle and stop. Make 03 more evenly separated cuts forming a 03 pie-shaped forms. Each cut should be 120-degree angle from the other forming 03 equal pie-shaped forms.

Step 03: Once you've made these initial 03 cuts, go to the same cuts and extend then 1/2-inch. Once you've done this, dissect the pie-shape form and make 03 more cuts the same length as the others forming a star. Now push the cut pie-shaped form inward till the center aperture is about 1/2-inch in diameter. As you look at it, it should look like a star.

Step 04: Repeat the same process of Steps 02 & 03 to the other circles.

Step 05: Now that have 05 star-shaped apertures in the plastic bottle, you'll notice the pointed pie-shapes are facing inward. This prevents the minnows from escaping once they do find the opening. They hit these pie-shaped fins and reverse their course. Now the last step is to attract the minnows to the Minnow Trap. Yes, they'll eventually end up in the trap on their own, but let's get it to work faster especially at night or in murky water. Take a small chem light and bend it to break the vial inside so 02 chemicals inside will react with each other so it will start glowing. Place it in the Minnow Trap and submerge it. The minnows should be compelled to the glowing light and so will bigger fish. See *"269+ International Fishing Tricks And More!"* at **www.survivalexpertbooks.com**

Important Note: It might not be a bad idea to anchor or secure a line to the *Minnow Trap* so the current or some critter doesn't take off with it. Again, if you want the real thing, see the POC below.

Now here's that POC so to get an exact replica *Minnow Trap* (as prescribed above) used decades ago by them old savvy anglers. And you can use it starting the same day you get it in the mail. See *The Sportsman's Guide* in the POC Section.

Montagnais Moose Vittles: Moose are some very dangerous animals once you have them cornered or if their younguns are threatened. But the hunters took a chance for the moose provided a lot of food and other natural supplies. Weighing in at 1,820 pounds and more than 07 1/2-feet tall, they are a potential threat that should be respected.

The Montagnais Indians of northeastern Canada had their own way to hunt moose. They stalked and waited till the moose grazed near water. Sneaking up on the moose, they forced it into the water where it couldn't defend itself. Once in the deep water, more Montagnais Indians in boats, closed and enveloped the doomed moose where it was repeatedly speared from behind.

Moose Tracking: Cree hunters didn't track moose by following directly behind their tracks. This may have been so to show respect for the moose by not walking in their tracks. They knew the habits of moose and tracked them from a parallel distance while staying downwind.

Cree stalked the moose using a semicircular loops downwind of the moose's trail. When the moose has doubled back or reversed their direction temporarily, its usually done after they eat. When the moose has doubled back, the Cree hunter makes his downwind tracking semicircular loops smaller and smaller till he encounters the moose.

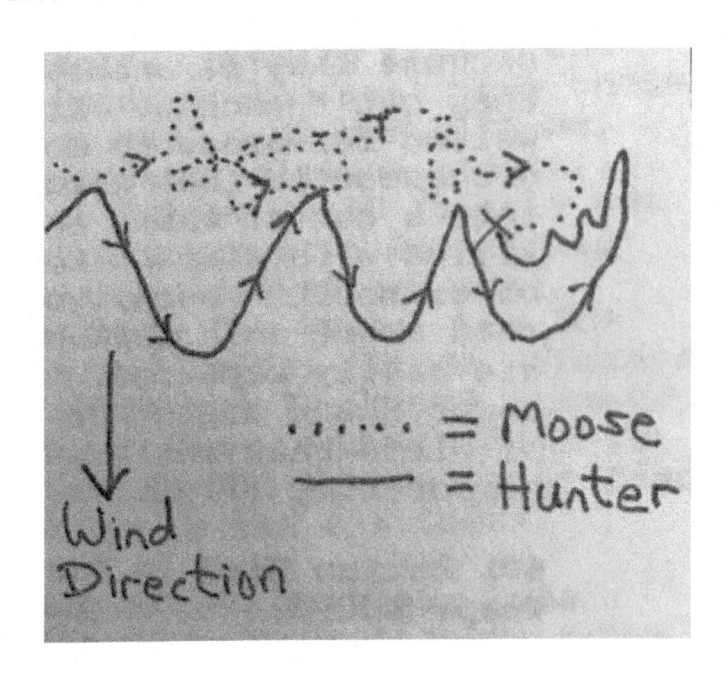

Musk Oxen: This REAL SURVIVOR of 20,000 years has even survived the last Ice Age and I want to tell you about this surviving critter - but first see *"Hotter Gear"* and then come back here. Did you read about *"Hotter Gear?"* Good, let's carry-on with this tough critter. The musk oxen resembles a buffalo with 03-foot long hair hanging from its body. Its fur is some of the warmest cold-repelling material on Earth which enables it to withstand bitterly frigid blizzard-blowing temperatures that would kill an unprepared survivor in seconds.

It roams Canada and northern Alaska and lives among the moist tundra of birch, blueberry, cotton grass, dwarf willow, ponds, muskeg bogs, lichen-covered rocks,... And it feeds on this enormous supply of birch, blueberry, cotton grass, dwarf willow,... And like caribou and reindeer during winter months it simply clears the snow to get at the nutritious inexhaustible supply of lichen (fungi - algae plant that can live in almost any environment even under snow).

360-Degree Security Perimeter!

The musk oxen have a military-type defense against their enemies - bears and wolves. The males would smartly form a tight shoulder-to-shoulder circle facing out against their predators. The young musk oxen and females would assemble bunched-up in the center. Once the 360-degree security perimeter is formed it's a stand-off. The bear or wolf or pack of wolves can not attack an isolated musk oxen, they have to attack the entire bunch and this is where they screw-up!

If a bear or wolf attacked the perimeter defense a male musk oxen would rush forward with head down and impale the attacker with its horn(s). The impaled predator would be thrown to the side and the male would not turn around to return to the perimeter defense but will smartly walk backwards taking his original position in the perimeter defense.

Eskimos considered musk oxen meat more tastier than whale and caribou. They also considered their blubber the best burning fuel. And they no doubt had many many uses for all parts of the musk oxen. The musk oxen were on the verge of extinction. They had no defense against the Eskimo's rifle. On the verge of extinction, the white man intervened and today the musk oxen are a protected species.

Can you learn from the musk oxen? Sure you can. That lichen don't sound bad at all when there's nothing else. And their military-type defense is the best! And believe it or not, their super warm fur is harvested and made into the warmest parka, gloves, boots you'll ever buy. Sorry, I don't have a POC for you at this time. Insure you see *Hot Gear* and especially *Hotter Gear*.

Naskapi Indian Blood Pudding: Here's another type of blood pudding you should know about. Blood from fallen caribou was often drank on the spot for the tired hunter who needed a fresh warm drink as an energizer. Blood was also gathered in a container. As time passed the blood would coagulate (thicken) into a blood pudding where it would be eaten later.

Noodling: Noodling is another name for "Hogging." Late 2004 or early 2005, Missouri passed a state law allowing fishermen to noodle. According to that state law, fishermen can catch up to 05 catfish via noodling. To noodle, fishermen simply catch fish with their bare hands. See *Hogging* and see **"269+ International Fishing Tricks And More!"** at **www.survivalexpertbooks.com**

No Weapon Duck Hunting: The following is a true story from a security officer working at a Federal Court House in Saint Louis, Missouri. This security officer related a true story (April 2002) of how his grandfather would sneak up on ducks and grab them at point blank range.

Being out of range of the ducks (sight, hearing, and smell,...), his grandfather would get a big pumpkin and clean it out. He'd then put a jack-o-lantern face on it like most folks do for Halloween. Then he'd put on the pumpkin head over his own head for a mask, get in the water and wade in the water slowly walking towards ducks. Nearing the ducks his entire body would be in the water (standing, squatting, crawling) except for the pumpkin head. Those duck critters would no doubt see the pumpkin head closing in on them but pay it no mind cause it demonstrated no threat to them. The *"floating"* pumpkin head had no signs of being human or of being any threat to them so they kept doing their duck business (feeding, resting, socializing,...). The grandfather wearing the pumpkin head closed in on the unsuspecting ducks and simply grabbed them. Was that easy or what?

Now I'm not sure how his grandfather secured the ducks, but to secure them quickly without those captured ducks alerting their duck buddies, I'd grab them by their webbed feet and pull them under water for a quick drowning.

Nowlin's Fish Stunner: Nowlin used a unique technique to stun fish so they floated to the surface for an easy catch. Nowlin placed his musket barrel just below the water's surface if the fish were swimming near the surface. If they were swimming 06-inches below the surface, the barrel was place 06-inches below the surface. Pulling the trigger, the underwater blast - concussion, stunned the fish having them float to the surface. See *"269+ International Fishing Tricks And More!"* at **www.survivalexpertbooks.com**

Warning: Unlike musket rifles of 150-years ago, modern weapons like the .45 calibre pistol have a very dangerous chamber pressure of around 45,000-pounds per square inch. That much chamber pressure should NEVER be tampered with beyond its intended design. Modern weapons are not designed to fire while submerged underwater.

I wouldn't recommend using this technique unless you had an *"open system"* weapon like a .38 pistol revolver or you have a musket weapon.

1st Note: Long ago (1976) at one of West Point Academy's training camps - Camp Natural Bridge, to stun fish, I've used blasting caps. But the blasting cap has to detonate in close proximity to the fish in order to stun it. See *Concussion Fishing* in this Special Report.

2nd Note: Up there in the mountains near West Point Academy on the way to Camp Natural Bridge, I've never seen such a dense population of deer in my life.

If you were a hunter wearing a blindfold, you could point your rifle or bow in any direction and peg a deer. Yes, that's an exaggeration, but the deer really were extremely plentiful the Summer of 1976 and I'm sure it remains the same if all that land is still part of a military reservation. Yes, depending on the military reservation, hunting is allowed. See your local Forest Ranger.

Nowlin's Pike Net Fishing: Nowlin and his father went fishing using a net made by Nowlin's father. The pike net was made of 04 hoops with each hoop smaller than the other. The 04 hoop formed the frame of a funnel. Around the 04 hoops was a net. The spread out pike net was placed with the widest hoop upstream and the smallest hoop downstream. The pike net was staked down so the current wouldn't take it downstream. The fish entered the wide hoop and were *"funnelled"* through the smaller and smaller remaining 03 hoops. The smallest hoop was as large as the biggest anticipated fish. The fish were funnelled through the 4th smallest hoop entering a bag net that was about 10-feet long.

The bag was tied to the 1st big hoop so the fish couldn't find their way to freedom. The Nowlin Pike Net can be used facing upstream or downstream depending which way the fish were swimming - migrating. See *"269+ International Fishing Tricks And More!"* at **www.survivalexpertbooks.com**

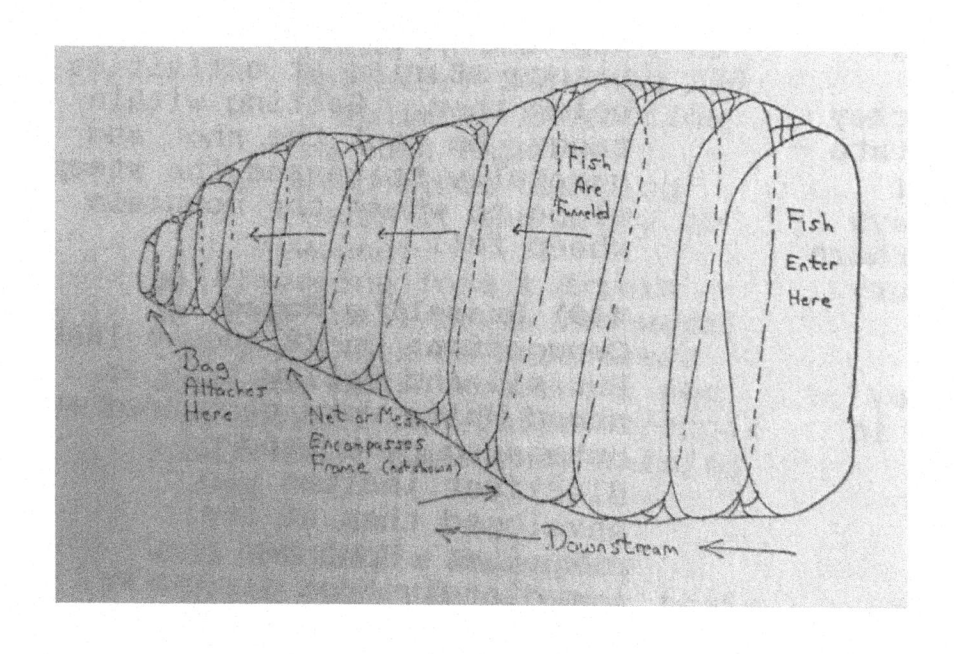

Nowlin's Fish Stunner: Nowlin used a unique technique to stun fish so they floated to the surface for an easy catch. Nowlin placed his musket barrel just below the water's surface if the fish were swimming near the surface. If they were swimming 06-inches below the surface, the barrel was place 06-inches below the surface. Pulling the trigger, the underwater blast - concussion, stunned the fish having them float to the surface. See *"269+ International Fishing Tricks And More!"* at **www.survivalexpertbooks.com**

Warning: Unlike musket rifles of 150-years ago, modern weapons like the .45 calibre pistol have a very dangerous chamber pressure of around 45,000-pounds per square inch. That much chamber pressure should NEVER be tampered with beyond its intended design. Modern weapons are not designed to fire while submerged underwater. I wouldn't recommend using this technique unless you had an "open system" weapon like a .38 pistol revolver or you have a musket weapon.

1st Note: Long ago (1976) at one of West Point Academy's training camps - Camp Natural Bridge, to stun fish, I've used blasting caps. But the blasting cap has to detonate in close proximity to the fish in order to stun it. See *Concussion Fishing*.

2nd Note: Up there in the mountains near West Point Academy on the way to Camp Natural Bridge, I've never seen such a dense population of deer in my life. If you were a hunter wearing a blindfold, you could point your rifle or bow in any direction and peg a deer.

Yes, that's an exaggeration, but the deer really were extremely plentiful the Summer of 1976 and I'm sure it remains the same if all that land is still part of a military reservation. Yes, depending on the military reservation, hunting is allowed. See your local Forest Ranger.

Ojibwa Bird Pole: A The Ojibwa bird snare consist of a pole six to seven feet long, a straight small branch about eighteen inches long that will be used as a perch, about twelve feet of cordage, and a five pound rock. The Ojibwa bird pole should be placed in an open area, watering holes, and feeding areas. Use deadfall for construction of the Ojibwa bird pole and/or mask all parts of the snare of human scent as prescribed. Firmly place the pole at the site intended. Drill a hole about six inches from the top of the pole. The hole should be almost the same size as the small branch. Tie a five pound rock to one end of the cordage. Feed the other end of the cordage through the hole.

Pull on the cordage so that the rock is hanging at least two to three feet from the ground and place the small branch in the hole of the pole just slightly in the drilled hole so that it doesn't fall out on its own. At the same time measure the placement of the overhand knot and the noose that will be placed on the perch.

The overhand knot is placed just outside the joint of the pole and the perch. This is to insure that the noose laying on top of the perch doesn't slip closed under the tension of the five pound rock.

On the other hand, once the bird lands on the perch, the perch will give under weight of the bird, the string will quickly pass through the drilled\carved hole and the noose will close around the legs of the bird because of the weighted rock. I use an end of rope bowline knot for a slip knot.

Let loose of the rock and tie the overhand knot in the proper place and tie the proper noose (slip knot). Now set the Ojibwa bird pole. You may have to play with it to get the right action.

You should construct the Ojibwa Bird Pole so that it is orientated so birds can land on the perch against the wind. 09 times out of 10, birds will always land into the wind!

Ojibwa Bird Pole

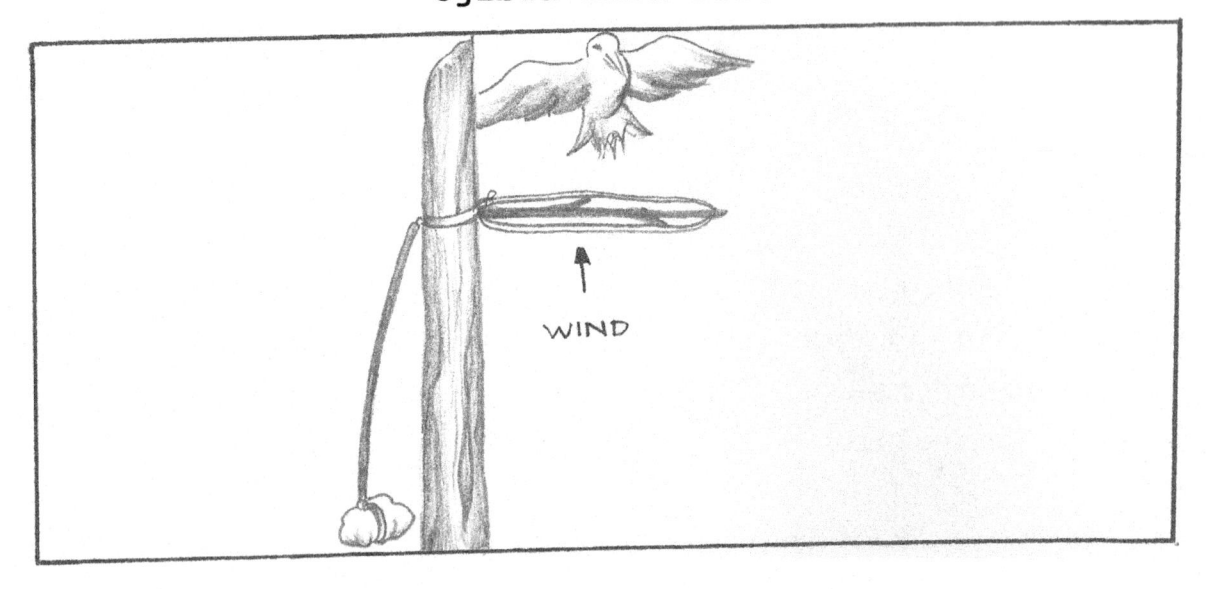

Ojibwa Deer Hunting: Ojibwa were cyclic hunters. They hunted and gathered food that was most abundant depending on the season(s). And they had different homes depending on the winter or summer season. Deer were most abundant during the late spring and summer months and hunted by driving them towards a fence made from natural vegetation. The deer ran into the fence and concealed at the fence were hunters with spears.

Now keep this in mind, those savvy Ojibwa already knew where to position the blocking fence and ambushing hunters. They already knew where to position their corralling hunters. How? Cause they already knew where the deer were going to be located. How? Cause they did a RECON! They studied those deer critters and they knew their habits, they knew their feeding grounds, and they knew their all-around schedule. They already knew all there was to know about the deer for a successful hunt.

Onoda Jungle Fowl Trap: The Onoda Jungle Fowl Trap uses channelization, bait, a couple rocks (raise string), and a string to snare the bird's feet. When the bird stepped over the loop, the evader pulled the string snaring the bird at its feet. Here's an illustration to show you how they caught them bird critters.

Onoda Rat Trap: Rats were plentiful on Lubang island and 2nd Lt. Onoda and evading comrades took advantage of them using 02 different rat traps. This 1st rat trap is very interesting because of the trigger used. And of course, channelization and bait are important. Here's a sketch of the *Onoda Rat Trap*.

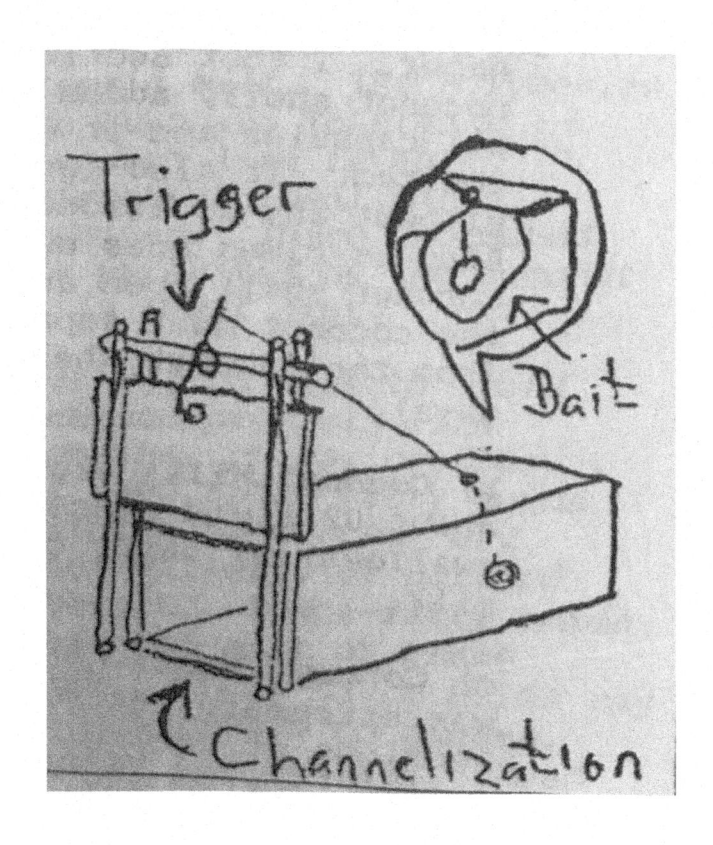

Onoda Sock Rat Trap: Here's a very simple trap using a sock with cans used to form a tunnel which channelize the rat. It was placed near the evader at night. When he heard the rat taking the bait, he simply reached over and closed the opening with his hand trapping the rat.

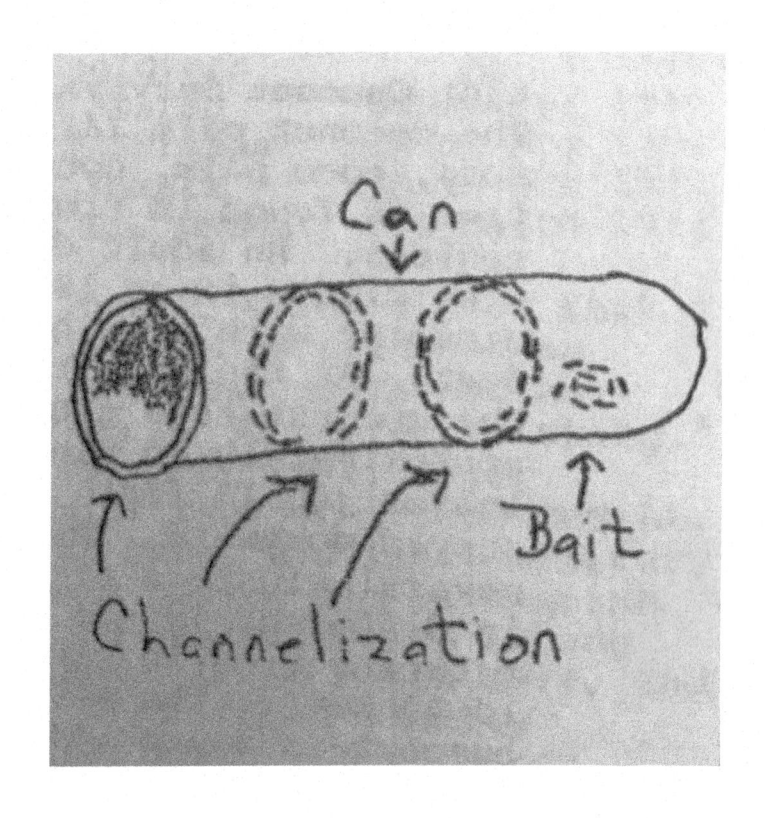

Onoda Wild Cat Trap: The *Onoda Wild Cat Trap* again requires channelization, bait, and a wire to secure the ornery wild cat. The wire noose is measured to the height of the animal's head & neck. When its head goes through the wire noose, it snares the animal around the neck as it moves through toward the bait. As the cat moves forward, the wire noose gets tighter and tighter snaring the wild cat.

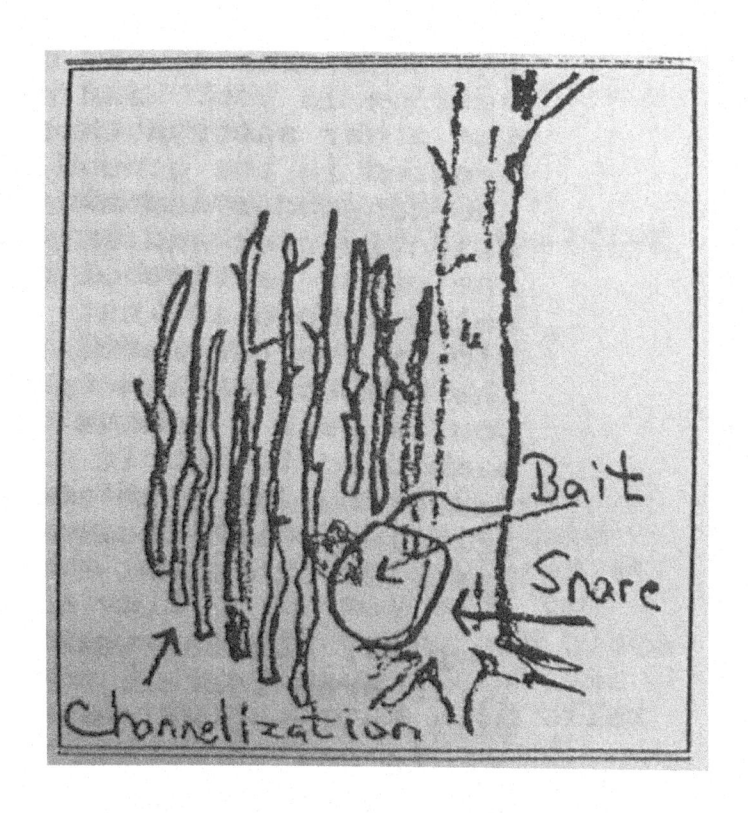

[Sketch showing a snare trap with labels: "Bait", "Snare", and "Channelization"]

Warning: When approaching ANY trap and snare, you better have a weapon or two to finish-off the critter, or at least defend yourself against the ornery critter that's really pissed-off!

Ostrich Imitation: Bushmen successfully hunted ostriches by imitating ostriches. They took the wings and feathers of a dead ostrich and disguised themselves as an ostrich. To imitate the neck and head they used a stick to mount the ostrich head while stick was placed through the neck. Wearing this disguise, they were able to close-in on other ostriches at point blank range. See *"99+ International Pied Piper Tricks To Compel All Types Of Animals To Come To You!"* at **www.survivalexpertbooks.com** .

WARNING: Imitating an ostrich is dangerous. Bushmen have been killed by hunters with rifles. Bushmen have also been attacked and killed by territorial ostriches defending their area. With their powerful claws they tore into the abdomen ripping it open, killing the bushman instantly.

More Ostrich Imitation: As you already know, bushmen imitated ostriches to close on and capture ostriches. They used this same trick to close on other big game like wildebeest. Closing in on the wildebeest, the disguised bushmen imitated the movements of an ostrich like pecking at bushes, rubbing its fake head against his fake body (getting rid of flies),... The wildebeest recognized an ostrich and had no fear of it and let the fake ostrich get closer and closer. Closing on the wildebeest at point blank range, the brave bushmen shot a poisonous arrow into the wildebeest. The wildebeest was soon doomed, within several hours it would be dead.

Note: American Indians have used the same technique hunting buffalo. Imitating animals that are not feared by buffalo. Or imitating deer to close on other deer. see *"99+ International Pied Piper Tricks To Compel All Types Of Animals To Come To You!"* at **www.survivalexpertbooks.com** and see *Faceless Hunter*.

WARNING: Imitating an ostrich is dangerous. Bushmen have been killed by hunters with rifles. Bushmen have also been attacked and killed by territorial ostriches defending their area. With their powerful claws they tore into the abdomen ripping it open, killing the bushman instantly..

Pacific Coral Fish Trap: Live coral was collected and heaped-up in shallow water forming a V-shape with a narrow passage leading to a tank (water). Fish were corralled (deliberately or naturally) into the weir and funneled into the tank where they swam and were contained till the fresh fish were easily collected and eaten. See *"269+ International Fishing Tricks And More!"* at **www.survivalexpertbooks.com**

Pacific Moa Snare: Moa are named for about 20 species of ostrich-like flightless birds that once roamed New Zealand. All species are extinct with the last species becoming extinct in the 19th century. Moas varied greatly in size from about 39-inches to 13-feet tall. Flightless, their legs were massive and relatively short providing them the means to evade predators. However, there was one snare that captured their massive legs. Moas were attracted to wild fruit of all sorts. A platform or perch was fabricated from wood so the moa could reach the tasty wild berries (bait). On top of the perch was loop snare with a long lanyard. Moas perched themselves on the wooden perch eating wild berries. A short distance away, the hunter waited for the right moment when both of the moa's feet were inside the snare loop. The loop was quickly pulled thus securing the moa's legs so it's unable to evade. The moa was then quickly finished-off and dressed for dinner.

Note: The hunter was probably at a slightly higher elevation than the moa so to insure when the lanyard was pulled, the snare loop tightened upward on the moa's legs. If the hunter was at a lower elevation once the snare loop was tightened, the moa could easily step out of the snare loop and escape.

Pacific Mutton Bird Trap & Snare: Also called puffins, whether habitating the Atlantic or Pacific regions, puffins are recognized by their large triangular-shaped, laterally flattened bills. Large numbers of muttons were captured as they flew close the ground from their nesting areas, feeding grounds, and breeding areas. Nets were set-up along their routes. Muttons flew into the nets thus capturing them.

Pacific Rat Traps: Rats in New Zealand chose the rural life of the forests rather than infesting the cities. And they were the chosen food for inhabitants back then. To capture the rats, 1st, their rat runs (rat paths) had to be located and they were easily located. Once located, 02 different traps & snares were employed. A pit was dug directly on the rat run which had the rats fall into pit. And that pit should be deep enough so the rats can't climb out.

And even if it is deep enough, I'm telling you, them critters will find a way out even if they have to sacrifice a few of their own. A another option to capturing rats were spring-loaded traps & snares. And you have PLENTY of options.

Now getting back to them rats, them critters were eaten like most folks eat chicken wings. The rats were skinned, cleaned and grilled over a fire. If rat food was to be preserved, the meat was preserved in its own fat.

Pacific Seal Hunting: Seals were also part of menu in the Pacific. The seals were easily captured by clubbing them (strike to their snout) as they lay soaking up the sun or a sealing expedition was formed and the seals were attacked in remote areas. All parts of the seal was used for food, fuel for fire, clothes, tools, weapons,... But one way the seal meat was preserved for up to 02 years was the meat was placed in a bag made of weaved kelp. The bag was filled with seal fat which preserved the seal meat for up to 02-years.

Pelican Fish Stunner: Them not so handsome pelican critters have an amazing fishing technique for some easy fish vittles. The pelican with its super keen eyesight from above spots a fish swimming just below the water's surface. It dive bombs directly over the fish. Speeding towards the water its wings are spread as it makes a devastating splash into the water directly over the fish. This splashing dive bomb is so powerful it creates an underwater concussion that temporarily stuns the fish which is easily captured by the pelican.

Can you copy-cat this technique? Sure you can. A flat non-penetrating instrument is used like a snow shovel, section of bark, large flat rock, your flat hand,... See *White Pelican Corral Fishing*.
And see ***"269+ International Fishing Tricks And More!"*** at **www.survivalexpertbooks.com**

Penguin Vittles: Explorers loved penguin eggs. They found penguin omelets delicious but didn't fancy hard-boiled penguin eggs for they tasted fishy and bounced like rubber balls.

Young penguins are very vulnerable and are easily captured and eaten by man, skua gull, sea leopards, and whales. When penguins and baby penguins are resting on a floe after eating krill (shrimp-like critter), those savvy whale critters jump on one end of the floe tipping it where the poor penguin slides into the water where it's doomed.

Penobscot Brown Bear Killing Trick: The Penobscot Indians were located in what is now Maine. They had a simple yet effective technique to kill or capture brown bear. Once confronted by the bear and it reared-up, an Indian would toss (not throw) a chunk of wood at it. The brown bear with its killer claws would catch the chunk of wood. The other Penobscot wasted no time and hit the bear repeated on the head with their clubs rendering it dead. The brown bear was placed on a toboggan where it was transported to their camp to be dressed and eaten.

Pioneer "Bark The Squirrel" Hunting: Depending where the squirrel was hit, pioneers knew that buckshot, birdshot or a rifle ball would destroy much of the squirrel - thus no meat to eat. So pioneers killed or stunned the squirrel without hitting it. They called it *"bark the squirrel."* The hunters lined-up their sights on a tree right next to the squirrel. When everything lined up, they shot at the tree trunk just inches from the squirrel. The impact of the bullet caused a concussion thus killing or temporarily stunning the squirrel - thus preserving all the tasty protein-laden meat.

Pioneer Beaver Trap: Here's another beaver trap to add to the collection so you're ready Anytime Anywhere.

Mountain men used pre-made iron traps to capture beavers. These traps secured the critter's paw, leg,... And in many cases, the critter would chew off their trapped paw, leg,... to escape. But in this case the beaver trap was set in shallow water but deep enough to drown the beaver.

The beaver trap was set in 02 - 04 feet of water, deep enough so that when the beaver is trapped, it couldn't reach the surface for air - thus drowning at the trap site. So the beaver couldn't swim off with the beaver trap, it was secured by a pole through its O-ring.

Plus the pole was tall enough (secured under water and above the surface) so to identify the exact location of the trap. A sturdy sapling was bowed over the beaver trap so the top of the sapling is above the water.

On the top of the bowed sapling, the bait is placed - castoreum. As you already know from previous AASNs, castoreum absolutely compels the beaver to the scent. And when it does, odds are the beaver steps on the rounded platform, thus activating the hair trigger and clamping shut on the beavers leg. See *Hypnotizing Castoreum*.

Note: Back in the pioneer days there were no hunting seasons nor hunting laws. However these are the modern days, check your local laws for lawful techniques for beaver hunting in your favorite hunting spots.

Pioneer Deer Hunting: Pioneers didn't cut any small or big game any slack. There was no such thing as giving any game a fair chance. You know this from the millions of buffalo that were slaughtered to almost extinction. Anyway, pioneers didn't cut any deer (buck, doe, fawn) any slack either. Here's a hunting trick that is no doubt against the laws in every state of this great country. But when your life is on the line, you gotta do what you have to do to survive Anytime Anywhere!

Deer needed water to drink. So hunters went to game trails where deer were known to drink. Whether a stream, river, pond, lake,... A dugout canoe is silently floating at <u>night</u> just off shore. One hunter propels and navigates the canoe with an oar. Another is set amidship (center) behind his home-made bark blind and protected from all light. The bait is a lit pine-knot torch. The deer is *"hypnotized"* by the bright light of the torch at night thus setting up the hunter behind the bark blind for an easy shot.

1st Note: Back in the pioneer days there were no hunting seasons nor hunting laws. However these are the modern days, check your local laws for lawful techniques for beaver hunting in your favorite hunting spots.

2nd Note: Deer were also hunted using artificial salt licks. Salt was placed on known game trails. The hunter layed silently behind home-made blinds and shot the deer at point blank range.

3rd Note: Deer were also tracked in snow. Depending on the depth of the snow, deer had a low Foot Load Index and so do humans. In deep snow, it was extremely tough and very slow travel for deer. However, with snow shoes, deer can be tracked down and hunted. See *Foot Load Index*.

Pioneer Wolf Trap: This wolf trap is actually a pitfall trap. A rectangle hole 08-feet deep is dug but the bottom is larger than the opening - like a bottle trap. It's dug this way so that the wolf can't climb out of the pit. The top of the pitfall trap has a wooden cover of boards.

In the center is a pole that allows the cover to pivot to the left or right. And this pole is secured by 02-sets of stakes loose enough so it's allowed to rotate left or right. On the center of the cover is a weight so when either side is pivoted down by the weight of the wolf, once the wolf falls in the pit, the weighted cover will recover itself to its original *"covering"* position. Bait is placed on the center top of the cover.

The Pioneer Wolf trap works by baiting the wolf. Its ultra-sensitive nose will pick up the scent of *"bloody"* bait. Once it finds your bait it will pounce on the covering platform. The platform will pivot from the wolf's weight thus dropping the wolf in the 08-foot pit. Since the pitfall trap is dug so the bottom is larger than opening, it's unable to climb out of the reversed walls. See *Bottle Trap*.

Note: Back in the pioneer days there were no hunting seasons nor hunting laws. However these are the modern days, check your local laws for lawful techniques for hunting in your favorite hunting spots.

Pounding Stick: Bucks hop and beat their hooves into the ground. It is believed they do this as an early warning of danger for other deer. When this is done, other deer are compelled to perk-up and investigate where the danger is. This may flush them from their hiding position or at least have them move a bit so you can locate them (movement attracts the eyes). You can imitate this hoove-pounding sound by pounding your *Forked Walking Stick / Staff*, or a good sized rock into the ground. If this doesn't work, you may get some worms. See *Worm Stick*.

POW Fly Trap: Those inventive American POWs (Korean War Prisoners Of War) made fly traps to win 01 cigarette for 300 flies. A fly trap was made of yarn from a sock. The yarn fly trap was made so the flies could easily enter but unable to leave (box, ball, cone,...??).

The inventor put his fly trap in the latrine. The very 1st day he got about 200 flies! Catching flies killed boredom and help block-out despair - both are enemies of survival.

Pronghorn Coyote Trap: Them coyotes are some smart critters. And like wolves, they hunt in packs. Coyotes will go after injured, old and young pronghorns versus going after healthy fighting pronghorn. Coyotes kill more fawns than all other predators combined. And one technique they use to go after fawns is to flush them out of hiding.

During springtime, water sources are near lower ground in draws and valleys. A pack of coyotes will work draws and valleys and flush out hiding fawns. The discovered fawn will evade but her speed has yet to be developed and the chase is a short one for the doomed fawn.

Pronghorn Snow Trap: The following snow trap is sure death to a trapped pronghorn. When the snow is fresh and deep, pronghorns do have some trouble traversing the fresh deep snow. However, when the temperature changes and warms-up a tad, the snow thaws and then at night the temperature drops and that thawed snows turns hard - it's a crust. Pronghorns dig for food in the deep crusted snow and they can't get out. Why? It's mostly due to their Food Load Index (FLI). What the heck is FLI? I already told about FLI. So see *Foot Load Index*.

If you're out in the woods in deep fresh snow and it warms-up that day, you know it's going to cool down at night and that deep snow will crust-up. You better get your snow shoes ready. You can bet somewhere, there are deer, pronghorns, elk,... (low FLI) stuck in-place, they're trapped and you (low FLI - you better have snow shoes) know it and so do all them ornery hungry predators (have high FLIs).

PRSC: PRSC is a military acronym that stands for Planning, Recon, Security and Control. PRSC are the US Army's *Principles Of Patrolling* and are just 01 of the tools to plan for combat missions (training and real world). PRSC is such an important tool, it could SAVE YOUR LIFE. I civilianized PRSC so YOU can AVOID problems, tragedies in the first place. Let me briefly explain PRSC.

- **Planning:** Write down on a few sheets of paper what you want to do in your outdoor adventure. Try to go in detail. Break it down day-by-day and each day break it down for morning, afternoon and before dusk activities. You should ALWAYS make camp 02-hours before sunset. NEVER go camping alone. Now you got your <u>tentative plan</u> on a piece of paper.
- **Recon:** Do a recon of your area of interest. Get maps of the entire area. Get books of the area. Go on the internet and get the scoop of the area. If you can talk to any people that have been there - that's good info too. Get multiple weather reports to the region / area you're venturing. Weather

itself could kill you. If proposed bad weather is present during your venture – ABORT your outdoor venture and go another day. Now that you did a Recon, you may want to adjust your plan.

- **Security:** Now for security, this is IMPORTANT. While you're out on your outdoor adventure, think of at least 12 things that will **HURT YOU, KILL YOU** and **CAUSE YOU LOSS OF EQUIPMENT.** Counter all 12+ of these before you go on your outdoor adventure. Let me give you an example. If you and your friends plan on fishing several spots over the next 03-days, one thing that could kill you is drowning. To counter this – EVERYBODY must know how to swim. EVERYBODY must wear a life preserver at all times. If you have anybody in your party that can't swim – ABORT your fishing trip all together or leave the non-swimmer behind. The non-swimmer in a water-laden environment is a threat to himself and all those around him. After doing Security, odds are you may adjust you Plan.
- **Control:** Now that you've Planned, Reconned, and implemented Security in your outdoor adventure, you're taking CONTROL. You're actually AVOIDING threats in the first place and you're far more flexible if any threats surface during your outdoor adventure.

I could go on for pages and pages to make you bullet-proof when venturing outdoors. PRSC is a great start and works so you're ready Anytime Anywhere! See *"Laydon's Emergency Survival Employment Instructions!"* at the end of this book.

Pueblo Indian Dead Falls: The Pueblo Indians had some dead falls that really worked in their desert environments and here's 03 of them I know you'll find interesting and useful when your life is on the line. Each dead fall is designed for a specific critter. Below are some sketches with notes.

A real quick reminder, when a critter is baited or channelized to your trap and snare, even though they are very smart (beyond instinct) they're not going say *"Hey, that's a dead fall"* or *"That's a treadle snare."* But they will say *"Hey, there's something wrong here"* and AVOID your trap and snare. Cause they smelled your scent, they smelled scent of the nearby freshly cut grass you used to camouflage it, or the scent of cut sticks, branches,... that alarmed it. You have to be careful with scent. Use mud, charcoal,... and mask your scent and everything you touch. Cut debris at a distance and downwind of your trap and snare. And last remember you have to compel that critter to go to your trap and snare via channelization and bait - even if it's part of you - a few drops of blood. Animals can smell blood at great distances. OK, let's start with the 1st dead fall, the coyote dead fall.

Pueblo Coyote Dead Falls: The main parts of the coyote dead fall are the platform to hold the weight, a trigger, and bait.

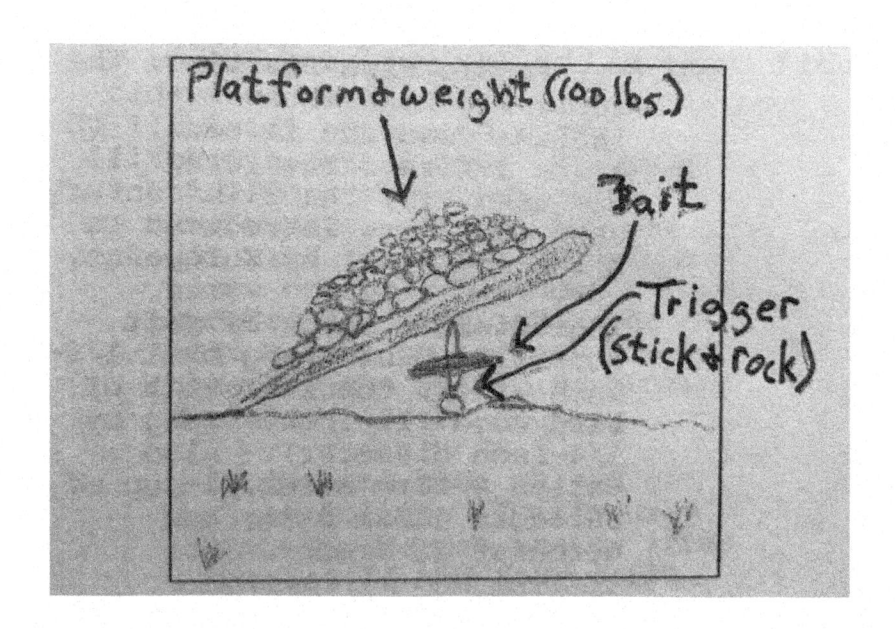

Pueblo Prairie Dog Dead Fall: The main parts of the prairie dog dead fall are the heavy platform (flat rock), trigger, string, and bait.

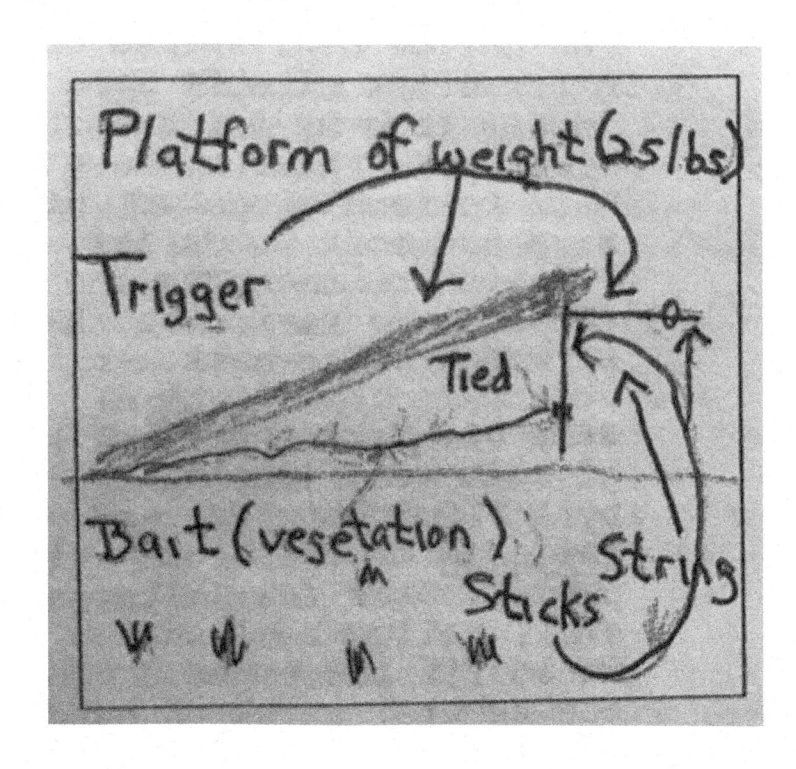

Pueblo Rabbit Dead Fall: The main parts of the rabbit dead fall are the heavy platform (flat rock), trigger, and bait.

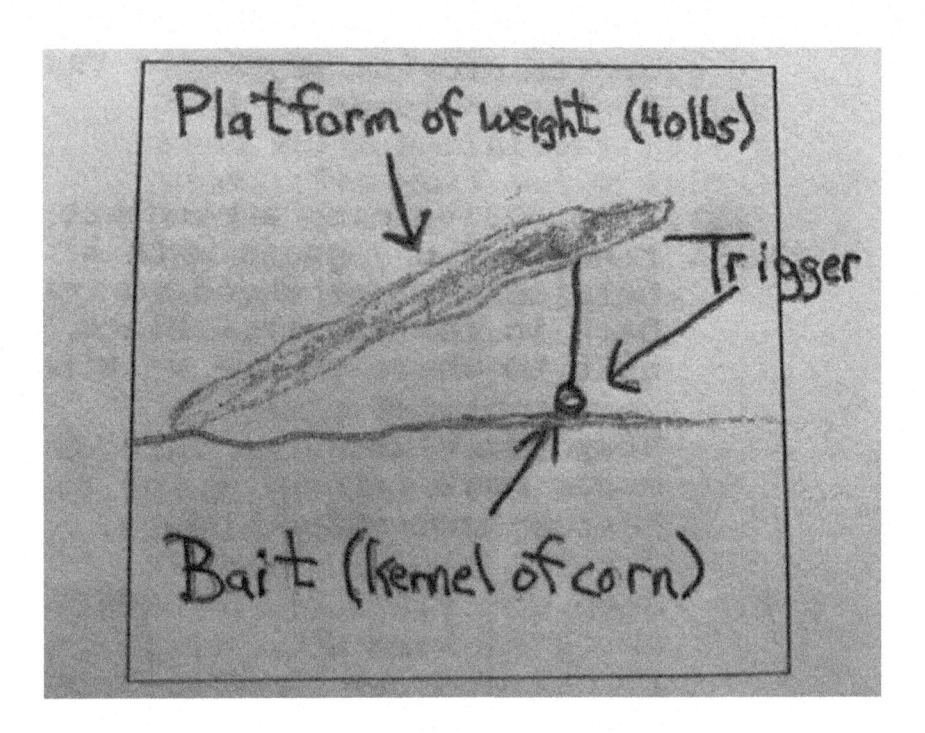

[Diagram: Platform of weight (40lbs) with arrow pointing to a flat rock propped up; Trigger labeled with arrow pointing to support stick; Bait (kernel of corn) labeled at base.]

Punji Traps: This next human boobytrap was probably derived from the VC (Viet Cong) during the Vietnam War (1960s and early 1970s). It may not kill you, but the painful stakes will surely incapacitate its victim immediately and for some time.

Ingredients: Enemy avenue of approach, shovel, twelve (12) 01-foot pointed sharpened sticks, defecation (human or animal scat), urination, natural vegetation for covering & camouflage, and vegetation & debris for channelization.

Step 01: A sight of probable avenue of approach of enemy personnel is chosen.

Step 02: A 05-foot pit is dug with the dimensions of 05-feet long by 03-feet wide. The pit is positioned in-line of the long-axis of the avenue of approach. In other words the 05-foot length is on the trail with the 03-foot wide section dug across the trail. The pit is 05-feet deep so when the victim steps into *"nothing"*, the victim's momentum has him accelerating & plunging into some or all of the 12 sharpened stakes so penetration is a sure bet.

Step 03: All 12 sharpened wooden stakes (punji stakes) are securely dug in-place throughout the punji trap. To cause disease to the victim to prevent quick recovery by the casualty; all punji stakes are smeared with human or animal scat or urination.

Step 04: Fresh vegetation is weaved together and placed over the punji trap. Attempt to match the punji trap covering to the surrounding ground and its vegetation. The punji trap may be identifiable during daylight hours but almost impossible to spot to the untrained eyes at night. A good idea is to sprinkle water on the covering. Then sprinkle everything with powdered dirt. Once it dries, it better matches - blends with the surrounding ground cover.

1st Note: Once the victim or victims become casualties to the Punji Trap, this should slow down the enemy pursuers. Since they already have your general direction of travel, it is highly advisable to alter course and employ several anti-tracking tactics and employ more non-lethal human boobytraps during the evasion if time permittable.

2nd Note: During the Vietnam War, much smaller punji traps were employed. They were just big enough for the victim to step into to cut into the foot, ankle, and leg.

Almost like a Cat Hole except with a wider diameter (about 01-foot) with punji stakes! The smaller punji traps were so successful and such a threat that metal shanks were placed in the soles of jungle boots to prevent penetration by punji stakes.

3rd Note: Once the punji stakes are sharpened, to get them to hardened state, place them into a fire just long enough to heat them up but not burn. Punji traps in Vietnam War were made from bamboo which sharpens real easily and hardens when heated.

You soldiers out there have just read some Human Traps & Snares that you can use during evasion to incapacitate (NOT KILL), incapacitate your enemy pursuers. Now your next question is: *"Can I use these same Human Traps & Snares for small and big game?"* Sure you can.

Pygmy Fat-Laden Termite Trap: Those savvy pygmies (Congo - Africa) had a technique to capture thousands and thousands of fat-laden, protein-rich termites. First the concrete-like termite mounds were located. The 03-foot high hard conical brown concrete-like mounds were made from earth and the termites saliva. In this case, a scouting party counted 20 termite mounds and the main body of pygmies moved in. The immediate area was cleared of debris around the mounds. Ditches were dug completely around each termite mound.

The ditch was used to capture fallen termites whether crawling or flying. A flat roof of sticks was made and placed over the mound entrance. A smoky fire was set near the base of the mound. Sensing fire, soon flying termites exited the mound entrance flying directly into the flat roof where their wings shattered - and the termites fell into the ditch.

Other termites crawled out of the mound falling into the ditch. Pygmies gathered the termites by the hundreds. Some ate as they gathered the crawling food. The thousands and thousands of fat-laden, protein-rich termites provided food for the entire tribe for 04 days. Termites were eaten raw or roasted. Termites tasted between a cross of lobster, snail, and a touch of mushroom.

Pygmy Human Meat: Cannibalism was once practiced throughout the Congo (Africa) by all tribes. It wasn't a ceremonial practice, just plain ol' dinner time. At some locations, live victims were auctioned off. Bidders would buy their favorite parts and those parts were covered with different colors of clay. Once the entire victim's body was sold, the live victim was dressed and separated like any big or small game. The human meat, organs, bones,... were considered delicious. When cannibalism was abolished, guards still had to be present at graveyards to prevent corpses from being stolen by neighboring tribes.

In my humble opinion (author), cannibalism is the very last resort after eating dirt, Mind-Over-Matter, and my most worst last resort - eating spiders. I'd readily make a burger out of thigh than eat a mouthful of spiders.

Quail: Here's a great survival trick to catch those quail that always surprised you into a near heart attack every time you unknowingly walked by them. The Choinumne Indians caught them by placing a low fence (natural-made a foot or so high) in the area of suspected quail. When the quail came to the low fence, they didn't fly over it (I don't know why) but ran along the short fence looking for an opening. When they came to a deliberate opening made by the hunter an awaiting basket trap was there to trap the fleeing quail. Neat uh! Critters like going in sheltered *"protected places"* like that *Den Trap*. One other matter, I have no sketches of exactly what the basket trap looked like but the *Basket Fish Trap* is a good idea cause they can go in but can't come out (notice the additional pointed sticks pointing inward) and once one quail bird is inside that critter will no doubt attract other tasty 02-legged quail vittles! See *Gambel's Quail*.

Rabbit Dead Fall: The main parts of the rabbit dead fall are the heavy platform (flat rock), trigger, and bait.

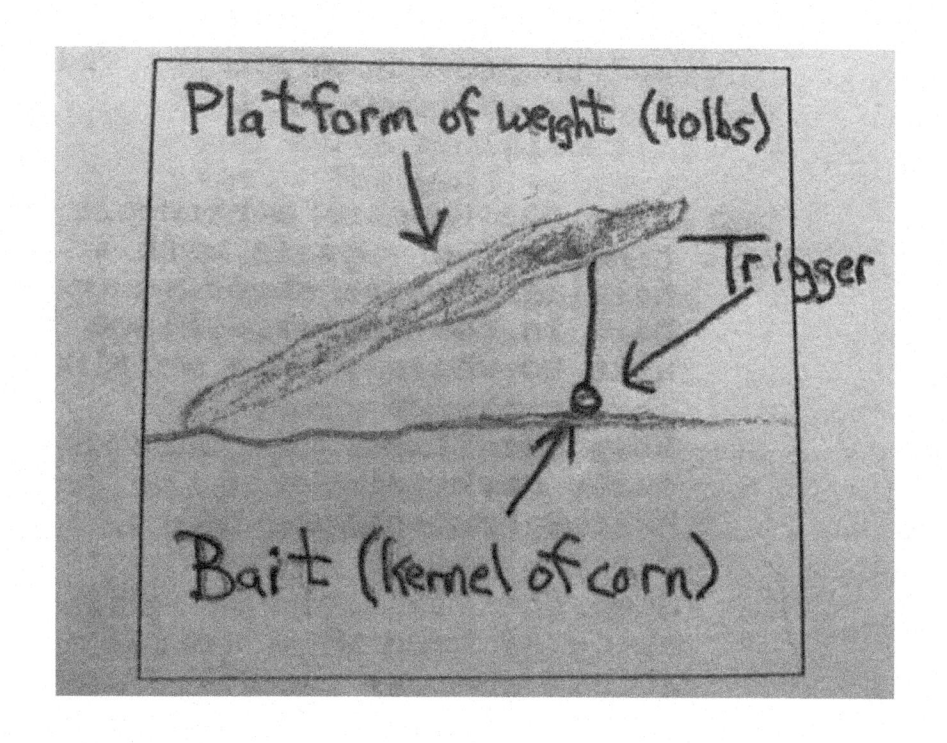

Rabbit Round-Up: Our northern friends had their own rabbit round-up. To successfully complete a rabbit drive, families throughout the area were brought together. And with them they brought a net made milkweed fiber which they joined to other nets. Families brought nets that were 02-feet wide and 200-feet long. When similar nets were joined together the net covered a wide area. The rabbits were corralled into this huge net down in the valley.

The drive began on the high ground at the ridges surrounding the valley. All available members formed a line on the ridges that enveloped the valley and began to corral the rabbits downhill by making noise with shouts and instruments.

The rabbits moved in the only direction available - downhill. As the advancing lines moved downhill closer to the valley, more and more rabbits were funneled toward the huge net. Near the valley waited others that clubbed the advancing rabbits. At the net, others clubbed the rabbits arriving at the net. When the advancing families arrived in the valley, closing in on the net, they too took part in clubbing the evading rabbits. In the valley the rabbits were dressed using the extremely sharp stone knives (keep reading)! The rabbits had several uses. They were used for valuable meat from their organs and flesh. Most of the meat was air dried or smoked for long term food stores. A lot of the their furs were used for clothing, rope, blankets,...

Rabbit Squealing Bloody Murder: If you ever heard a rabbit screaming bloody murder - it's a very high pitched squealing sound. If you can learn to copy-cat that sound - great! It reminds me of the sound a squirrel makes when a 9-life critter has it cornered! If you don't know it, rabbits are just about on EVERY CRITTERS DINNER MENU from snakes to birds to cats (9-life & big felines) to canine species! Once that rabbit starts screaming, you can bet any critter within hearing range (animals have great hearing) will be compelled to investigate in hopes of a tasty meal.

Rabbit Sticks: Rabbit sticks are a proven weapon used to kill or immobilize small and used to slow down big game. Rabbit sticks are simple to make and in many cases already waiting for to grab throughout most wilderness areas.

Rabbit Sticks

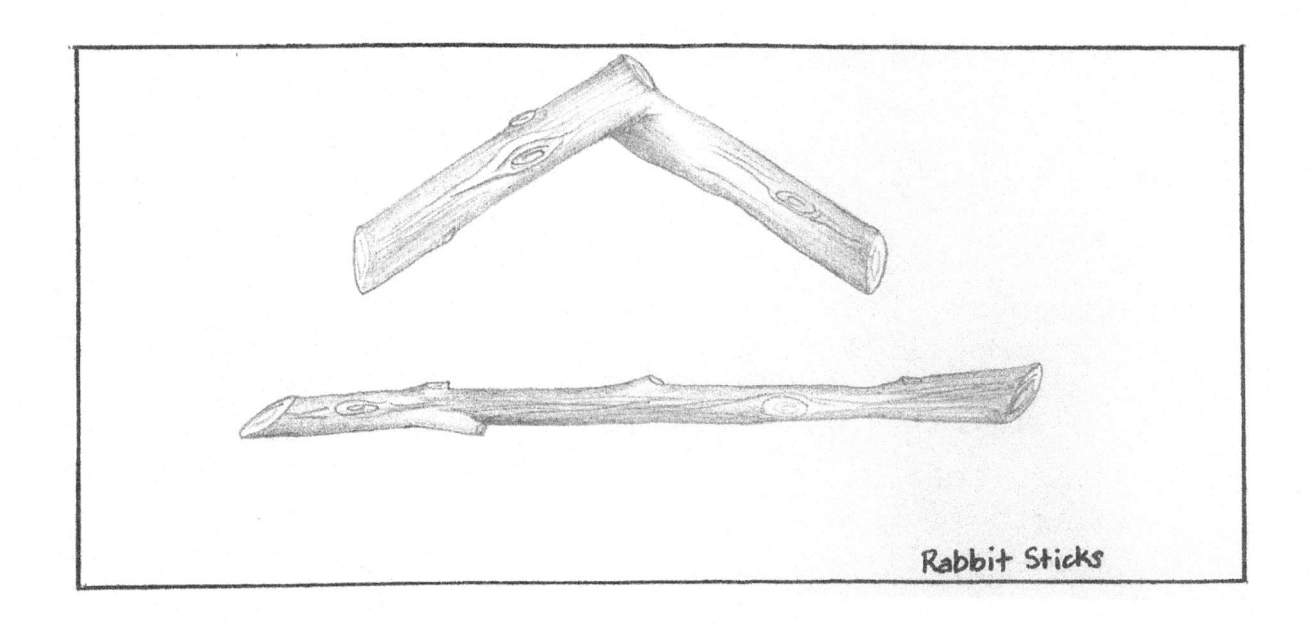

Ingredients Needed to Build Rabbit Sticks:
A curved stick about 12 to 24 inches long. Or a 12 to 24 inch straight stick that is slightly weighted on one end.

How to use the Rabbit Stick:
The Rabbit Stick is best used for small game. However, Catawba Indians were able to break the legs of running dear. This would slow it down so they could eventually kill it later on.

The Rabbit stick is best thrown side-armed. This is to give it a horizontal flight so to give it the best opportunity to engage a weak spot on the intended wild game while it's standing, walking or running.

The curved portion Rabbit Sticks and weighted Rabbit Sticks gives the stick additional momentum - thus higher velocity for a more forceful impact on the intended wild game.

Practice should be included to insure effectiveness in capturing wild game using either type of Rabbit Stick. See *Aztec Duck Stick* and *Long-Range Boomerang*.

Rabbit Stopper: Here's a neat trick Indians used to literally immobilize rabbits in their tracks. First they found a small game trail used by those hopping critters. They'd identify the rabbit trail by their tracks, fur, scat,... Then they'd take a pile of sharp pointed burrs from a variety of plants and place the burrs in the small game path. The next morning they'd check the small game trail. And sure enough the poor critter was literally stopped in its tracks unable to move because of the painful multiple burrs stuck in its four paws.

Rat Dinner: The 1,500 POWs at Woosung POW camp were on a starvation diet. Each POW was given a small bowl of rice, a small bowl of stew, and some tea that added up to 500 calories max. To supplement their diet, POWs captured rats and ate them. According to starving POWs, the rats were very tasty. Rats were plentiful, and the supply never ran out.

Rat Vittles: American POWs captured rats to supplement their meager diet but the Japanese feared the rats would spread disease and cut into their slave labor so they brought in a 9-life critter to hunt down rats. The POWs knew if the cat hung around their extra food supply was gone so they made the cat *"disappear."* The POWs captured the rats by making a trap that formed a complete box. Bait was put in the box and placed in a dark place with no human traffic.

The mouse would enter the box and take the bait. Once the bait was taken it would trip a trigger that would release the door that closed the opening entrance. POWs caught plenty of rats and provided nourishment they badly needed.

Salmon Harpoon: The salmon harpoon is a 06 to 07-foot spear that has 02 01-foot prongs (sharp pointed projections) secured to it. The sharpened pointed prong were made from animal bones or horns. The Yahi employed their salmon harpoons by taking a position on a rock in the middle of a river. More times than not it was thrust into the fish and not thrown so to accidently lose it floating down river.

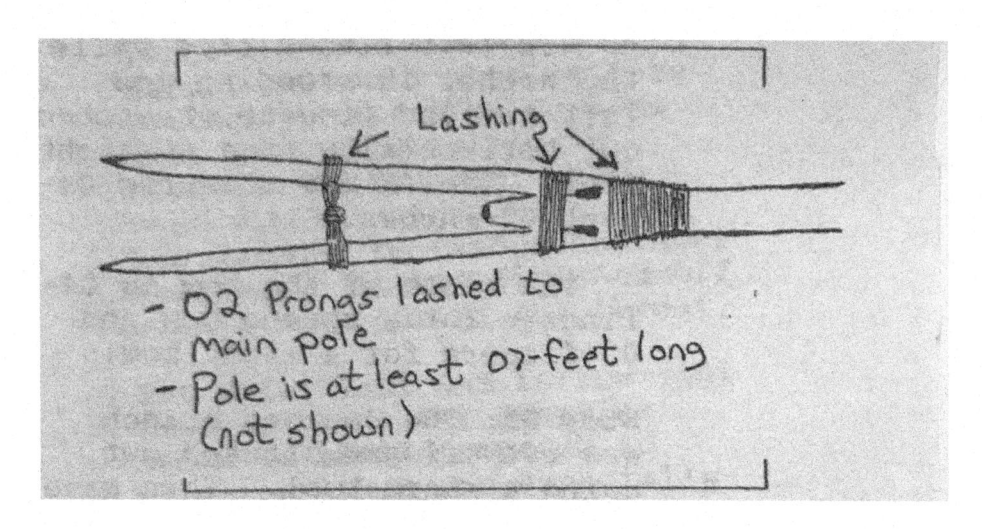

- 02 Prongs lashed to main pole
- Pole is at least 07-feet long (not shown)

The Salmon Harpoon also had detachable horned toggles with a weaved line of hemp rope. The horned toggles were used to play or bait fish to come in close for the kill. The Salmon Harpoon was used as the fish swam upstream, so the fish were harpooned from behind. As a matter of fact, the Salmon Harpoon was actually used when Ishi and fellow hunters were tired of catching fish by hand.

Ishi and fellow hunters also used other means to fish namely using a specific plant to stun fish. It's unknown exactly which plant he used. However, in ***"269+ International Fishing Tricks And More!"*** at **www.survivalexpertbooks.com**, I've named several plants found in North America and all over the world that stun fish for easy fishing. Fish weirs were also used.

The Yahi tribe didn't waist anything. After eating fish, they gathered the fish bones, dried them out, and pulverized them into a powder. The fish powder was eaten as a calcium supplement for strong bones.

Note: Ishi was the last surviving member of the Yahi tribe located in what is now northern California.

Salt Lick Ambush: Daniel Boone ambushed deer at *"licks"* - salt licks. Salt licks are natural deposits of exposed salt and animals are compelled to them. And here's a quote from one of my AASNs (Newsletters): *Daniel taught his young son James one neat deer hunting trick. He told him to always stay downwind of deer. Daniel showed James where to find natural salt deposits called "licks" near riverbanks because deer would always go to the licks to get the minerals their diet needs. All you had to do was lay in wait downwind from a lick and the deer would eventually show up for an easy kill. Plus you can bet they go for some water too! So monitor riverbanks for deer activity and stay downwind.*

How did Indians and pioneers find salt licks to ambush deer? It's simple, they tasted fresh water streams, rivers for a salty taste. Once they found the salty taste they knew they were near the salt lick which was upstream - upriver.

Closing on the salt lick, they looked for deer tracks that led to the salt lick. Once the salt lick was found, it was a waiting game. The Indians and pioneers waited in ambush downwind from the tasty salt lick.

I'm not sure if this is legal, but I've heard of hunters chamming - if you will, baiting deer with salt blocks. A salt block is placed in an isolated area, weeks, months, before deer season. Deer are accustomed to getting their ration of salt. Then when deer season opens up - the hunters hunker down around the salt lick at a distance pegging deer as they close in from surrounding areas enroute to the salt block. Salt blocks are available since farmers, cattlemen,... use them to supplement the nutrition of their cattle, sheep,...

Note: You don't need a salt lick or a block of salt block to compel deer to come to you, see *Delicious Peanut Butter Deer Bait*.

Sauna In A Can: The following is a life-saving survival trick I learned as a young know-nothing soldier while serving with the U.S. Army's 82nd Airborne out of Fort Bragg, North Carolina.

Here, let me give you some background information first - so you can better appreciate this life-saving survival trick when your only life is threatened by killer cold weather.

I entered the service (US Army) right out of high school in the early summer of 1973. The Vietnam war was still going on but they were already pulling troops out of Vietnam by then (March 1973). But all the teachers I had from Basic Training till I arrived at A Co. 2nd Bn. 505th Infantry - 82nd Airborne - were all fresh out of Vietnam.

The training and actions by my superiors above me by today's standards would be called training abuse. But I feel I got the BEST TRAINING in the world compared to the military training conducted today. There was a saying I heard over and over again and I still believe it today: *"What you do in training, you do in combat."* In other words if you half-ass it in training, you half-ass it in combat - thus soldiers die unnecessarily. I've talked about this in my Newsletters but we'll carry-on.

Anyway, this training was no sissy training. I was brought up and raised in one of the most least desired and most miserable jobs in the Army - Airborne Infantry. The word infantry just brings miserable thoughts to the mind even to those that never served in the military.

Here I was jumping into drop zones in the middle of the night with all this heavy gear, nauseated sick as hell from the rollercoaster plane rides and in some cases bitterly cold and already soaking wet from sitting there in the dirt at Green Ramp waiting to board the plane at one o'clock in the morning and that C-130 or C-141 was hundreds of meters away. The rain never let up and here were a couple hundred paratroops all miserably shivering cold just like I was but NOBODY quit, NOBODY planned on quitting, NOBODY,... We all carried-on like the miserable, soaking wet, shivering paratroops we were - for God and Country!!

Anyway, as a young know-nuthin' soldier in the Airborne Infantry, I was put into environments where I was miserable for several days at a time. The time dragged-on so so s l o w while we were in the field.

Our only shelter were the foxholes we dug and the bottoms were often filled with super cold water. I'm telling you, those 03 1/2 years with the 82nd Airborne, many times I thought I was going to die from the miserable cold and many times I was scared to go to sleep, fearing I'd never wake-up.

Well, here and there we did some neat survival tricks to stay warm even if we were soaking wet. And one that I learned was what I named - *"Sauna In A Can!"*

As a young know-nuthin' soldier, I had the opportunity to attend a school called 82nd Airborne Recondo School. It was a baby 03-week U.S. Army type Ranger Course. But as it turns out after I attended and completed U.S. Army Ranger Course several years later, I felt pound for pound, the 82nd Airborne Recondo School was more intense.

Probably because back then I didn't know anything about patrolling, tactics, or leadership. It all hit me cold in the face.

As it turned out, like all the other schools I attended, this was a great NO SISSY school. It was taught by a cadre of all Army Ranger qualified instructors. My class - we had about 07 Marine Force Recon Marines attending the course - the elite of the Marine Corp but mostly made-up of Army soldiers from the 82nd Airborne.

And from the 1st seconds from the *"Duffel Bag Drag"* from the hardtop of Manchester Road thru the deep sand leading to the base camp that seemed 10-miles away - it was all out - one ass whoopin' after another complimented with the bitterly cold wet weather.

In the patrolling part of Recondo School, it seemed we walked from one end of North Carolina to the other and everybody was hallucinating from lack of sleep. Plus we were all hungry, we'd often look to the ground for food in C-Ration cans tossed away months or years before. And throw-in the stinging cold in our hands & fingers, feet & toes, and the unthinkable of failing,... And the revolving student chain-of-command from the Patrol Leader (PL), Assistant Patrol Leader (APL), Squad Leaders (SL) were constantly kicking butt on the super tired, super hungry, hallucinating,... Recondo students.

And when it came my turn in the leadership position, here I was an APL. We were static in a 360-degree position pulling 50% security at night. The PL was under his poncho, shiverring non-stop with his red lens flashlight writing an OPORD (Operations Order) for our next mission. It was after midnight and super stinging cold. I was constantly walking around kicking people to make sure 1/2 of the patrol was awake pulling security like they were supposed to.

And I kept walking by this one position with this one soldier who kept smiling up at me every time I walked by his position. Here he was wrapped-up in his poncho in his foxhole and he smiled at me every time I walked by his position. *"What the hell is wrong with him?"* I asked myself. He's supposed to be miserable, shivering, cold,... just like the rest of us. Why does he keep smiling?

Well the next racetrack I did, I was going to ask him what was wrong with him. Approaching his position, there he was looking up at me smiling again!! I said something like *"Hey, what are you doing?"* He told me he was staying warm!!!!!!!!

"How?" I asked him. How can you stay warm in this miserable penetrating wet cold of North Carolina? This is what this young Private was doing. With only his head sticking out of the hood of his poncho, below him he had a small can of sterno burning away.

The heat it put out was plenty of heat to keep him warm (keep reading) in the bitterly cold weather but the burn was so low it didn't violate Noise & Light Discipline. I couldn't see any light at all coming thru the poncho so I let him carry-on. The burning heat from the can of sterno was contained within his poncho.

So after Recondo School, I copycatted his technique and used it several times while in some very cold weather. All I did was sit down up against a tree with my heavy poncho wrapped around me. I lit the small can of sterno and regulated the heat by placing a portion of the lid on the opening of the can (1/4th covered, 1/3rd covered, ½ covered). I adjusted the heat by how much the lid covered the opening.

I'm telling you, I've used this technique in miserable *"cussing"* cold weather even when I was soaking dripping wet. I even had my head tucked under the hood instead of my head sticking out of the hood itself. There were no ill effects to me at any time. And I'm quite sure the many times I used *"Sauna In A Can"*, it kept me from suffering from life-long cold weather injuries and probably to a sleeping death!

And YES YES YES - it feels so good from the miserable shivering cold to a super comfortable heat - it really feels like a soothing warm sauna!!!!!! That's why I named it *"Sauna In A Can"* and it can really save your life Anytime Anywhere!

But be careful, it can really get hot - real hot so you have to regulate the temperature (keep reading). And in my book it's safe. Like I've said, I've had my head tucked under the poncho with the burning sterno for several hours and had no ill effects. Heck, those chefs use sterno all the time to keep food warn in enclosed indoor environments and you don't see anybody having any ill effects over the burning sterno and fumes. Well, there you go!!!

WARNING: <u>Never never never</u> use any type of military or civilian heat tabs using this technique or in any enclosed environment. Heat tabs are extremely toxic. Remember, back in the 1970s and 1980s, the training was superior compared to what it is today. When the weather is kicking your butt, the war doesn't stop. That should give you an advantage to kick butt on your enemy cause he's hunkered down feeling sorry for himself. And *"Sauna In A Can"* provided me a 2nd, 3rd, 4th,... chance to refit real quick and carry-on with the mission.

Here's a "Sauna In A Can" Follow-Up:

Depending on the size of sterno cans you use, regulating the size of flame,...them *"Saunas In a Can"* can last a long long time and at least help you recover and PREVENT killer hypothermia. I've used it when I was soaking wet, shivering cold, cussing and hating life!!

I hunkered down, got under that poncho - my head too, and lit that baby. Boy did it feel good. And the temperature rose so much inside the poncho, I was steaming steaming cause I was soaking wet. You'd think I was cooking vittles under the poncho!!

Boy it felt good every time I used it I didn't want to come out from underneath that poncho (thick poncho - heavy) is best). Heck just about any cover will do. And yes, if you have a casualty going hypothermic, this would be a great remedy when no professional medical attention is around.

Let me get back to the burn duration of sterno. I currently have an 08-ounce can of "STERNO" made by Candle Corporation of America. It advertises that this 08-ounce can of sterno will burn for 02 1/2 hours (150-minutes). And its temperature output is 205-degrees Fahrenheit.

Remember I said you can regulate the heat by placing the lid over the top of the can to cover 1/2, 1/3, or 1/4. I'm telling you, **205-degrees** Fahrenheit will get you toasty warm real quick. Oh, before I forget, for packing purposes, I always used the small sterno cans and I still had to regulate the heat output so those big cans should definitely be regulated.

Here are some approximate times you should know about concerning the burn times for this 08-ounce can of sterno:

Wide Open------------------02 1/2 hours
1/2 Covered----------------05 hours
1/3 Covered----------------07 1/2 hours
1/4 Covered----------------10 hours
I hope *"Sauna In A Can"* has you more ready Anytime Anywhere!

See Ya, - Joseph A. Laydon Jr.
Yes there are more neat survival tricks like this. You must see http://www.survivalexpert.com

WAIT WAIT - HERE'S AN UPDATE: 15 January 2014 (Wednesday)"

Last night I was watching a TRUE story on Netflix. The movie was called *Bravo Two Zero*. I won't give up the story but it's about them badd ass British SAS (Special Air Service) soldiers on a live mission. In a couple parts of their mission they were hurtn' bad cause it was sooo coooold. Watching this movie I thought *"Too bad they didn't know about Sauna In A Can!"*

Secret Mountain Man Caches: Jedediah and his fellow mountain men / trappers accumulated hundreds and hundreds of beaver pelts. The accumulated number of beaver pelts couldn't be carried throughout their long 08-year trek through the wilderness so they had to be cached throughout their expedition.

The caches of beaver pelts were later recovered and transported to Saint Louis for cash sale. The caches also hid the valuable beaver pelts from marauding Indians. Here's a step-by-step process for their secret caches.

Step 01: Locate a cache site that has a feature that can't possibly be forgotten or confused with any other area. Must be a site that can pinpointed down to the very exact spot of the cache. I don't believe they used <u>very detailed maps</u> but YOU should. Site should also be void of water drainage or prone to a water table.

Step 02: Lay-out buffalo robes skin-side up near the cache site. All dirt dug-up from the cache is placed on the buffalo robes so to leave no sign that any hole was dug.

Step 03: The initial aperture of the hole was narrow. But the deeper the hole, the hole was excavated wider and wider resembling a giant *"Bottle Trap.* See *Bottle Trap.*

Step 04: Once the cache was dug-out, a buffalo robe was placed on the bottom. All beaver pelts and supplies were tightly packed (lack of air) in the cache. Another buffalo robe was placed on top of the beaver pelts and supplies. Dirt was packed tightly (lack of oxygen) on top of the cache till level with the surface.

Step 05: Remaining dirt on the buffalo robes were carefully dragged away to a stream and discarded. At the cache site there should be no sign of any digging.

They returned early from scuba school failing the course and they were traumatized. NO, not because they failed the course but what happened to them and all scuba students. Scuba School puts the students through swimming drills that are so rigorous that scuba students end up floating unconscious underwater.

No they didn't drown – not yet. It's called *Shallow Water Blackout*. As told to me by multiple scuba students, they're swimming underwater and its LIGHTS OUT. What happens is they suck-in water and go unconscious. During the next few minutes it's called *Shallow Water Blackout*. The water is stopped from going into the lungs by some muscles in the throat. This is *Shallow Water Blackout*. The scuba students are retrieved and easily revived. And are asked if they want to quit. A scuba student told me all scuba students have a *Shallow Water Blackout* at least once during scuba school.

Now after approximately 03-minutes, the muscles in the throat relax and the water goes into the lungs – now you're drowning. Returning scuba students after experiencing *Shallow Water Blackout* 01 or more times, are traumatized. So traumatized that they're scared to take showers or take a bath in their own house. Whether these soldiers passed or failed the US Army Special Forces Scuba School, they're better & safer swimmers paid for by your hard-earned tax dollars. See *Swimming Cramp Remedy Point* and *Cold Water Diving Reflex*.

Shining: Shining is an illegal technique used at night to locate or stun wildlife by shining a very bright light in their location (eyes). Once the wildlife is located (shining - glowing eyes) or stunned, the prey is shot. This activity is very effective but is absolutely illegal in non-survival situations. Also known as Headlighting. Texas Rangers in the 1930's used shining to hunt before it became illegal. One Texas Ranger stated how he could always tell he was shining a coyote: *"...I sometimes hunted varmits in the brush with a headlight. You can readily tell when you are shining a coyote. These sneaking animals will never come at you straight, but will circle around and show you only one eye."* Shining works so good it's illegal in non-survival situations. Plus you know when a coyote critter is in your light if you have to use this hunting trick. See *Jacking*. See **"269+ International Fishing Tricks And More!"** at **www.survivalexpertbooks.com**

Simple Snare: A simple snare consist of a noose placed over a trail or den hole and attached to a firmly planted stake. If the noose is loosely placed over the trail or den hole, use some twigs or twist blades of grass around it to hold it up.

Insure that the noose is large enough to fit over the intended prey's head. As the prey moves through the noose it will become tighter around its neck. The animal will struggle and the noose becomes tighter.

Wire is the best material to use for this type of snare because it will not loosen up like cordage. The bait for this snare is the prey attempting to leave or enter the den, and using it's run/game trail.

Simple Snare

Small Game & Fish Paralyzing Stunner: There are plants all over the Earth and probably under the oceans that are sure death to humans and animals. And there are plants that won't kill but will absolutely stun its victim. One such plant is a highly poisonous berry called the Levant Nut (*Cocculus Indicus*). It can be found in India and can be identified by its large climbing shrub.

Here's how to use this absolute stunner. Take several berries and pulverize it. Mix it with many small flour dough balls. Place the tainted flour dough ball on game trails for small game and in still water to stun fish.

Once the small game and fish are stunned, it's safe to eat the small game or fish. Just make sure the small game and fish are thoroughly cleaned-out with fresh water. For a *Cocculus Indicus* product, see *Herbal Advisor* in the POC Section. See **"269+ International Fishing Tricks And More!"** at **www.survivalexpertbooks.com**

Snake Alert: What's a good warning sign that a venomous snake (black mamba, boomslang, puff adder,..) are nearby? Look for birds raising hell! With their super keen eyesight, odds are if a venomous snake is near, birds will congregate above it in a nearby tree squawking up a storm and they may not quit till the snake is killed or evades out of the area. Now this is known to work in the Kalahari but maybe not in North America, Europe,... I know certain species of monkeys do the same thing, raising hell to alert others of venomous snakes.

Warning: Even though birds warn of a venomous snake, the hiding snake may be well hidden from an ignorant searcher so BEWARE! Remember the birds are warning you, but not telling you exactly where the snake is located.

Other animals throughout the world give their warning sounds to other animals of different species. Like both chimpanzee and white-tailed deer stomp their feet to warn of danger in general.

Snake Fence: Some small game desert critters like to imitate the porcupine and make their homes among the super sharp thorns of cacti which protects them against most or all prey to include all snakes. And so thorns can be made into a fence to deter them slithering fanged venomous snakes. Next time you make camp in snake country, consider making perimeter around your tent, camp,... of thorns from cacti or other thorny plants. Why? It's proven that them snake critters hate crawling across thorns. Most likely to prevent injury. Animals know once they're injured, they're very vulnerable to other prey, so they go out of their way to avoid injury. See *Snake Trap* below.

Snake Trap: A snake trap can be made by encircling the already found snake with thorns from cacti, and other plants bearing thorns. The snake may attempt to crawl over the wall of thorns but will back-up to avoid injury. Animals know once they're injured, they're very vulnerable, so they go out of their way to avoid injury.

Snow Drift Traps: Those savvy Indians took advantage of every of everything Mother Nature provided to survive and they took advantage of the weather. When hunting, they corralled big game into snow drifts. The snow drifts not only blocked their escape but the deep snow trapped them in place. They were stuck, they couldn't go anywhere.

Cree Indians reigning in Ontario, Manitoba, and Saskatchewan, Canada maneuvered buffalo on ice where their movement was stopped *"cold."* The ice had them slipping, sliding, and falling and having them at their most vulnerable position - off their feet. Easy pickens even for a novice! And where do you think the Cree learned this survival trick? From wolves. They also maneuvered buffalo into rivers where there were like *"fish out of water"* and easy pickens.

Squirrel Pole: A The squirrel pole consist of a pole approximately ten feet in length, and wire for several wire nooses. A large branch free of leaves or smaller branches can be used. Remember to mask the scent of a freshly cut branch. Place the pole on an incline to a tree where squirrels are known to be. Construct and secure several wire nooses along the pole so that the squirrels must pass through one of the wire nooses.

Secure the noose so that when the squirrel is caught in the noose, it will eventually be strangled because the noose is secured to the underside of the pole and not to the side or top. Squirrels are curious, and with time will eventually be caught in the wire nooses. The bait for this snare is the squirrel attempting to leave or enter the tree.

Squirrel Pole

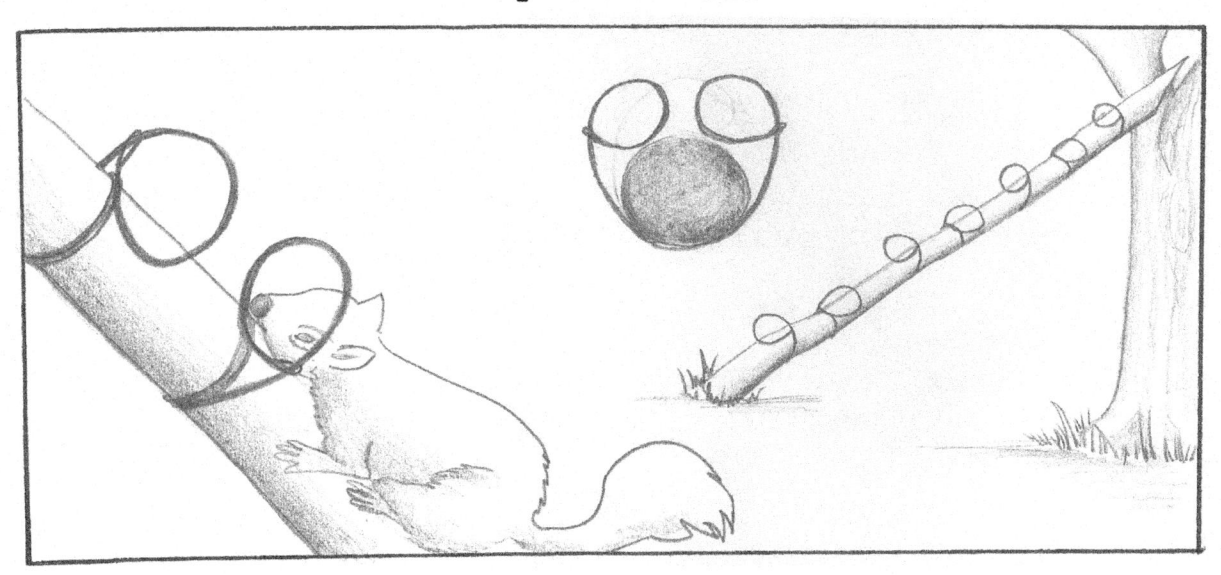

Super Duck Decoys: While we're talking about ducks and geese, let me tell you about a duck decoy that works so good, it's already BANNED in some states. On 131728M January 2003, CBS News did a segment on robot duck decoys that worked so good, many folks were calling *"fowl"* and they're already banned in several states!

Down in St. Bernard Parish, Louisiana, duck hunters are using an electric look-a-like duck that has flapping wings. It's suspended by a 04-foot iron rod above the water's surface, at the water's edge, or on land. Flocks of flying ducks see the electric flapping decoys and are compelled to close on their duck friends, thus falling into an ambush of duck hunters hidden in their blinds. These electric decoys work so good, they're already banned in several states. See *Mojo Mallard* in the POC Section for more information on these super duck decoys.

Note: Ducks are tasty and find themselves on dinner tables and restaurants. One species of duck that are very common in the waterways of Brazil and Europe, especially on dinner tables in Europe are the Muscovy ducks. It's found wild from Mexico to Brazil but actually domesticated throughout the world. Its meat is known to exceptionally succulent.

Swimming Cramp Remedy Point: Somewhere in North America and the world, water obstacles (rivers, lakes, ponds, oceans, ice - falling through,...) kill people each and every single day. And one cause of death are swimming cramps in the legs. The legs hurt very painfully and refuse to work and something else might happen when the legs fail to work - FEAR & PANIC! If you're alone, and FEAR & PANIC overwhelm you, odds are you're a weak swimmer, non-swimmer, or you're in very frigid water and your fate is already set. However, here's an emergency acupressure application that could save your life.

Anyway, let's say you're doing OK and leg cramps suddenly set in and are really hurting to the point your legs become paralyzed. A quick remedy may be a simple acupressure hold. Using your thumb and index finger, pinch the skin right under your nose and above your upper lip - this area is called the philitrum (GV 26). Pinch the philitrum for 30-seconds, you should get relief real quick. GV 26 is also used to remedy cramps, dizziness, and fainting.

Warning: NEVER swim alone, NEVER go without a life preserver (if in a boat), and if you're a weak swimmer or non-swimmer - STAY THE HELL AWAY FROM ALL WATER OBSTACLES. You're a threat to yourself and those around you.

Tangling Bird Catcher: I already talked about the effective weapon called the bola. Bolas were used by tribes located throughout the Louisiana area. Their bolas weren't used to tangle the legs of evading big game but to *"wrap-up"* and down flying ducks and other birds. Their bolas had pear-shaped weights. Why? Probably the pear-shaped weights were more apt to go different directions once the bola came in contact with the prey thus effectively *"wrapping-up"* its wings and legs and downing the evading duck, bird,...

Remember, the bola is thrown at the target by rapidly swinging it in a circular motion (building up centrifugal force) and letting it go in the precise direction and trajectory of the prey. And once it makes contact, the weights that are attached to the thongs, string, babiche,... change direction circling the target which wraps the thongs, string, babiche,... around the prey's legs, wings,... tangling it, thus preventing it from fleeing.

Note: Geese, ducks,... tend to migrate at the <u>west side</u> of streams, lakes ponds,... when breeding.

Tapping: Squirrels, raccoons, owls, and other critters that use trees for dens can be made to come out by tapping the trunk of the tree with a hard stick.

The Deer Is Over Here: The Paiute used a unique trick to locate deer. One critter they never hurt or killed was the grey jay. While tracking the rare big game they were after (deer, antelope, elk), they'd pinpoint the big game location by listening to the loud call of the grey jay.

The gray jay would sound the alert letting everybody know that big game was in the immediate area. So next time you're out hunting, listen for those loud jay bird sounds and all the other critter sounds too! You can bet deer listen to them too. Some critter is probably alerting the deer of your presence. See *White-Tailed Deer*.

The Wrath Of Mother Nature - Blizzards: Since you're out hunting, I thought I'd add this segment in here to give you a better respect for Mother Nature and all She possesses.

First, let me give you some record snowfalls that occurred here in the US. This should give you an idea of the killer wrath of Mother Nature when it comes to snowfall.

Feb 13-19 1959, **189-inches of snow** fell on Mount Shasta Ski Bowl.

April 14-15 1921, **76-inches of snow** Silver Lake, Colorado.

Feb 19, 1971 - Feb 18, 1972, **1,224.5-inches of snow** fell on Paradise, Mount Rainier, Washington.
March 11, 1911, **37.5 feet of snow** fell on Tamarack, CA.

You see, Mother Nature can whoop you good if you don't prepare or aren't ready to react to the unexpected like killer snow. But add wind to that snow and you got a killer blizzard.

The US Weather Service defines a snow blizzard as a storm with winds of more than 35 miles per hour and a visibility of only 500 feet or less (flying snow). A severe blizzard is defined as having winds exceeding 45 miles per hour and visibility is 1200 feet or less (flying snow) with temperatures of 10 degrees Fahrenheit or less.

Now that you know what a blizzard is, let me give you some *"cold hard facts"* about killer blizzards.

The combination of snow and wind chill winds is a deadly combination. Blizzards will steal your body heat sending the *"clueless"* survivor into *"sure as dead"* hypothermic conditions. Once the body core temperature begins dropping below its optimum core temperature of 98.6, the survivor is doomed unless the he takes immediate action.

Also called *"white storms,"* blizzards are flying ice crystals that freeze everything in place - even the tears in your eyes. It steals your body's heat at a high rate.

One of the greatest killer blizzards in US history occurred 11 - 14 March 1888, on the east coast from Maine to Chesapeake Bay. They called it the *"Great White Hurricane."* Sources stated that 50-inches of snow fell in Connecticut and Massachusetts while 48-inches of snow fell in New York and New Jersey. Killer snowdrifts as high as 40 - 50 feet were recorded. The blizzard literally snapped telegraph & telephone lines, immobilized traffic, incapacitated rescue and rescue efforts, froze ships in place. More than **400 deaths** were reported and damage estimates ran up to $25 million dollars. Because of this killer blizzard, the creation of the New York subway was born.

Other killer blizzards in the US and elsewhere include:

7-8 Jan, 1996, Northeastern US - 100 killed.

13-14 March 1993, Eastern US - 200 killed.

22 August 1996, Himalayas-Northern India - 239 killed.

12-20 December 1967, Southwest US - 51 killed.

15-16 February 1958, Northeastern US - 171 killed.

26 December 1947, NYC & N Atlantic states - 55 killed.

11-12 November 1940, Northeast and Midwest US - 144 killed.

Have we forgotten about the wrath of Mother Nature when it comes to killer blizzards? Are we to dependent of fire-rescue to save our lives if it should happen to us? Are we sure electrical power will always be there to warm our water, food, houses, bodies...? Are you ready for the next killer blizzard Anytime Anywhere?

So what about you? What are you going to do when and if a killer blizzard strikes your home town, state, region...? What about when you're out camping, hunting, hiking... alone or with family members and friends?

Without getting paranoid, HAVE A PLAN! Take a re-look at **PRSC**. Even if you got some lousy candles, a few good sleeping bags and some water and chow stored-away in your house, you at least did something! Think about killer blizzards! What if one would strike your hometown, state, region at the same time? Are you gonna be ready? You gotta read about *Sauna In A Can* to fight off the killer cold.

Trash Basket Decoys: Yep, believe it or not those 05-gallon white trash baskets are used as decoys to lure in snow geese. White snow geese with black wing tips are found in northern regions. The white plastic trash baskets are cut in-half lengthwise and anchored to the ground (wind) with the open side down. They don't resemble a white goose but from flying altitude, the white geese think they're snow geese buddies are down there eating, watering, resting,... - it must be safe! The hunter is among the decoys in plain view but wearing white.

Note: Do not look up, NEVER show your face unless you're wearing a white mask or other full-face camouflage. Once a critter sees a human face they're outta there at a full sprint.

Treadle Spring Snare: A The treadle snare consist of several (at least twelve) stripped sticks small in diameter and approximately fourteen inches in length; two forked sticks about six inches long; some cordage approximately 30-feet in length; and a small stick approximately half an inch in diameter and about an inch and a half in length; a shallow hole about one foot square; and a large enough branch (near the treadle snare site) to apply enough tension or hold the weight of a weighted object to spring the snare once the trigger is activated.

First pick the location of the treadle snare which should be on a run or game trail. Insure to mask the scent of all working pieces of the treadle snare, including your hands. Dig a shallow hole approximately one foot square on the run or game trail.

Secure in the ground, the two six inch forked sticks at each corner of the shallow hole on the side of the branch. The forked ends will face away from the snare and towards the sapling or large branch.

Next, place one of the a fourteen inch sticks up against and centered on the two anchored forked sticks. This stick will be placed on the side of the sapling or branch.

Next place all but one of the remaining sticks over the shallow hole so that they completely cover the shallow hole and are resting on the perpendicular stick just previously placed against the two anchored forked sticks. Place the remaining fourteen inch stick on top of and centered on all the sticks covering the shallow hole.

Next, tie-in the cordage onto the sapling or large branch (you may also use a weighted object with the cordage over a branch). Pull down on the sapling\branch or weighted object and measure the placement of the trigger, and the noose.

Now set the trigger between the two horizontal sticks (you'll need to lift the bottom stick thus raising the platform of sticks) and so that it on the branch/sapling side of the two horizontal fourteen inch sticks. The top horizontal stick is placed up against the forked portion of each anchored fork. Also it will be pulled on the platform side by the branch\sapling.

If you have trouble setting the trigger, you may have to modify it by carving it, burning it... Next place your noose so that it is placed on the outer edges of the treadle platform. Camouflage, bait, and channelize as necessary.

The treadle snare will capture its prey once it steps on the treadle platform. The stick or sticks that are pushed down, will drop the bottom horizontal stick which activates the trigger. The tension of the snare pulls the cordage which collapses around any part of the prey that happens to be caught in the treadle snare. The tension pulls the prey up so that it is suspended at least two feet in the air and hasn't a chance to escape.

Treadle Spring Snare

Twitch-Up Snare: A The twitch-up snare consist of a sapling or larger branch, two forked pieces of wood that will be used as a stake and a trigger, and a fifteen to twenty foot piece of cordage. Remember to mask the scent of not only yourself, but all parts of the twitch-up by rubbing mud or charcoal on all parts of the snare to include your hands.

First find a run, or game trail in which to position the twitch-up snare. Insure that there is a sapling or large branch near the game trail to provide the tension for the snare. Bend the sapling or branch over the run or game trail and mark the trail. Place the stake (forked stick) firmly in the ground so that the short end of the fork is parallel to the ground. The short end of the stake (forked stick) should be cut to one to two inches to effectively have contact with the trigger.

If there are any jagged edges on the forked stake, smooth them out with a file or rub it against a rock.

Next take the other forked piece, the trigger and marry up the short end with the stake and insure that they slide away from each other without too much problem. Now take a the fifteen to twenty foot piece of cordage and tie it to the sapling or large branch. Pull on the cordage, pulling down the sapling/branch towards the run/game trail. Measure how much tension you'll need for the twitch-up and measure where to tie the cordage to the trigger.

You may want to cut a groove in the trigger so that the cordage doesn't slip off of it. Also insure that you have enough cordage to tie the noose on the run/game trail. Once everything is measured, let up on the tension of the cordage and tie-in the trigger and the noose. Once everything is tied-in, set the twitch-up. Bind the trigger against the forked stick, and set the noose. Camouflage as necessary. The bait for this snare is the prey using it's run/game trail.

Twitch-Up Snare

Waiting Snake Trap & Snare: This next human boobytrap is evil. It was used by VC (Viet Cong) in underground tunnels against American soldier - tunnel rats during the Vietnam War (1960s - early 1970s).

Ingredients: Enemy avenue of approach, venomous snake, 07-foot forked stick, 01 tree, 1 1/2-feet of string, nail, and natural debris for channelization.

Step 01: A sight of probable avenue of approach of enemy personnel is chosen. A small or big tree right next to the avenue of approach is chosen.

Step 02: Fresh vegetation and deadfall debris are placed to channelize the approaching enemy to the exact site of the Waiting Snake Trap & Snare.

Step 03: A venomous snake is secured using a forked-stick. While the snake is secured by the forked stick, a nail and string are secured to the tail-end of the snake's tail so to secure the snake but prevent excessive bleeding. A nail is pierced through the tail and a line is secured to both sides of the nail to prevent escape. The snake is carefully dragged to the Waiting Snake Trap & Snare. The other end of the line is secured to the bottom of the tree on the side of the avenue of approach.

1st Note: Camouflaging the lines of the Waiting Snake with wood ash blackens the line making it undetectable.

2nd Note: Once the victim or victims become casualties to the Waiting Snake, this should slow down the enemy pursuers. Since they already have your general direction of travel, it is highly advisable to alter course and employ several anti-tracking tactics and employ more non-lethal human boobytraps during the evasion if time permittable.

Wampanoag Deer Snare: The Wampanoag (modern day areas of Massachusetts and Rhode Island) knew deer ate the leaves of certain trees. They'd cut down a single tree which deer would eventually find and eat its leaves. The deer would eat its leaves and when it came round the top of the tree a snare was set up at ground level.

The deer would trip the snare and be pulled up by its leg via a pole. If you didn't catch it - the fallen tree itself is being used to channelize the deer into the ground snare. This Wampanoag trap and snare deserves RFIR. But take another look at the *"Deer Snare."*.

White Pelican Corral Fishing: Old West cowboys noted that white pelicans work together to get more fish than they could eat. During the warmer summer months you'd find them in the waters of Nevada Territory. They be offshore, side-by-side forming a semi-circle and closing on the shore herding and corralling hundreds or thousands of different species of fish. Closing on the shore, they'd dive to easily capture their meal. Fishermen throughout history have used this same technique in water and on land catching fish and small & big game complimented with weirs (water & land) and other hunting tools and I've annotated many many hunting applications throughout the AASNs. Browse through the A-Z Index now for HUNDREDS of hunting and fishing applications that really work Anytime Anywhere!

Hold the phone. Thousands of miles to the south in South America, groups of Great White Pelicans there execute the same exact strategy as stated above. Side-by-side or in a horse-shoe formation, the pelicans herd the fish towards the shallow waters of the shore or cul-de-sacs (dead ends) where they're easy pickens' for the pelicans. See *"269+ International Fishing Tricks And More!"* at **www.survivalexpertbooks.com**

Woodrat Food Cache: A woodrat is found west of Rocky mountains and can be identified by its hairy tail. It's identifiable colors are buff & black on top and white below. Its nest and cache site can be identified by its dome-shaped nests that are 03-feet high or more. The exterior of its nest may be smartly studded with cactus needles and thorns for protection from predators.

Indian tribes living and roaming in southwestern North America gathered the very tasty and fat pine (pinyon) nut. They also sought out the woodrat for those smart critters gathered a bounty of pine nuts and stored them in their shelters. Just one cache of pine nuts would be a fattening meal. So next time you're outdoors in the area where pine trees and woodrats live together, get your eyes to search for shelters and caches of the woodrat.

WARNING: Never never never put your hand in any hole unless you just dug it yourself just minutes before. That includes hollow logs, under rocks, logs, pile of debris (woodrat shelter),... You just never know what ornery critter is hiding in there and will strike whether its venomous or not. Even the non-venomous critters can still pass on a variety of sickly and deadly diseases from their scratches and bites. YES, that includes them ornery critters in water like dangerous snapping turtles. See *Hogging (catching giant catfish and snapping turtles)* in the 2003 AASN.

Note: The pine nut is rich in nutrients, and especially fat,... and in my (author) humble opinion, the pine nut saved the remaining survivors of the Donner Party. Here's a quote from that segment: *"the chief of one Indian village gave Eddy a handful of **pine nuts!** After eating them, Eddy "felt wonderfully refreshed!"*

The Donner Party – entire write-up is annotated in the February 2001 AASN (Newsletter). Read that entire segment (full subscribers) and the survival tricks used by the Donner Party.

Worming: You ever heard of worming? Probably not. Worming is a technique to find Earth worms for fishing. And this technique requires no digging. All you have to is look under rocks, small rocks. Under these selected rocks you'll find a few to several Earth worms just under the pried-up rock. But what kind of rocks should one look for to find hiding Earth worms. First of all worms hate water, they'll drown. That's why they come to the surface when it rains. So to take advantage of their tunneled homes in the Earth and have protection from the rain, they tunnel to the surface directly under rocks.

Plus the sheltered rocks give them 24/7 protection from getting eaten from them pecking hungry birds and other hungry small game critters. I know what your question is – *"Which rocks provide hiding Earth worms?"* I have some ideas but no solid proof at this time. This subject requires some R&D. But in the meantime – go Worming and find worms for fish bait and try to find commonalities in which rocks (location, size, terrain,...) them worms prefer to hide under. See *"269+ International Fishing Tricks And More!"* at **www.survivalexpertbooks.com**

Worm Stick: A The Worm Stick is simply made up of two green sticks about 02 feet long and an inch wide. One of the sticks has several notches carved into it. The Worm Stick simulates rainfall and gets worms to come to the surface. These worms can be used to eat or as fish bait.

Take one of your sticks and carve a sharp point to it at one end so easily drive it in the ground. At the other end carve about 12 notches in the stick about 01 inch apart.

Find a place in which to draw-out worms. Look for small holes in the ground, live or dead worms, trails...

Take your staked Worm Stick with the notches and drive it in the ground to the first notch. It should be about 01-foot in the ground. Rub the other smooth stick against the notched stick.

The vibrations of the smooth stick rubbing against the notched stick is sent into the surrounding ground. Worms think the vibrations are rain drops hitting the ground. They don't want to drown so they come to the surface and are easily gather. See *"269+ International Fishing Tricks And More!"* at **www.survivalexpertbooks.com**

Worm Sticks

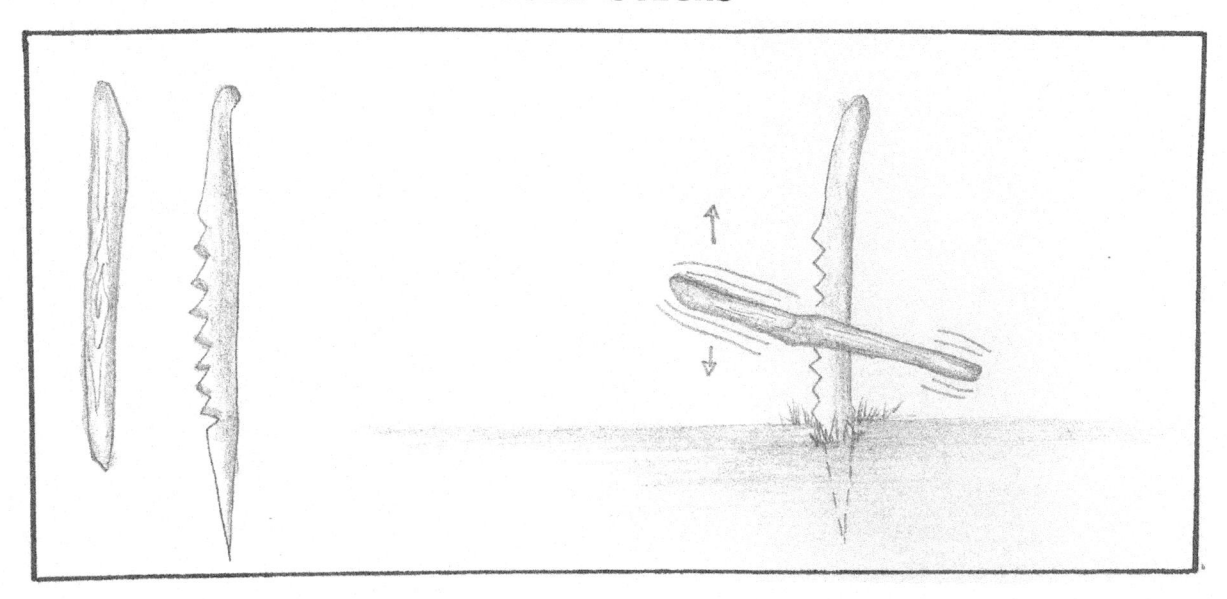

Zuni Crow Snare: Zuni knew crow birds were after their corn crops and they had several strategies to keep the hungry birds from eating their crops. They built different types of scarecrows, they stationed the younguns out there to scare them away, the younguns threw rocks at them, and the adults took their turns as human scarecrows too. But the Zuni had an ingenious trap and snare to protect their crops and get some crow vittles at the same time!

They took string (sinew) and stretched many lines like a clothes line but very close together over the crops. On these lines they places thorny cactus leaves to prevent the crows from squeezing through. Also on these lines they secured slip nooses made of hair. The crows would land on the string and get caught in the slip nooses.

Note: There's no evidence they used channelizing but I'm sure those very savvy Zuni placed those cactus leaves in such a way so to channelize crows into the hair snares.

Zuni Hunters: Small and big game it didn't matter, they knew what they were doing. Young Zuni boys as young as 04-years old were taught to hunt those hopping black-tailed jackrabbits with their powerful sling shots. Traps and snares and rabbit sticks were used to capture small game. They even used "drives" to herd - corral rabbits and antelope.

The largest land weir ever recorded that I'm aware of was 75-miles long! This 75-mile long land weir eventually came to a funnel where the antelope were controlled, captured and dressed by the Zunis. Near this funnel were pits where the animals would fall into and break their legs. This giant land weir and pit traps beats running 20-miles uh.

Crows Can't Count: The crow species are exceptionally intelligent but they have a little trouble with their subtracting. Here's a true hunting story that was related to me (08 Nov. 2007). Respecting hunters know crows ain't stupid. So four (04) armed hunters overtly and loudly go into the crows area and of course all the crows will fly off to safety staying out of range of their shotguns.

Watching their area from a distance, the crows see a single human hunter finally leaving their area. *"It's safe to go back boys"* caws the boss crow. So the bunch of crows head back only to get ambushed by the 03 hiding hunters that stayed behind. Now you know crows can't count.

"Laydon's Emergency Survival Employment Instructions!"

You opened this *Survival Kit* cause you are now in a serious survival situation.

Step 01: <u>YOU TAKE CHARGE RIGHT NOW</u>. Announce to everyone that *"I Am In-Charge"* cause YOU ARE THE SURVIVAL EXPERT. Assign duties & responsibilities and pair-up everyone. Instruct everyone that *"We Are Now In A Life Or Death Survival Situation. Follow My Orders And We Will Get Back To Safety."* Even though you're already in a survival situation, why get in worse trouble. Employ PRSC (Planning, Recon, Security, and Control). Especially Security - always think of 12 things that will hurt, kill the survivors, and cause loss of equipment and constantly counter them. If by chance you have a 02-way radio or satellite phone use it this second - NOW. Cell phones are usually useless in a wilderness environment (no towers).

Step 02: Go static (stay where you are) and the ground you are currently occupying right now - *"Take It By Force."* In other words you now <u>own this land</u>. Unless this parcel of land is a threat to you and those under your care or doesn't satisfy all the *8 Elements Of Survival* (Fire, Water, Shelter, First-Aid, Signal, Food, Weapons, and Navigation), then you may re-locate if there is enough daylight. A search party will look for you at your LKP (Last Known Point) and branch out from there. So go static, stay where you are now.

Step 03: Assign duties and satisfy the *8 Elements Of Survival* (Fire, Water, Shelter, First-Aid, Signal, Food, Weapons, and Navigation).

- **TAKE INVENTORY:** Assign a Supply Sergeant to go through <u>everyone's gear</u> to find essential supplies that satisfy the *8 Elements Of Survival*.
- **BUILD A FIRE:** Gather large stacks of tinder, <u>kindling, and sustaining fuels</u>. Build a large fire for protection (wildlife), warmth, beacon (survivors & search party), cooking,… Use **THIS PAPER** to help you fire-up your kindling. This Survival Kit has other ignitable items to aid you in emergency fire-starting.
- **BUILD SHELTERS:** Whether everyone brought tents or not, build shelters before it gets dark. Build shelters in a circular fashion around the firepit.
- **BUILD WEAPONS:** Assign 01 or 02 survivors to build a sturdy 08-foot spears for each survivor and a short dagger as a secondary weapon. ALL survivors must carry these weapons at all times.
- **RECON FOR WATER:** You can go 03-weeks without food but you can only go 03-days without water before your body goes to crap (mentally & physically). So water is a priority over food. Assign 02 survivors to recon for water if no water obstacle is nearby. Use walkie-talkies for comms if you have them. Assign them an exact magnetic azimuth and exact distance to travel. They are <u>never</u> to wander the woods for water. Weapons, comms, compass, and a map are required. They must return within 01-hour. Future patrols will procure water
- **FOOD PROCUREMENT:** The Supply Sergeant should take an inventory of ALL FOOD and WATER and a meal plan should be established. As a back-up plan for food, use the **300,000 Plants On Earth – Edibility Test** (page 02) to procure emergency food.
- **FIRST-AID:** Assign a medic (preferably trained). The medic must check ALL survivors for all possible health threats and attempt to remedy them. Medic assigns a location to build a latrine (50 meters downwind).
- **NAVIGATION:** Recon your surrounding area and set-up natural beacons (logs, large etching in the ground,…) in open areas pointing to your survival site. Plan for an evasion to safety. If a rescue party doesn't arrive in 05-days, you and your party may have to evade to safety.
- **KEEP BUSY & INFORMED:** Keep your subordinates <u>busy</u> and keep them informed so to avoid the *02 Greatest Enemies of Survival* – FEAR and PANIC. Constantly satisfy & improve on the *8 Elements of Survival* (Fire, Water, Shelter, First-Aid, Signal, Food, Weapons, and Navigation).
- **24-HOUR SECURITY:** One or more of your survivors may not cooperate. Take them off to the side and attempt to make it clear that <u>YOU ARE IN-CHARGE</u> and they must follow all your orders so everyone makes it back to safety. If he or she is still a problem, secure them (gag & bound them) for their own good and the good of all survivors. 24-hour day & <u>night</u> security must be established for constant accountability of all survivors and early warning of any and all threats to the main body of survivors.

This is just a general guide to help you out if you find yourself in a survival situation.

IRISAP Copyright 2015 – All Rights Reserved

"300,000 Plants On Earth – Edibility Test!"
(There's Food All Around You)

300,000 Plants On Earth – Edibility Test: Depending what you read, there are approximately 300,000 to 350,000 plants on this Earth. OK, let's **STOP** right there. There's no way 300,000 plants are within your reach to test for edibility. So let's do some math. Odds are you're located on land. At the high end, the Earth is covered with 70% water (oceans, seas, lakes, ponds, swamps, rivers, streams). So 70% of 300,000 is 210,000. 300,000 minus 210,000 comes to 90,000 plants. <u>YES, I know most plants are on land and not on or under water. I'm just doing a worst case scenario</u>. OK, let's carry-on. And since you're located at one specific spot on the Earth let's divide that 90,000 divided by 10,000 which comes to 09. Odds are no matter where you're located on land, <u>there are 09 plants within walking distance that may be edible to your body type</u>. OK, let's carry-on.

Plants that are located below water (fresh water & salt water), on surface water, below ground, on the surface and growing on rocks and other plants. Plants are at the bottom of the food-chain and are the MOST EASIEST to procure in emergency food procurement situations. Eating plants could save your life. Plants provide a host of needed nutrients like protein, minerals, sugars, vitamins,.... But not all plants are edible to humans and when a specific plant is edible, one plant may be good for one survivor but harmful to another survivor. So how does each survivor find edible plants, insects, small game, big game,…? Each survivor must conduct an *Edibility Test* for each and every plant, insect, small game, big game,… and here it is the *Edibility Test*:

STEP 01) Inspect for prickly thorns, fine hairs, bright 'WARNING' color. If evident, it is likely inedible. Try another plant. If there are no prickly thorns or fine hairs, proceed to STEP 02. **YES**, this Edibility Test can be applied to all other consumables.

STEP 02) Place (pinch or rub) a small portion of the plant to your lip and test for burning or itching. If evident, it is likely inedible. Try another plant and re-start at STEP 01. If not, proceed to Step 03.

STEP 03) After three minutes, place the plant on your tongue for fifteen minutes and test for any discomfort. If evident, it is likely inedible. Try another plant and re-start at STEP 01. If not, proceed to Step 04.

STEP 04) Thoroughly chew the plant and hold it in your mouth for fifteen minutes and test for any discomfort. If evident, it is likely inedible. Try another plant and re-start at STEP 01. If not, proceed to Step 05.

STEP 05) Swallow the plant material and test for any discomfort. If evident, it is likely inedible. Try another plant and re-start at STEP 01. If not, proceed to Step 06.

STEP 06) Wait eight hours and test for any discomfort. If evident it is likely inedible. Try another plant and re-start at STEP 01. If not, proceed to Step 07.

STEP 07) Eat 1\2 cup of the same plant and wait another eight hours and test for any discomfort. If evident, it is likely inedible. Try another plant and re-start at STEP 01. If not, proceed to Step 08.

STEP 08) If there are no signs of any type of discomfort or internal disorders, the plant is safe for eating. INSURE you mark that specific plant, tree, bush... for safe eating for future procurement!

1st WARNING: A plant may be acceptable to one survivor but may not be acceptable to another. It is <u>highly advised</u> that each survivor in your survival party conduct their own edibility test for each and every plant to insure the safe consumption of each plant.
2nd WARNING: Avoid all mushrooms unless you're a qualified **EXPERT** (Mycologist) on identifying edible and poisonous mushrooms! **USE THIS PAPER FOR EMERGENCY FIRE-STARTING**

IRISAP Copyright 2015 - All Rights Reserved

Survival Acronyms!

Here are the acronyms I used in this book. THANK YOU for getting this book. If you're not a full subscriber. You may not understand the acronyms I used in this book. So here's a quick description.

I'm going to cover the following acronyms and Survival Terms:
- **PRSC**
- **WET**
- **8 Elements Of Survival**
- **Priorities Of Work**
- **Task Organize**
- **Go To Sh!+ Plan**
- **Go To Sh!+ Azimuth**

Let's start with *PRSC*.
- **PRSC:** PRSC is a military acronym that stands for Planning, Recon, Security and Control. PRSC are the US Army's *Principles Of Patrolling* and are just 01 of the tools to plan for combat missions (training and real world). PRSC is such an important tool, it could SAVE YOUR LIFE. I civilianized PRSC so YOU can AVOID problems, tragedies in the first place. Let me briefly explain PRSC.

Planning: Write down on a few sheets of paper what you want to do in your outdoor adventure. Try to go in detail. Break it down day-by-day and each day break it down for morning, afternoon and before dusk activities. You should ALWAYS make camp 02-hours before sunset. NEVER go camping alone. Now you got your <u>tentative plan</u> on a piece of paper.

Recon: Do a recon of your area of interest. Get maps of the entire area. Get books of the area. Go on the internet and get the scoop of the area. If you can talk to any people that have been there - that's good info too. Get multiple weather reports to the region / area you're venturing. Weather itself could kill you. If proposed bad weather is present during your venture - ABORT your outdoor venture and go another day. Now that you did a Recon, you may want to adjust your plan.

Security: Now for security, this is IMPORTANT. While you're out on your outdoor adventure, **<u>THINK OF AT LEAST 12 THINGS THAT WILL HURT YOU, KILL YOU AND CAUSE YOU LOSS OF EQUIPMENT</u>**. <u>Counter all 12+ of these before you go on your outdoor adventure</u>. Let me give you an example. If you and your friends plan on fishing several spots over the next 03-days, one thing that could kill you is drowning. To counter this - EVERYBODY must know how to swim. EVERYBODY must wear a life preserver at all times.

If you have anybody in your party that can't swim - ABORT your fishing trip all together or leave the non-swimmer behind. The non-swimmer in a water-laden environment is a threat to himself and all those around him. After doing Security, odds are you may adjust you Plan.

Control: Now that you've Planned, Reconned, and implemented Security in your outdoor adventure, you're taking CONTROL. You're actually AVOIDING threats in the first place and you're far more flexible if any threats surface during your outdoor adventure.

I could go on for pages and pages to make you bullet-proof when venturing outdoors. PRSC is a great start and works so you're ready Anytime Anywhere!

- **WET:** WET stands for Weather, Enemy and Terrain. ALL are obstacles to your outdoor adventure and should be known about, reconned to improve your plan. Let's talk about each part of the WET formula.

  Weather should ALWAYS be considered in your planning. In this AASN and others I talk about different weather problems that can destroy your property, injure you, and kill you. Weather is the most powerful force on this Earth. From hurricanes to tornadoes to floods to earthquakes to blizzards... you have to know and plan for the weather.

Yes fire is included too! Try wandering into the forest in California and it hasn't rained in months? Perfect conditions for a fire that can surround you and cook you well done - may be not? There are fire blankets you can purchase - see POC Section.

The area you're going into and the time of year could help you plan for probable weather that may be a problem. Equipment like the weather radio POC I gave you last issue could save your life by giving you an early warning!

I gave you at least 30 weather forecasting techniques so far in your *Survival Program* and more are coming! Learn these weather forecasting techniques applications and "tricks" to insure you're safe Anytime Anywhere!

Enemy includes everything from plants to insects to critters to even humans, yes your closest friend - hunting buddy! Do a little research or ask your buddies who have been there before and know what kind enemy is in the area you're about to go into.

Know about the plants that you're allergic to or at least know what they look like. Is there a lot of poison ivy, poison sumac... in the area and what does it look like?

What about the insects, any problems with army ants, regular bees or even killer bees? What about the critters, any bear attacks lately, alligator or crocodile attacks or mountain lion attacks...? What about snakes, are there any poisonous snakes in the area and what kind are they?

What about temperatures, are the ground temperatures steady at 125 degrees in that desert environment at this time of year?
What about accidental shootings by hunters, have there been any lately? Is **your hunting buddy** properly trained to use his weapon and not accidently shoot and kill you? Lots of hunters are killed each year by fellow hunters! Why? They NEVER identified their target and shot at what they thought was a deer, or some other game. Or they flagged (accidently aimed their weapon at their partner) their hunting buddy and the weapon fired. You have to know your enemy and plan & prepare for it prior going into the area. Now let's talk about terrain.

Terrain like Weather and enemy can whoop you real bad and even worse kill you. When I talk about terrain like mountains, valleys, swamps, desert, cliffs, open area, jungle..., I'm including all the natural and manmade elements that go with that terrain like water obstacles, snow, boulders, loose rock formations, volcanoes, manmade barriers, toxic areas, power lines...

With respect to your terrain, your physical health comes into questioning. For example if you plan on walking the Appalachian Trail or wandering through the killer Mohave Desert in mid-summer, and you're out of shape - you know you are (you have trouble walking up a flight of stairs), you have no business taking on such a task. To do it by yourself is suicide, you're asking for trouble and you're gonna get it! If you go with friends you'll soon become a casualty and a now a rescue is inevitable. So know yourself first.

If you're out of shape, get in shape prior to such a physical demanding task. With your doctor's OK, walking is a good start along with a good healthy fruit, vegetable and juicing diet.

Now terrain all by itself can whoop you real good! Try walking the TVD (Tennessee Valley Divide), a great workout if you're in-shape or a potential heart attack if you're not! Try walking through a very hot & humid jungle environment without all the other problems in the jungle, you're in for a real "somebody shoot me" treat! Try walking through a desert environment like the Mohave Desert in California or White Sands in New Mexico in the dead of summer - you'll be cussing at yourself for doing something so stupid! You'll know what the words "death march" really mean!

You have to properly plan and prepare, I'm telling you from experience! I've been severely whooped in all sorts of terrain, weather, critters all over the US, Central South America, Great Britain, Mid-East, and I'm telling you a little planning and prep (preparation) will go a long way! I wish I had a $100 for every time I thought I was really going to die from WET!

So please use WET with PRSC when you anticipate any outdoor trip!

- **8 Elements Of Survival:** The *8 Elements Of Survival* are Fire, Water, Shelter, First-Aid, Signal, Food, Weapons and Navigation.

01) Fire: Fire no doubt will give you that <u>sense of security and well-being</u> in a survival environment. Helps AVOID the 02 Greatest Enemies of Survival - FEAR AND PANIC! Fire can be used to:

a) Cook your prey (that you've caught in one the traps and snares you'll soon learn about).
b) Keep you warm.
c) Keep wild animals away.
d) Signal a rescue party (smoke during the day - fire at night).
e) Purify your water.
f) Dry your clothes.
g) Smoke meat.
h) Prepare parts for all your traps and snares.
i) Much more...
See **www.survivalexpert.com/fire**

02) Water: Water is ABSOLUTELY ESSENTIAL in a survival situation. Gathering water, filtering it and purifying it should be a continuous process. You could never get enough water.

Water next to immediate first aid (in a life threatening situation) should be at the top of your list. You can go about three weeks without food but you can only go three days without water.

Remember lack of water DULLS THE MIND! You're going to be "CLUELESS", if you're not continuously hydrated.

Drink, drink, drink and drink water. When in doubt DRINK!! Once you're dehydrated, you'll have trouble remembering how to do very simple math problems (35 divided by 07 equals daaaahh!!). Your short-term memory will become even shorter! Remember this: When in doubt DRINK WATER - even if you're not thirsty, drink water!!!

Below are some good reasons to keep gathering water, filtering it and purifying it on a continuous basis! Also later in this section I've listed a few items you might consider for your survival kit to procure water.

a) Hydration (minimum 04 to 05 quarts a day, depending on your activity, temperature and injuries).
b) Hygiene (complete or partial).
c) Cleaning and preparing small game.
d) Cleaning clothes.
e) Preparing herbal teas.
f) Cooking vegetation.
g) Cooking insects.
h) Sterilizing bandages.
i) Much more....

03) Shelter: There's nothing like *"Home Sweet Home!"* A shelter will definitely give you that added feeling of security and contentedness in your survival environment!

Once you've picked your survival site - a site that satisfies all the elements of survival, make an assessment of your priorities of work and you may begin building a shelter as your first priority (no injuries, water nearby...). Initially, construct the easiest shelter. Later, dictating your situation, you may construct a more elaborate shelter to suit your needs!

Shelter also pertains to the protective clothing you are wearing. Below are a few benefits of shelter.

a) Protection from the elements (cold, wind, sun, rain, snow...)
b) Place to construct survival tools listed throughout this book.
c) Gives a sense of security.
d) Helps AVOID FEAR AND PANIC!
e) May be identifiable by air or ground rescue.
f) Place to store and safeguard food and water.
g) Much more...

04) First-Aid: First of all, I feel EVERYONE should be familiar with basic first-aid.
a) Four life-saving steps (Clear the airway, Stop the bleeding, Treat the wound and Prevent shock.
b) CPR.
c) Heimlich Maneuver.
d) Treating fractures and broken limbs.
e) Psychological first-aid.
f) Treating heat and cold casualties.

At the same time, a good healthy diet and the correct supplements will go a long way towards your survival if you find yourself in a survival situation. A good survival kit could save your life. Later in this section, I've listed a few items you might consider for your survival kit.

05) Signal: Is anybody out there? Don't count on getting help instantaneously once you find yourself in a survival situation. Make an assessment of your situation and begin your priorities of work. Depending on your situation, you may want to build a quick shelter from the cold rain, give yourself first-aid and sleep prior to contemplating building any signaling devices. Here are some hints to enhance your signal efforts.
a) TELL somebody EXACTLY where you are going and when you should return.

b) Walkie-Talkies within your group (NEVER venture alone) enhances your adventure. If separated deliberately or accidently - use the Walkie-Talkies.
c) Satellite phones will get you out of jam and could save your life.

06) Food: If there is one thing that will boost your morale in any situation - survival or not - it's food! You can go three weeks without food before you're in serious trouble. But food is all around you. From the lowest part of the food-chain (plants), yes to even the human body if it comes to that! See the *"300,000 Plants On Earth - Edibility Test!"* at the end of this book.

07) Weapons: The Right to Bear Arms (2nd Amendment)! I hope you seriously consider this Right. Not only to AVOID The 02 Greatest Enemies Of Survival - FEAR AND PANIC in a survival situation, but to protect yourself! Why? Now that you're in a wilderness environment \ a survival environment, you're now IN the food chain!!! Congratulations!!!

This book will hopefully HELP YOU AVOID A SURVIVAL SITUATION and if you find yourself in a survival situation, HELP YOU SURVIVE IT!!! Remember: IMPROVISE, OVERCOME and ADAPT!!!

I always advised my subscribers to ALWAYS carry a primary weapon (rifle) and a back-up weapon (pistol). A high caliber is recommended depending on the threats out there. A .22 caliber pistol is worthless against an attacking bear. Also consider carrying pepper spray. See *Counter Assault* and *Universal Defense Alternative Products* in the *POC* Section. Also consider field-expedient weapons.

Listed below are some good reasons to build, carry and use field-expedient weapons. Later in this section, I've listed a few items you may want for your survival kit.

a) Self-protection.
b) Capturing small game.
c) Neutralizing captured game.
d) Psychologically it gives a sense of security and confidence.
f) Helps AVOID FEAR AND PANIC (the 02 Biggest Enemies of SURVIVAL)!
g) Used to build other survival tools.
h) Much more...

08) Navigation: I've said this once already and I'll say it again: The last thing you need to do is wander off in your survival area and get lost. All that work you've done is for nothing. Remember me telling you about the lack of water?

Lack of water DULLS THE MIND! I'm telling it's so true. You must consider navigation as part of your survival kit. Not only making a field-expedient compass but markers to help you find your way back to your survival site! Why? Because your mind will deteriorate while you're out there (dehydration, hunger, depression, despair...). You will forget!

Listed below are some things you need to do right away once you find yourself in a survival situation.

a) Build a field-expedient direction Shadow-Tip Method as soon as possible as well as a bottle-top compass. The shadow-tip will be your "BIG Compass" and should be near your shelter - preferably next to your "BIG CLOCK". You can also build a compass - see Section 08. Both should be clear of your regular foot traffic in and around your survival site.

b) Start drawing a sketch map of your survival site and immediate surroundings. Insure you record directions, distances, and descriptions. Try to be as specific as possible. Why? Because you're gonna be more forgetful as time goes on!

c) Make beacon markers throughout your survival area to guide you "home." Make sure each beacon is different and is recorded on your sketch map with direction, distance and its unique description (branches, sticks, animal skull, etched markings in the ground...).

See **www.survivalexpertbooks.com/navigation**

- **Priorities Of Work:** Priorities of Work are actions that need to be done according to their urgency. Here's a survival scenario. Say for example you and 07 of your buddies are out in the middle of Yosemite National Park (1,200 square miles).

01) You and your party went off the trail a few hours ago, you're now lost lost.

02) You have 02 in your party that are hurt. One survivor has a severely twisted ankle & immobile and the other is severely dehydrated.

03) In 02-hours it will be dark.

04) A storm is moving in from the west.

You're now in a survival situation. **YOU are now in-charge so take charge**. You must establish Priorities of Work and in my humble opinion, here are my Priorities of Work:

a) Go static: You're lost, you have 02 injured survivors, a storm is on its way and it will be dark in about 02-hours. Make camp with your tents in a semi-circle with the openings facing east (downwind of the coming storm). Have 02 people (have previous medical training??) care for the 02 injured survivors. All the others stay together and gather enough kindling and especially sustaining fuel to keep the fire going all night.

b) Security: Once all the firewood is gathered, if you don't have firearms, start making weapons. Each person should have a 07-foot long spear-like weapon and a short sharpened stick for a secondary weapon. These weapons must be with each survivor every second. Establish a rotating 02-survivor fire guard. A fire guard is to insure all survivors are secure (no survivor wanders off), the fire is kept going all night and into the morning hours.

c) Inventory: The individual property of each survivor is now the property of all survivors. Take inventory of all foods, water, first-aid supplies, medicines, communications / signal type equipment, special clothing, knives, tools, containers, cooking utensils, flashlights, batteries,…

d) Food & Water: Using the inventory, distribute a portion of water and food to each survivor. Try to spread out the rations for an entire week. Extra rations may be given to the 02 casualty survivors.

e) Navigation: Since you are now in a survival situation, your original outdoor adventure is out the window. Seriously consider staying static and have a search party find you plan to navigate your way to safety. If you have a map, pinpoint your exact location. Then plan a very detailed route to the nearest safe site. If you don't have a map, get everyone together and make a map annotating all the details from your last safe position to your current location. If you have a compass use it for magnetic readings to safety. Plan to navigate to safety together. Make a stretcher for the survivor with the twisted ankle. See *Go To Sh!+ Azimuth* below.

If you have serious doubts about navigating to safety - consider staying static till search parties find your location. If this is the case make multiple BEACONS in open areas near your location pointing to your location so aerial searchers can find you.

Can you see what was just done with all these Priorities Of Work? It satisfied the *8 Elements of Survival* (Fire, Water, Shelter, First-Aid, Signal, Food, Weapons and Navigation).

- **Task Organize:** The Priorities Of Work you just read, have your buddies do some of the work. For example if you have a nurse, doctor or anyone with previous medical training, have them care for the casualties. Have somebody make a fire guard roster. If you have somebody in your group that is ex-military, have them navigate your way to safety. If you have somebody that worked with inventory, have them consolidate all supplies, inventory it and re-issue it out according to the needs of the group. You see how to task organize? You being in-charge, you should spot check and supervise.

- **Go To Sh!+ Plan:** The *Go To Sh!+ Plan* is done before you go out on your outdoor adventure. When there's trouble in your outdoor adventure, your original adventure is out the window and now you're in a survival situation. Now before you go outdoor's IMAGINE you have to get to safety like right now. What is your plan? What will you do to get everybody to safety real quick. Here are a few examples:

    a) Satellite Phone: You break out your satellite phone and call for help. Give them your situation. Your friends may show up in trucks or you may call the local law enforcement and they'll arrive via vehicles and / or helicopters depending on your situation.

    b) Go To Sh!+ Azimuth: See *Go To Sh!+ Azimuth* below.

    c) Go Static: If extraction isn't possible like severe weather is about to hit you, then go static. Then employ your Priorities Of Work. See *Priorities Of Work* above for an example.

- **Go To Sh!+ Plan Emergency Package:** The *Go To Sh!+ Plan Emergency Package (GTSPEP)* is assembled and packed before you go out on your outdoor adventure. When there's trouble in your outdoor adventure, your original adventure is out the window and now you're in a survival situation. The *GTSPEP* is packed in its own backpack. The *GTSPEP,* like true Survival Kits must satisfy the *8 Elements Of Survival* (Fire, Water, Shelter, First-Aid, Signal, Food, Weapons and Navigation). PLUS the *GTSPEP* has items in it to psychologically help the survivors. Here's a general list of items that could be pack in the *GTSPEP*.
    - **a)** Satellite phone & extra batteries
    - **b)** Flint lighter and electric lighter
    - **c)** Fire-starting tinder
    - **d)** Canned foods loaded with liquids
    - **e)** Silverware
    - **f)** Plastic tarp (shelter)
    - **g)** First-Aid supplies
    - **h)** Mace
    - **i)** Water filtration & purification devices
    - **j)** Playing cards
    - **k)** Prophylactics (water containers)
    - **l)** Weapons (pistols, knives)
    - **m)** Compass & Map (your area)

- **Go To Sh!+ Azimuth:** The *Go To Sh!+ Azimuth* is calculated before you go out on your outdoor adventure. When there's trouble in your outdoor adventure, your original adventure is out the window and now you're in a survival situation. The *Go To Sh!+ Azimuth* (magnetic azimuth) is calculated so that no matter your location on your adventure, that magnetic azimuth will lead you to a linear feature (road, trail, river,…) that will lead you and your party to safety.

Points Of Contact!

American Camping Association Inc.-----------1-800-428-CAMP
American Camping Association Inc., 5000 State Road 67 North, Martinsville, IN 46151-9984. Camping and anything related to camping is undoubtedly related to ***developing successful children into mature & wise adults and adults into more mature people & better leaders***. If there is one catalog that could open up the doors to the many other outdoor activities that can improve your life, it's the American Camping Association Book Catalog. Their 46-page catalog offers so many outdoor informational - educational products, I couldn't even begin to list and describe each product. Outdoor Adventure Programs are also listed. Get your family, your organization out of the house and call or write for your **FREE** catalog today!**

Arc'Teryx-------------------------------------1-800-985-6681
bird@arcteryx.com   1-604-985-6681
                                               1-604-985-3643(fax)
Arc'Teryx, 170 Harbour Avenue, North Vancouver, BC, Canada V7J 2E6. Arc'Teryx has some very impressive outdoor gear. Remember in *Section 17 Field-Expedient Water Crossing*, you learned how to build rafts and rope bridges? Remember I asked you to get yourself a good rappelling harness? Well Arc'Teryx has some rappelling harnesses for you and that's not all! They have 6 different types of rappelling harnesses as well as several different small and big backpacks, cool bodywear -jackets, pants, bibs, pullovers, sleeveless jackets... They'll also include a directory of distributor throughout the US!

Art Of The Decoy, The---------------------by Adele Earnest

Cabela's--**1-800-237-4444**
1-800-496-6329(fax)

Cabela's, 812-13th Avenue, Sidney Nebraska 69160. If you're a couch potato, turn-off that TV and see the outdoors! You'll leave your toxic home and finally breathe some fresh air as well as burn some extra calories! Cabela's 274-page, all-color catalog offers some really good hunting, fishing and outdoor gear to enhance your safety as well as your outdoor pleasure! Call today for your **FREE** catalog today!**

Camping World--------------------------------**1-800-626-5944**
1-800-334-3359(fax)

Camping World, Three Springs Road, P.O. Box 90017, Bowling Green, KY 42102-9017. If you own an RV and love to travel the country or desire to purchase camping\travelling associated equipment then this is the catalog for you! Camping World Catalog includes products like awning & accessories, covers, storage, bike & carriers, boats, outdoor lighting, outdoor accessories, tables & chairs, grills, kitchen accessories & appliances, furnishings, vacuums, water accessories, toilet - chemical & sanitation accessories, bath accessories, vents, air conditioners, generators, electrical accessories, maintenance & repair, wheels & tires, towing, CB's & detectors, compasses, travel accessories, travel comfort items, clothing... You don't have to own an RV to enjoy camping or purchase many Camping World's products that will come in real handy when you're venturing out in Mother Nature's back yard! Call or write today for your **FREE** 243-page, all color catalog. Look into this company and "Get out of the house!"**

Campmor----------------------------**Orders**---**1-800-CAMPMOR**
1-800-230-2153(fax)
Customer Service---**1-800-525-4784**

Campmor Inc, P.O. Box 700, Saddle River, NJ 07458. Folks if you step one foot outdoors, you gotta get Campmor's catalog. They have hundreds and hundreds of products for an enjoyable and say outdoor's adventure whatever it is! Call Monday through Friday from 8:00 a.m. to midnight and 8:00 a.m. to 6:00 p.m. Saturday EST!

Cascade Designs, Inc.------------------------1-800-531-9531
www.cascadedesigns.com

Cascade Designs, Inc., 4000 First Avenue South, Seattle, WA 98134. I was impressed by Cascade Designs catalog! They have World Class outdoor equipment based on real world experience to insure you have a safe and enjoyable adventure! They offer Therm-a-rest self-inflating mattresses, Platypus hydration systems, SweetWater water filters and purifiers, PackTowl camping towels, SealLine waterproof bags, Tracks walking staffs... They even give you a directory of the closest dealer to you!

Cheaper Than Dirt------------**voice orders**---1-800-625-3848
www.cheaperthandirt.com   1-800-596-5655(fax)
                          Customer Service---1-800-625-2506
                       technical questions---1-817-624-6104

Cheaper Than Dirt, 2520 NE Loop 820, Fort Worth, Tx 76106-1809. Folks, don't let the name fool you! Cheaper Than Dirt has some very high quality outdoor products at some great prices!! Their catalog is PACKED with everything you'll need to insure your next outdoor venture is fun, safe and satisfying! They must have a 500 or so different products from A to Z. Call today for your **FREE**, color, 72-page catalog!

Counter Assault---------------------------1-800-695-3394
                                  1-406-257-GRIZ

Counter Assault, 120 Industrial Court, Kalispell, MT 59901. Counter Assault offers a life-saving "PepperSpray" that may come in handy if confronted by an attacking bear, or other animals! They offer several **"Pepper Spray"** to deter everything from human assailants to vicious attacking bears! Counter Assault's products have been featured in numerous magazines and news articles! My recommendation is to look into Counter Assault for your safety and protection today! Call or write today for your FREE informative brochures!

Dahlgren Footwear, Inc.----------------------1-800-635-8539
                                    1-626-334-7119
                                    1-626-334-4689(fax)

Dahlgren Footwear, Inc., 16016 Foothill Blvd., Azusa, CA 91702. Folks when you're outdoors, you have to take care of your feet! Especially if you plan on staying out there more than a few days! Daily foot maintenance (hygiene, massage, first-aid...) is a given and should be in your outdoor schedule. In cold weather environments, frostbite checks should be conducted not only for your feet but for your face too! To keep your feet warm and comfortable, Dahlgren offers a variety of toasty warm socks like the *Expedition, Alaskan, Trail Fitness, Skiing, Walking, Hiking*...! Call or write today for your **FREE** brochure!

Dana Designs----------------------------------1-888-375-3262
                                    1-800-972-4066(fax)

Dana Designs, 19215 Vashon Highway, Vashon, WA 98070. Dana designs has been offering their very impressive Backpacks for more than 13-years! Dana Designs has very well designed and proven backpacks like ArcFlex, Astralplane, Terraplane, Terraplane X, Alpine AV, Swiftcurrent, Glacier, TerraFrame, T1, Longbed, Shortbed, Flatbed, Bombpack, Bridger, Bighorn, Shadow Peak, Dynamo...! Very impressive line of backpacks, but there is more! Too many products to annotate here. Call today for your **FREE**, all-color, 29-page catalog!

Decoys - The Art Of The Wooden Bird--------by Richard
                                    LeMaster

Edge Company Catalog, The-------------------1-800-732-9976
                                    1-802-257-2787

The Edge Company Catalog, P.O. Box 826, Brattleboro, VT 05302. The Edge Company catalog will give you the "edge" with their tools, knives and hi-tech action gear! For all you outdoor types, The Edge Company Catalog has a bunch of goodies you ought to look into to enhance your safety and planning for your next outdoor trip or vacation away from home! OK, you want a taste of what they have waiting for you? OK!

They offer laser lighters, super-power astronomers scope (only 7 1/4 inches), micro-revolver flare pistol, air pistols\rifles, miniature stun guns, night vision devices, universal socket tool, micro-torch, knives, micro-radiophones, electronic dog dazer, battery re-charger (for non-rechargeables)... Get the feel for what they offer? Get the "edge" and call today for your **FREE** 75-page, all color catalog.

Emergency Essentials------------------------1-800-999-1863
Emergency Essentials, 165 South Mountain Way Drive, Orem UT 84058-5119. This is the only company that I've come across the last four years of research for this book that is orientated towards "outdoor preparedness!" An emergency can surface anywhere at anytime so be prepared! Look into this company today. Emergency Essentials offers a wide variety of products that may prevent that potential emergency as well as remedy one! They offer a One Year Unconditional Guarantee! Call today for your **FREE** 57-page catalog!**

Garmin, International Inc.------------------1-800-800-1020
www.garmin.com   1-913-397-8200
                                                1-913-397-8282(fax)
Garmin International Inc., 1200 East 151st Street, Olathe, Kansas 66062. In *Section 08 Field-Expedient Direction*, I give you several techniques to find direction and help you find your way where ever you are. But I wouldn't be a good instructor if I didn't tell you to go out and get yourself a good reliable compass! Along with a compass I want you to look your own GPS (Global Positioning System). A compass and a GPS can literally save you money, time and your life! Garmin International Inc., has several GPSs and accessories. Like the: GPS 12 Personal Navigator (for camping, hiking, hunting...), NavTalk (GPS & cellular phone), GPS-III (electronic map), Garmin's StreetPilot (simple trips cross-country), GPS 89 (moving map for pilots), GPSCOM 190 (moving map & VHF transceiver), GPS 90 (moving map & planning features for pilots), GPS 92 (moving map pilot data...), GPS III Pilot (pilot GPS)...

Yes there is more, but you can get **FREE** color brochures by calling or writing today! I highly advise you that you get your own compass (wrist & handheld) and GPS before your next outdoor adventure.

Herbal Advisor--------------------------------www.herbaladvisor.com

Hitchcock Shoes-----------------------------1-781-749-3571
                                    1-781-749-3576(fax)

Hitchcock Shoes, Inc., 225 Beal Street, Hingham, Massachusetts 02043. If you're a man and need those hard to find **W I D E S H O E S**, this is the company to order from. From **EEE to E E E E E!!!** All kinds of footwear!!! After looking and looking for wide shoes for my feet (author), this is the **ONLY** company that had my size. I've ordered shoes from Hitchcock for several years now. Call or write for their free, all color, 48-page catalog. ***STOP the pain*** and get the correct pair of footwear. Call their Customer Service at the number above.

Hunting Whitetails By The Moon-----------by Charles J. Alsheimer

Intensive Research Information
Services And Products (IRISAP)------------www.survivalexpert.com

Long Life Food Depot----------------------1-800-601-2833
www.longlifefood.com   1-765-939-0110
                                    1-765-939-0065(fax)

Long Life Food Depot, P.O. Box 8081, Richmond, IN 47374. I think you already know what this company offers - *Long Shelf-Life Food Rations For Outdoor & Emergency Preparedness*. Whether you want just enough for you a week of outdoor adventures or enough for you and everybody you know for a couple years, this company can get it for you at some decent prices!

Their variety of MREs are too numerous to annotate here so you have to get their latest list prices. Call or write today for your **FREE** informative price list on their MREs!

Major Surplus & Survival------------------1-310-324-8855
www.MajorSurplusNSurvival.com   1-310-324-6909

Major Surplus & Survival, 435 West Alondra Blvd., Gardena, CA 90248. Major Surplus & Survival offers several hundred outdoor items you may consider using on your next outdoor trip or just to prepare for any contingency or emergency. Their **FREE** 64-page color catalog is packed with everything, like outdoor clothing, sleeping bags, rucksacks, tents, survival foods, knives, parachutes, ropes, GPS devices... Call or write for your **FREE** catalog today.

Marin Mountain Bikes---------------------1-800-222-7557
www.marinbikes.com   1-415-382-6000
                                        1-415-382-6100

Marin Mountain Bikes, 84 Galli Drive, Novato, CA 94949. Marin Mountain Bikes are top of the line and are known internationally! That's all they do - Mountain Bikes! Technology is behind every Marin Mountain Bike! Every mountain bike is lightweight, proven superior suspension, stiffness and reliability. Marin offers many mountain and racing bikes too numerous to mention here! So call or write for your FREE two-sided, all-color, fold-out brochure! If you want the best, look into Marin Mountain Bikes!

Mojo Mallard--------------------www.mojooutdoors.com

Moss Tents----------------------1-800-859-5322
www.mosstents.com   1-207-236-9490(fax)
E-mail: mosstent@acadia.net

Moss Tents, P.O. Box 577, Camden, ME 04843. Folks if you want World Class equipment like a tent, you have to look into Moss tents! Moss Tents protect you from KILLER blizzards to bitter cold winds. Use what the expedition explorers use Moss Tents! They offer 21 world-class tents and para-wings (add-ons).

Their 16-page, all-color, informative catalog will show you everything! Don't risk you lives on a store-bought tent, get the best - get a Moss Tent! Call or write today for your **FREE** catalog!

Most Famous Lion Hunt Of All Time----See *The Ghost And The Darkness*.

Murray's Lures-------------------**www.murraylures.com**

Pioneer Gourmet Food Provisions--1-800-814-0289
Pioneer Gourmet Food Provisions, 300 North 597 West, Manti, Utah 84642. Pioneer Gourmet Food Provisions offers long shelf-life foods. They offer their food products in big 1-year supplies which means you SAVE BIG BUCKS! They also award you by referring your friends to them! For every customer you refer to them, they'll send you $150 worth of their gourmet foods! and speaking of which, I received a FREE SAMPLE! They sent me a packet of *Broccoli & Cheese Soup*! I think I'll put it in the survival kit (50-calibre ammo can) I have in my truck! Call or write today and get your **FREE FOOD SAMPLE** and **FREE** catalog! Tell them I referred you to them!

Project Peanut Butter-----------**www.projectpeanut Butter.org**

Ranger Joe's-------------------1-800-247-4511
                                   1-706-689-3455
                                   1-706-689-0954(fax)
Ranger Joe's, 4030 Victory Drive, Columbus, GA 31903-3903. Ranger Joe's has been in business since 1963! It's known for its "World Famous Military & Law Enforcement Gear." Get out of your toxic house and see what Ranger Joe's has to offer for your outdoor adventures! Call today for your **FREE** catalog today!**

```
    R.E.I. Camping--------------------1-800-426-4840
                                1-800-443-1988(TDD)
                                1-206-891-2533(fax)
                Outside U.S.---1-206-891-2500
```
Recreational Equipment Incorporated (R.E.I.), 1700 45th Street East, Sumner, WA 98390. REI has been involved in offering "Quality Outdoor Gear and Clothing since 1938." They offer over 700 choices of quality outdoor gear and clothing. REI offers back-packs (all types), clothing, footgear, navigation equipment (compasses and global positioning equipment), sleeping bags (all types), tents, (all sizes), optical advanced sunglasses, watches and more...! So look into this company and over 700 of their great products. Get out of your toxic house! Call for your **FREE** catalog today!**

Sportsman's Guide, The-------------1-800-888-.30-06
www.sportsmans-   1-800-333-6933
                Customer Service---1-800-888-5222

The Sportsman Guide, 411 Farwell Avenue, South St. Paul, MN 55075-0239. The Sportsman Guide offers "Field Tested Outdoor Gear." They have "special buys", "close-outs" and "new items" at great prices! I bought my 50-calibre ammo cans for my survival kits at really great prices! At last count they have about 100,000+ great products to support all your outdoor adventures! Call or write today.

Suunto USA------------------------1-800-543-9124
www.primus.se   Sweden---+46-8-629-22-00
info@primus.se   Sweden---+46-8-629-22-66(fax)

Suunto USA, 2151 Las Palmas Drive, Calsbad, CA 92009. Folks if you want some very high quality portable stoves, look to Suunto. Primus offers portable stoves that can be used for a simple campout to proving themselves at altitudes of 12,000 feet! World Class to professional explorers use the best and most dependable equipment and I bet you can find Primus gear in their packs!

Primus offers their *Himalaya EasyFuel, Alpine EasyLight, Himalaya VariFuel, Alpine Titanium, Alpine PowerCook, Alpine MiniDuo...* Primus also offers high-tech & lightweight lanterns, cookware, windshields, and fuels. If you want dependable and proven portable stoves... look into Suunto! Call today for your **FREE**, all-color, 19-page catalog! **NOTE:** I received a second packet from Suunto. I thought I should tell you about some great products brochures they sent me this time! You know how I've told you how important it is to monitor the weather before and during any venture; well Suunto has some wristband computers you gotta know about! The *Vector, Altimax, Navitec* and the *X-Lander*!

All of these neat devices not only tell you the time, but they have other built-in features like: digital navigational features (bearing in degrees, cardinal direction, declination adjustment, N-S arrow, level bubble) memory functions, records ascent and descent data, altitudes, temperatures, records and compares barometric pressure data (**great for weather forecasting**), calendar programmed to the year 2089, stop watch, daily alarms, countdown timer,...

These gadgets could save your life! INSURE you ask for them when you request your **FREE** information packet! I also got some great data on their Katadyn Water Solutions! Call today for your **FREE** catalog and brochures!

Terrelogic------------------------1-888-MY-DRYAD
www.terrelogic.com   1-416-703-8018
                              1-416-703-8019(fax)

Terrelogic, 590 King Street West, Suite #403, Toronto, Ontario M5V 1M4, Canada. Terrelogic offers the only "penthouse" shelter that I've seen. It's called drYad! It's a shelter that you can hang from a heavy duty branch or hang it in a well established tree. It can shelter two people of up to 400 pounds!

There are many advantages and situation where you would want to have your shelter off the ground. Look into Terrelogic and their drYad. For a **FREE** brochure and Q/A sheet, call the toll-free number today!

The Ghost And The Darkness----------This movie is based on the Tsavo Man-Eaters - a pair of lions who attacked construction workers on the Kenya-Uganda Railway between March - December 1898. Approximately 135 victims were attacked and eaten by the pair of lions. Both lions were eventually killed by professional hunters.

Universal Defense Alternative Products (UDAP)--------------------1-800-232-7941
www.udap.com   1-406-763-5052(fax)

Universal Defense Alternative Products, 13160 Yonder Road, Bozeman, MT 59718. What are you gonna do when your faced with an attacking bear, cougar... and don't forget about a big angry mother moose! Whether you're armed or not, try industrial size pepper spray! Yes, pepper spray! Not that sissy stuff for those muggers, but the BIG pepper sprays for the BIG critters! UDAP offers quality pepper spray products for your outdoor protection. They also offer pepper spray holsters, and videos. Call or write today for
FREE information!

U.S. Calvary----------------------1-800-333-5102
                                1-502-352-0266(fax)
          Charge Orders---1-800-777-7732
       International Orders---1-502-351-1164

U.S. Calvary, 2855 Centennial Avenue, Radcliff, KY 40160-9000. U.S. Calvary offers the "World's Finest Military and Adventure Equipment." Their 142-page, all color catalog is packed with great products to enhance your next adventure! So get out of your toxic house & call or write U.S. Calvary to receive your **FREE** catalog!**

Walrus------------------------------1-800-550-8368
www.walrusgear.com   1-206-763-4689(fax)

Walrus, 8300 Military Road South, Seattle, WA 98108. Walrus offers durable and proven sleeping bags, accessories, tarpology and tents. Their very informative catalog tells you all about their outdoor products so you can make a better buying decision. Call or write today for your **FREE**, all-color, 20-page catalog.

Wiggy's Bags------------------------1-970-241-6465
                                  1-970-241-5921(fax)

Wiggy's Bags, 2482 Industrial Blvd., Grand Junction, Colorado 81502. Wiggy's Bags *"Simply The Best Since 1986"*, offers you guessed it - toasty warm sleeping bags! Sleeping bags to keep you warm in just about any environment. One is rated down to 80 degrees below zero! Is that cold enough for you! Wiggy's also offers hypothermia bags, gloves, backpacks, tents, parkas, sweaters, and more. If you want to stay warm, call or write Wiggy's for their **FREE** catalog today!

More Kindle E-Books And Paperback Books For YOU!

Joseph A. Laydon Jr. (MSG Ret. Army) is the author and owner of Intensive Research Information Services And Products (IRISAP). Joseph has been writing "self-reliance" orientated data since 1991 and since July 2012 has been re-publishing his works via Kindle E-Books and CreateSpace Paperback Books. He has self-published more than **80 Survival Books** (Kindle E-Books and Paperback Books). Below is a list of all his Survival Books and you can see these books by simply going to the 02 websites listed below for detailed descriptions and videos.

- **Kindle E-Books:**--------------------www.survivalexpertebooks.com

- **Paperback Books:**-----------------www.survivalexpertbooks.com

139+
SURVIVAL
Expert Products
Catalog!
JOSEPH A. LAYDON JR.

35
INTERNATIONAL
WILDERNESS
Survival Tricks!
JOSEPH A. LAYDON JR.
100%

179+
INTERNATIONAL
KILLER HOT DESERT
SURVIVAL TRICKS AND MORE!
100%
JOSEPH A. LAYDON JR.

55+
TRUE
INCREDIBLE
MYSTERIES!
100%

89+
EMERGENCY
COLD WEATHER
Survival Tricks And More!
JOSEPH A. LAYDON JR.
100%

339+
INTERNATIONAL
EMERGENCY FOODS,
EMERGENCY WATER,
LOST HOME-MADE RECIPES AND MORE!
When The Crap Hits The Fan You Just
Gotta Have Food And Water Or
YOU'LL BE DEAD REAL QUICK!
100%
JOSEPH A. LAYDON JR.

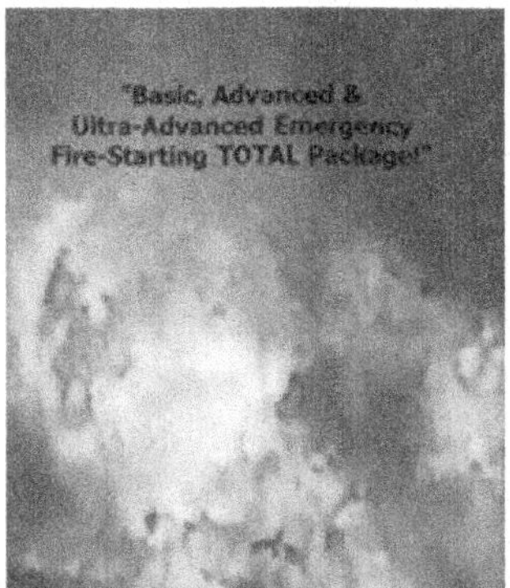
"Basic, Advanced &
Ultra-Advanced Emergency
Fire-Starting TOTAL Package!"
Joseph A. Laydon Jr.

99+
INTERNATIONAL
PIED PIPER TRICKS
To Compel All Types Of
Animals To Come To You!
JOSEPH A. LAYDON JR.
100%

Exodus
To
Genesis!
Joseph A. Laydon Jr.

JOSEPH A. LAYDON JR.
THE GETTYSBURG PROGRAM
WHAT YOU DON'T KNOW MAY BE KILLING YOU...
YOUR COMPLETE GUIDE TO BETTER HEALTH AND VIBRANT LIVING!

169+ Lose It Or Else
ACCELERATED WEIGHT-LOSS
Facts, Tricks And More!
JOSEPH A. LAYDON JR.

199+
INTERNATIONAL
EMERGENCY FIRST-AID
APPLICATIONS AND MORE!
JOSEPH A. LAYDON JR.

77+
INTERNATIONAL
FORECASTERS
OF WEATHER, EARTHQUAKES, TORNADOS AND MORE!
JOSEPH A. LAYDON JR.

900+
JOSEPH A. LAYDON JR.

JOSEPH A. LAYDON JR.
THE GETTYSBURG PROGRAM
WHAT YOU DON'T KNOW MAY BE KILLING YOU...
YOUR COMPLETE GUIDE TO BETTER HEALTH AND VIBRANT LIVING!

839+
INTERNATIONAL
WILDERNESS
SURVIVAL TRICKS USED BY
REAL SURVIVAL FROM WORLD CLASS REAL SURVIVORS!

169+
JOSEPH A. LAYDON JR.

SIX
HEALING
OILS
AND MORE!
Super Dirt Cheap Healers You
Just Have To Know About Today
JOSEPH A. LAYDON JR.

375+
INTERNATIONAL
PRISONER
SURVIVAL TRICKS AND MORE!

FOURTEEN
HEALING
OILS
AND MORE!
Super Dirt Cheap Healers You
Just Have To Know About Today

269+
INTERNATIONAL
FISHING

ANYTIME
ANYWHERE
Survival Program!

How To Learn Spanish Fast!
(3,399 Ways To Speak Spanish Instantly)
Joseph A. Laydon Jr.

259+
INTERNATIONAL
SMART CRITTER
Survival Tricks And More!

239+
TEXAS RANGER,
PIONEER,
OLD WEST
SURVIVAL TRICKS AND MORE!

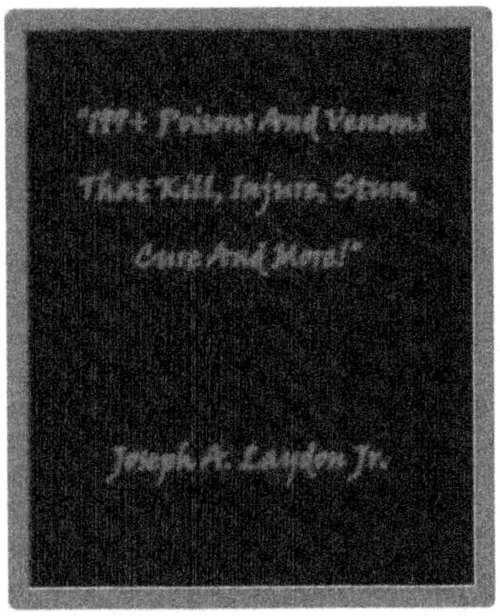
Joseph A. Laydon Jr.

199+ Emergency Traps & Snares And Other Hunting Tricks To Capture Any Game!
Joseph A. Laydon Jr.

99+ International Cancer Preventers, Cancer Fighters, Cancer Killers And More!
Joseph A. Laydon Jr.

179+
EMERGENCY
COLD WEATHER
Survival Tricks And More!
JOSEPH A. LAYDON JR.
100% Satisfaction Guarantee

How To Learn French Fast!
Joseph A. Laydon Jr.

The Many Benefits Of Coconuts, Peanuts, And Other Tasty Nut Foods!
Joseph A. Laydon Jr.

"72+ Fantastic
Mind-Over-
Matter
Joseph A. Laydon Jr.

179+ International Emergency Wilderness Shelters And More!
Joseph A. Laydon Jr.

Basic & Advanced Navigation Workbook And Videos!
Joseph A. Laydon Jr.

Anytime Anywhere Survival Program A - Z Index Guide! (10,000+ Survival Entries)
Joseph A. Laydon Jr.

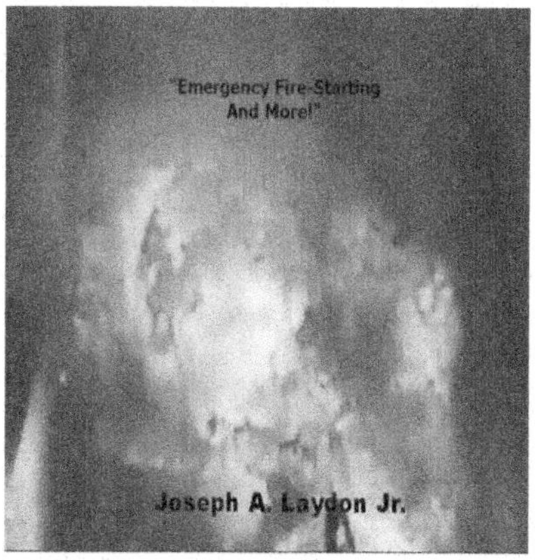
"Emergency Fire-Starting And More!"
Joseph A. Laydon Jr.

About The Author

Joseph A. Laydon Jr. (MSG Ret. Army - 18Z5V) is the author and owner of *Intensive Research Information Services And Products (IRISAP)*. Joseph is a well-qualified instructor in international wilderness survival and the other 03 Survivals he teaches (Health, Crime, and Money). He is a 20-year US Army veteran (Master Sergeant E-8 - 18Z5V) associated with all Special Operations units in the US military, as well as Special Ops units in the Mid-East and Central & South America.

He's a qualified SERE Instructor (Survival Evasion Resistance & Escape) and has **taught wilderness survival** at the college level for 03 years. He's a qualified instructor in basic & advanced pistol marksmanship, basic & advanced rifle marksmanship, CQB (Close Quarter Battle), basic & advanced cross-country navigation, basic mountaineering techniques, and self-defense. Since 1994, he's published many self-improvement Survival Programs, Survival Videos, SPECIAL Reports, Intelligence Reports, monthly Newsletters, <u>**80 Survival Books**</u> (Kindle E-Books & CreateSpace Paperback Books) and more in the works.

He's an inventor, he *"sideways engineers"* new survival tricks that can SAVE YOUR LIFE! An example: On 17 August 2000 - 1417 hours, at Scott Lake, Scott AFB, IL, Joseph made international history! He is the 1st in the world to replicate the mysterious fires of Africa using a single drop of water! On 05 January 2001, he discovered how to start a life-saving fire in just 02-seconds using a beam of light from a flashlight in pitch black *"blind man"* darkness! On 06 April 2005 - 1810 hours, he invented delicious & tasty Solid Fuel Rolls and several Trail-Mix Cookies that are used as emergency foods and used as long-burning emergency fire-starting kindling.

And recently - <u>**50+ MORE TOP SECRET INVENTIONS**</u> of advanced & ultra-advanced fire-starting like starting EMERGENCY FIRE-STARTING using personal care products and first-aid products you already use like:
- Shampoo
- Toothpastes
- Mouthwashes
- Breath Drops & Breath Sprays
- Salves
- Ointments
- Over-The-Counter Medicines
- Drink Enhancement Products
- Other ingredients like your spit (saliva), your urination,...

See **www.survivalexpert.com/fire**

He also teaches Advanced Navigation (*Basic & Advanced Navigation Workbook And Videos* [includes Workbook, Videos, maps, protractors,…]) so you're ready Anytime Anywhere! Only from IRISAP and only for privileged IRISAP subscribers - YOU! See *Basic & Advanced Navigation Workbook And Videos* at **www.survivalexpertbooks.com/navigation**

Below is a sample of his military achievements & qualifications (<u>**not in chronological order**</u>) which reflect his unique & superior ability to teach basic, advanced & ultra-advanced survival applications, techniques and "tricks" that could help you AVOID serious killer survival threats as well as SAVE YOUR LIFE when you get in life or death situations. His trade secrets, Programs, and Videos are only offered to IRISAP subscribers-YOU!

- US Army Airborne School
- US Army Special Forces Qualification Course - SFQC (Green Beret)
- US Army Master Parachutist Wings
- Uruguayan Parachutist Wings
- British Parachutist Wings
- Kingdom of Jordan Parachutist Wings
- Expert Infantry Badge - EIB
- 82nd Airborne Division Recondo Course
- Adverse Weather Aerial Delivery System Tests - AWADS (01 of 386 volunteer paratroopers)
- US Army Special Forces Weapons Course (US & foreign pistols, submachineguns, assault rifles, rifles, machineguns, mortars, anti-tank weapons, anti-aircraft weapons,…)
- Weapons Armorer Course
- Indirect Fire Course (60mm, 81mm, & 4.2 inch *"four deuce"* mortars)
- Jumpmaster Course
- Basic French Language Course
- Combat Infantry Badge - CIB
- US Army Ranger Course
- Advanced Navigation Course
- Special Forces Sniper Course (02)
- Survival Evasion Resistance and Escape Instructor Course (SERE Level B)
- Wilderness Survival Instructor (College level - 03 years / 1991 - 1994)
- Rappell Master
- Fast Rope Master
- International Sniper Instructor
- International Close Quarter Battle (CQB) Instructor
- Participated In Multiple Combat Actions

- Special Forces Operations And Intelligence Course (O&I)
- Good Conduct Medal (06)
- Army Commendation Medal
- Army Achievement Medal (02)
- Meritorious Service Medal (02)
- Armed Forces Expeditionary Medal
- Letters Of Commendation (13)
- Letters Of Appreciation (08)
- Held **SECRET and TOP SECRET Clearances** for 20+ years

Featured on FOX-2 (24 August 2000). Joseph now resides in Illinois. He offers products concerning Wilderness Survival, Health Survival, Crime Survival, and Money Survival so to greatly enhance the lives of all IRISAP subscribers - YOU! Any questions, write to Joseph today.

Sincerely,
Joseph A. Laydon Jr. (IRISAP)
P.O. Box 48
Cutler, IL 62238-0048

You And Yours Have A Safe One
Anytime Anywhere,

Joseph A. Laydon Jr.

E-Mail: wwwsurvivalexpert@yahoo.com

WEBSITES

- Main Website----------------------------www.survivalexpert.com
- 40+ Survival Paperback Books------------www.survivalexpertbooks.com
- 40+ Survival Kindle E-Books-------------www.survivalexpertebooks.com
- Anytime Anywhere Survival---------------www.anytimeanywheresurvival.com
- Weight-Loss----------------------------www.loseitorelseweightloss.com
- True Scary Videos----------------------www.truescaryvideos.com
- Exodus To Genesis----------------------www.exodustogenesis.com

<u>IRISAP Copyright 2017 – All Rights Reserved</u>

Take Notes

Take Notes

Take Notes

Take Notes

Take Notes

Take Notes

Take Notes